9|14

Early reviews:

"A terrific new book by Suzanne Gilbert. Tapioca Fire is moving and fascinating....It kept me on the edge of my seat and I had difficulty putting it down. Suzanne Gilbert has a wonderful style of writing and I highly recommend her new book."

~Sandy Musser, Author and Activist for Adoption Reform, November 17, 2013, Amazon Review

"A great read! This was a fascinating story of international adoption and intrigue. Once I started the book, I had to finish it in almost one read! The world of international adoption is almost like an alternate universe...secret...[sometimes] full of lies and deception and shame...and joy and reunion. Tapioca Fire sheds light on this hidden part of our world....Keep writing Suzanne!"

~ Pamela Kathryn Smith O'Brien, Ontario Reunited Adoptee, November 14, 2013, Amazon Review

"We all search for love and acceptance; for adoptees that battle is fraught with so much more. Suzanne Gilbert brings that struggle to life in a saga of a search and discovery that crosses continents and generations."

~Elaine Durbach, Journalist, October 9,

2013, Facebook

"Tapioca Fire is a rich journey through the landscape of connection and loss. We hear the story from all sides as Susan attends a support group that includes other adopted searchers as well as adoptive parents and birth mothers.... Her depiction of urban and rural Thailand is also solidly grounded....It is clear that you can trust her accuracy as she writes with understanding about human trafficking and other contemporary forms of slavery. ....I recommend this book to anyone who is involved with adoption, including professionals who work in this field. The many possible outcomes of searches like Susan's, with both uplifting and distressing aspects, and the complexity of people's intertwined lives, make this book worth your while."

~Mary Gilbert, Quaker Earthcare Witness representative to the United Nations, December 28, 2013, Amazon Review

"She endeared me immediately by paying tribute to her adoptive family and the many memories they have given her. That also rings true with me. Regardless of all the family that I have found and will continue to find since my search came together, I will always be indebted to the family that raised me, the love, the memories, and

the constant support they have always given me, even when it came to finding my roots. You have a great work of art here."

~ **Gina Lauren Gynn, Reunited Ohio Adoptee and Mother, October 30th, 2013, Facebook,** *shortly before the state restored adult adoptees' access to original birth certificates (OBCs).*

SUZANNE GILBERT

Tapioca Fire

~A novel~

By Suzanne Gilbert

This novel is a work of fiction. The characters,
incidents and dialogue are drawn from the
author's imagination and are not to be construed
as real. Any resemblance to actual persons or
events, living or dead, is coincidental.

CONTENTS

AUTHOR'S NOTES & ACKNOWLEDGEMENTS

With thanks to my beloved first reader, Mark Furman.

Thanks also to the late Betty Jean Lifton, Elaine Durbach, Pam Hasegawa, Jonathan Schonfield (a birth relative and son of Rabbi Solomon Schonfield) and the women of my writers' group for their close reading of passages that would become part of this book. To them much credit is due while any shortcomings in this telling remain my own.

I explored some of the ideas and emotions in this book on Maine Public Radio's "Maine Things Considered," Lilith Magazine, the ICEA Journal, RitualWell.org by Mayan and RRC, Midwifery Today, The Birth Gazette, the CLAL newsletter Sh'ma, Moment Magazine and through two Seders co-hosted at Temple B'nai Or and the Morristown Presbyterian Church.

I have mentioned that one character is autobiographical. These people buoyed me on my quest: my birth mother, Ellen Gilbert, my birth father, Bill Ray, my half-brother Tiernan Ray and family genealogist Martha Cahn Pellegrino. I am thankful to my mother, Carolyn Kriegman, for her lifelong honesty and engagement, and to all my adoptive relatives for our memories.

Spiritual mentors include my Wellesley College professors Elinor Grumet and Reverend James T. Kodera, Father Thomas Brosnan and his writing on spirit and body in adoption, and the many teachers unnamed here who may think I don't remember.

I based English renderings of psalms and Hebrew prayers on Jewish Publication Society translations with liberal adaptation. I am indebted also to Michelle Cameron, Diana Grayson, Joyce Maguire Pavao, and Jeroen Sikkema for their encouragement and wise words along the way.

During the final stages of editing, I found crowd-sourced support from members of the adoption triad, genealogists and others who contributed posts and pictures to the Tapioca Fire and Suzanne Gilbert pages on social media.

In gratitude to my final reader, Mark Furman, always.

~ PART I ~

"Steward: I know, madam, you love your gentlewoman entirely.

Countess: Faith, I do: her father bequeathed her to me; and she herself, without other advantage, may lawfully make title to as much love as she finds: there is more owing her than is paid; and more shall be paid her than she'll demand.

Helena: Mine honourable mistress.

Countess: Nay, a mother:....I say I am your mother:
And put you in the catalogue of those that were enwombed mine. 'Tis often seen adoption strives with nature; and choice breeds a native slip to us from foreign seeds:"

> *~ Shakespeare*
> *'All's Well That Ends Well'*

1 TAPIOCA FIRES
1991

Daubs of indigo, scarlet and purple broke the pale blue night with the ardor of a county fair at summer's end. Susan and her guide, Kun Sompan, walked a new route back to the hotel at her request. This might be the last chance to understand the world of the person whose disappearance almost a quarter of a century ago changed her life forever.

She only had a day to explore sprawling Bangkok before heading up north where her mother had fled years before.

Kun Sompan told Susan they would avoid the notorious red light districts of Patpong Road and New Petburi and instead head to the local night market. Yet as they continued down even this street she was overwhelmed by the jaded miasma, shot through with neon and mirrors. A musical babel of techno, American, Japanese, Chinese and Thai pop assaulted her. It mixed with the low hum of single unit air conditioners that bothered the tropical air.

This was not the red light district, but its impression was slick: the sheen of wet pavement, lip gloss on girls standing in the street in stilettos. Flashing billboards above entrances left ajar to pole dancing places. Glimpses inside of rose colored lights and body oil on thighs and shoulders. There was a warmly private odor that mixed with the smell of rice wine and beer.

Susan and Kun Sompan turned a corner and a small boy with a smudged face held out a handwritten note that he pushed toward her in his open palms. It was something in English. She smiled down at him before accepting it. She read, "Little boys, men, women, little girls," and then dropped it in horror. He looked at her, angelic. She looked over at her guide. He kept them moving. She was relieved when they turned another corner and saw their hotel door.

~

The next morning Susan had the breakfast that came with her stay, rice porridge simmered with fresh chicken broth. Kun Sompan arrived soon after to drive them the six hours north.

The first hour would encompass the crowded streets of Bangkok and its inner suburbs. She wouldn't be here in the capital long enough to differentiate neighborhoods but she tried to take in as much as she could from the passenger window. There were motley pedicabs and motorized carts called *tuk-tuks* everywhere, colored like ponies on a carousel. They clogged the streets and flowed along sidewalks, streaming with people in traditional sarongs, or black capris with cheap sandals, or Western-style clothes.

The rush hour smell of diesel exhaust overwhelmed the fresh food sold by vendors and the incense from shops along the Chao Phrya River and its canals. Music poured from storefronts and *tuk-tuks*, and even motorbike riders tied makeshift radios to their handlebars.

Concrete buildings painted in swimming pool blues and pastels made up the banks of this human river. The homes were narrow and deep like two-car garages. Inside most buildings they passed she could see a cement room on the ground floor used either as a shop front or a sitting room, with a second room behind beaded curtains that must be the kitchen.

Like any city, first floors had roll down

metal doors. Above them wrought-iron grills covered windows and balconies with twizzled banisters all the way up their full three or four stories. Susan marveled at the hammered metal displays of starbursts, spirals and scalloping that looked like they had been cut with giant pinking shears.

Eventually the slow pace of the traffic and the steady rumble of the car engine lulled Susan to sleep under brilliant tropical sunshine that poured in through her window and sun roof. Hours later she awoke to a strange, vast landscape.

"The rice basket of Asia," Kun Sompan offered.

Rice paddies stretched out on either side of the road, in soft greens that reminded Susan of springtime. She saw them blanketing the countryside in gradual terraced fields whose flooded basins caught the noon sun.

She daydreamed them into some leviathan beached green fish. Scale upon scale of silvery wet paddies covered the earth, ending far off with copses of trees and small tin-roofed hamlets. When they caught rays at certain angles they momentarily reflected flashes of light into her eyes. These jolts kept her awake for a while, but east to west jetlag was the worst. Later in the day she wouldn't mind giving in to what felt as strong as a drugged sleep.

Hours passed and as the sun headed down toward the earth, the earth seemed to rise up to meet it where it was setting behind a stand of trees on a far off ridge. The sun reddened the sky, and she thought she saw smoke rising, too.

Kun Sompan looked around a little when the acrid smell of smoke started filtering in through the car's air conditioning. The road had reached the top of a bluff and he pulled off to get his bearings. He walked up a ways and then stopped and turned around to gesture through the windshield for her to come out, too.

She took a deep breath as she opened the car door and her mouth filled with dry, heavy, bitter-tasting air. Joining Kun Sompan in front of the car, she looked down at the bowl shaped valley in front of them.

It was filled with smoke, like what she imagined the crater of a volcano must look like. Ugly red-orange flames glowed in black-scorched fields. The entire valley was a patchwork of red and black acres and only a few squares were untouched. There the withered stumps of what he explained were cassava root still clumped in dry, pale soil. The afternoon of dazzling sunlight was obscured by brownish puffs of soot and smoke that garlanded the valley like a woolen shawl. Her eyes started to smart.

"Tapioca fires," he said.

She could make out about a half dozen or so men and women holding blue plastic pails standing on a narrow raised path between two fields. An ember rose and landed near the sandals of one man who doused it with some water from his bucket. The fires seemed to have been set deliberately and then contained within each field by the farmers.

As she watched, two men and a boy carried a smoldering stick over to a threshed field, stooped down and set one corner ablaze. As smoke rose, yellow fire crept along the rows. In a neighboring field the tongues of fire had cooled to red and left the edges of the field a singed, black thatch.

At the far right end of the valley, the fields were still untouched and there was a hamlet of homes that looked like others she had passed on the road out here. They stood on stilts beneath rusted corrugated metal roofing.

As they got back in the car, he explained, "That over there is the village. We'll drive down to it. It's the end of the tapioca season. Some villagers burn the cassava fields that tapioca comes from. It makes the earth better. Some go to the town to sell tapioca, barter tapioca, go to market. The woman's husband went to the fair they have in town, children gone, too."

"Should I call her Ms. Prichittakorn?"

"In Thailand we don't call people by last names. Even the Prime Minister, even a General in Armed Forces. So you call her by her first name."

She paused, considering what he said, and then asked, "How is it you say 'mother' again? I'm not sure I'll use it, but..." and her voice trailed.

"*Kun-mae.*"

Susan was still repeating the two syllables to herself when they pulled up alongside the stilts of one of the houses. The walls were some kind of broad, dried, brown fiber woven in basketry and each raised platform seemed to have a main structure with two smaller sheds rising near it.

Chickens watched and a pig lolled in the shade between the smooth, unpainted pillars supporting this house. She heard creaking on the boards overhead and a woman, whose features she couldn't yet take in, came to the edge and looked down at them before lowering a ladder.

2 FILM NOIR
1990

Susan's mystery-solving began like many a 1940s detective movie. She was the Oriental woman waiting outside an office to see the private investigator. His address took her to the section of the city that was called the Ironbound because it was surrounded by rail tracks. Known for good, cheap seafood and Portuguese. Either on the verge of being discovered or forgotten.

He called her in and she opened the door that, almost unbelievably, had a huge eyeball stenciled on it right over the letters advertising, "Fred Kouyoumjian, Private Eye."

After shaking hands Fred Kouyoumjian offered Susan a seat. There was nothing in this office to be frightened of, she reminded herself. It was only a first conversation, not a commitment to proceed.

She was opposite his desk facing a wall of hunter green file cabinets. Everything about his office spoke fluently male–deep blue walls, municipal league baseball trophies and a mohair Morris chair in the corner. There was no overflowing ashtray or blue cigarette haze like the movies, but the daylight did come in filtered and refracted through heavy air that sparkled with dust.

"How can I help you?"

"Well, I'd heard you locate missing persons and what I have is kind of like that."

She couldn't compare it to the requests of any film noir client. No one, based on what little information she had, was murdered. There had been no kidnapping so far as she knew. She did not know if extortion, fraud, or counterfeiting were involved.

There was a sense that an identity had been switched, that someone who should never go missing was gone, that an inheritance had indeed been lost, but none of this in the conventional sense.

The identity theft was that of the vanished woman whose name it might be on a slip of paper in Susan's purse. The inheritance was the cultural one that Susan might have had if things had been different over two decades ago. The missing person was the woman who had given birth to her and left no trace.

~

Six months earlier Susan was riding a bus when she overheard two women talking about something they called "adoption search and reunion". She'd never heard the term before. They talked about "adoption reform" because with adoption, once "everyone"–social workers, attorneys and adoptive parents–agreed on an adoption, they sealed the adoption records from the adoptee.

Now, according to what Susan was hearing, adult adoptees were challenging that agreement made without their consent. They, as well as some adoptive parents and birth parents, were pressing the courts and state legislatures to restore to adoptees their original birth certificates. Original birth certificates have the true place of birth and the biological parents' names on them.

Susan was stunned. She leaned across the aisle and introduced herself.

It turned out the women were facilitators of what they called an "adoption search self-help group". One was an adult adoptee named Lisa and the other was an adoptive mother named Christine.

Christine told Susan, "The group meets monthly and we have everyone from the triad there."

Susan asked, "Triad?"

Now Lisa leaned across the aisle, "We've coined the term 'adoption triad' with meeting facilitators from each side in the geometry: an adult adoptee, a birth parent, and an adoptive parent."

They seemed intrigued when they learned she was an international adoptee. There were rumors that some Korean adoptees had tried searching, but an international adoption was pretty much a cold case in those days. Nevertheless, the two bus riders wrote out Fred Kouyoumjian's name and number on a paper napkin for her.

"So," Susan marveled, "there are reunions between adoptees and their birth relatives!"

She had never hoped for this. She hadn't rejected the idea either; she just never considered it because it was impossible. Now she dared to hope that the detective and this community of searchers could help her.

~

Susan found herself in Fred

Kouyoumjian's office saying, "I want to conduct a search for my birth mother. I was adopted so, of course, they won't give me my real birth certificate. But I did get a name that I think is hers."

"That's excellent. How'd you do that?"

"Well, one of the Buddhist nuns gave it to my parents–wrote it on a piece of paper and passed it to them but they couldn't understand what she was saying."

"Whoa, Buddhist nun?"

"Y-yes. I was adopted in Bangkok, Thailand."

Fred Kouyoumjian waited a beat before continuing. He seemed satisfied with this new fact as he took in her Eurasian face. Long, brown-black hair. The bridge of her nose gracefully flattening into wide, dark, delicately lidded eyes. Medium complexion that could also have been Latina or Mediterranean.

"This wasn't an agency adoption?"

"No, they went themselves to an orphanage there. Most of the kids weren't orphans. They were left there by poor unwed mothers so I think that name might belong to my birth mother. Suwan Prichittikorn."

"Excuse me?'

"The name was Suwan Prichittikorn. I'll

write it for you. And the orphanage. And the year. No exact date. Sometime early fall near the end of the rainy season. My parents went in October when it's cooler there but not too wet."

"The hottest month is April, isn't it?"

"I don't really know."

"Oh, so you've never been there? Since the adoption? I went there for some R and R after doing a couple of searches and reunions in Korea...."

He began discussing their options: visiting the orphanage, hiring an interpreter, checking provincial registries. His voice sounded reassuring and she felt herself relax into the back of her chair. She focused more clearly on what the detective was saying and found she had been clasping a pen lightly in her fist, copying down a few odd words.

Fred recommended going after the low hanging fruit first and asked Susan to draft a one paragraph missing persons ad, describing what she knew of her birth mother, herself. Any birthmarks? Had the orphanage given her adoptive parents any clothes or gifts from the girl?

They would hit the English language press and the local Bangkok press. But—he seemed proud of this insight—Susan's birth mother may have moved away from the capital, "so to get the most effective coverage, we'll use trade magazines to target the Rice Growers Association, the Society of Shrimp Fisheries, the Tapioca Cooperative Network, the Silk Weavers Guild and the Rubber Tappers Federation."

"That's creative," Susan said and decided she would hire him.

Fred looked down with a show of modesty that warmed her, even if it was false.

Susan put her palm on her notepad, "Mr. Kouyoumjian, within the next six months I'll be traveling to Tokyo for work. That would probably be the easiest time to visit Bangkok. Do you think you could find her by then?"

"Many adoptees never even clear these first hurdles for any information. It's not unheard of that they're left in the capital by someone traveling there with no name, no region they came from, no photos or real birth date. It's always a long shot with international adoptions. I'll tidy up your missing persons ad but, honestly?"

Susan looked at him.

"Very rarely do you hear of someone responding to the ads, but they're your best first move. Whether they're a match or not is still another long shot. I'll be more proactive than that, have my people reach out directly. I've got a pretty good record but sometimes with private adoptions like yours, especially with international ones, the trails go cold. Records are discarded. People forget or just won't talk. All the trap doors are shut," and he clapped his hands together, startling her.

He continued, "I can give it a try and if there is any chance of finding her, I'm as good at international searches as anyone. You at least have a possible name of your birth mother, or maybe it belongs instead to one of the nuns still there. The name of the orphanage may actually be a cloister that happens to take in unwed mothers, not a true orphans' facility. It would help if you can get more about your birth mother's own place of birth from your parents. She may have returned to her native province."

Susan smiled, "I guess I have some homework to do. Draft that ad. Talk to my parents to see if they have anything more. Especially around geography or from my birth mother."

He started to rise from his desk and added, almost as an afterthought, "The time this takes me to tackle could be a blessing in disguise. I'm not discouraging you at all, but meeting your birth mother could send you for a bigger loop than you expect. I think adoptees should have access to their records just like anyone else, but you might want to figure out how much you'd want this woman in your life. How it'll make things between you and your adoptive folks. Sometimes things can get pretty rocky for a while."

Susan swallowed and waited.

"On the other hand, in my experience, parents and adoptees grow beyond that. A reunion with birth parents is just a process that takes some adjusting by everyone involved. It'll probably be okay but it's something to keep in mind."

Susan was surprised when he pulled open a file cabinet drawer and handed her two pieces of paper about a search self-help group in a town only ten miles away. Consciously polite, she took both, glancing at them to confirm that they were the facilitators she met on the bus.

"Susan, it would be good for you to hear the stories of others who are either searching or were found, and you'll hear it there. I'll tell you what they would tell you anyway: that self-help and support are two different things. They're a self-help group that would put someone in touch with an investigator like myself, or get them access to resources. You'll meet others who are also on this quest, working out the nuts and bolts."

"That's all I want."

"They try to keep themselves from going too far into being a support group, you know, providing counseling on the fly."

"Counseling?"

Fred paused to look up and try to read her face.

Susan nearly squirmed in her seat, "I think 'counseling' carries the connotation of there being something wrong with us and that's not why I'm searching. It's not because there's something wrong with me–or my adoptive parents."

"That's not what I meant. It's an emotional event, like a birth or a death or a wedding or a divorce. Normal people go through all of them. Normal adult adoptees go through search, and search can succeed or fail, or be denied. Then meaning gets assigned to it. There's something to be said to having others in the same boat while you're going through any emotional event. If I may, why are you searching?

"As I told you, I have a business trip to East Asia anyway in six months."

"Have you ever been to East Asia before?"

"I did some of my MFA work in Japan."

"So, you've spent considerable time in the region," he was making a statement not a question, "It's only now that you want to visit your birth country."

Susan fought off a defensive tone, "It's for my daughter, to give her some medical history."

"Is there a particular condition?" Fred persisted.

"No."

He paused, looking in her eyes before he said almost apologetically, "This isn't like counseling for a gambling addiction or substance abuse where you're trying to address a problem that's only a symptom or a reaction to a deeper problem. There doesn't have to be something wrong with you or your parents for you to want to discover what you lost through being surrendered."

"I'm just curious."

"Then go for the stories."

"The stories?"

"Everyone has a story. There will be birth mothers there telling their stories."

"Really."

"They're more than saints or sinners, and each is unique. It's good to hear how a reunited adoptee, and her birth parents, and her adoptive parents could describe the same reunion differently."

"Thanks for these flyers. I'll check one or two out."

It was for her little daughter, Lily, that Susan was embarking on this search, she told herself. She told that to her husband, too. They owed it to Lily to find out her medical history, any inheritable diseases in their biological family.

Then again, sometimes Susan would look in sweet Lily's clear, bright eyes and get the eerie certainty that the woman who bore her had done this once, too, with her. What had that woman seen, looking in my eyes decades ago in the nuns' orphanage? Was she sad to leave me?

How did that woman feel in labor? Susan's own labor had been tough and she only got through it by grabbing mentally for any rope–thinking she finally shared something, childbirth, in common with her biological mother.

The need to find that woman and to finally see someone who shared her eyes or her chin, the need had grown as miraculously and as inevitably as her own unborn child until her desire to search was undeniable, like a homing instinct.

Until then there had only been the fantasy of the swan.

When she was an infant and her parents Al and Masha were choosing her name they weren't sure what to do with the name, Suwan Prichittikorn, which seemed to belong to the poor birth mother. They weren't even sure how to pronounce it, but they somehow wanted to honor it. Was it more like Sue-Anne or Swan? Her father had suggested the names Shana or Shayna, and her mother had wanted the Hebrew name Shoshona, and they finally settled on Susan.

As Susan got older, around eleven or twelve years old, people began complimenting her on her long graceful neck and hands, and one day an old man told her she had "the beautiful neck of a swan."

That was it.

Even though she knew enough about linguistics to understand that Suwan probably meant something else in Thai, still, from that day forward she was sure that the name and her swanlike neck were a clue. She had daydreams that maybe one day she would even recognize her birth mother by her smooth graceful throat.

As a teenager, while her chest stayed as flat as an airport runway and her nose always seemed flanked by eruptions of acne, she could always look in the mirror, dreamily fingering a chain necklace around her throat, watching how her knuckles could fold and unfold her fingers like graceful wings.

~

Susan was back down on the street hailing a cab. After she gave him the address she sank back into the vinyl seat cushion and simultaneously lifted one leg to clasp her knee. She could feel her shoulders and her jaw tighten as she thought about the indefinite wait ahead. Fred Kouyoumjian had given her no estimates on how long this would take.

Her mood might be okay for now, she thought, as she tried to loosen her shoulders by rolling them back, but she could imagine herself growing irritable and tense as the days, weeks or, months might roll by. She let out a sigh.

She would give this search until her business trip to Tokyo. Six months. If he found anything she could keep it casual and tack on a few days to fly down to Thailand after she finished her business in Japan. Better than making a special trip that would burn up the family vacation budget and possibly turn up nothing. Her shoulder muscles were softening now. She'd wait six months and then just forget it.

Looking out the window, she turned her thoughts to her parents. The waiting wasn't like the wait when you get a baby through your own pregnancy, she thought. You are given a due date to mark on your calendar and then tell to friends. With search there was no ultrasound or fetoscope to listen to the other's heartbeat. No quickening to tell you things are progressing, no reassuring kicks to tell you the other will be in your arms soon.

Poor Mom, she thought with no clear reason. At the end of the day she would remember to give her mom a call. She headed home to the quieter suburbs and her little daughter, the one and only flesh and blood relative she had ever known.

~

Susan almost sleep walked through the next six months. There was Lily's waking up at night, and getting to know their family caregiver, a mother of teenagers named Terry, whom Susan genuinely liked. Nevertheless, every time Lily seemed clingy or got a bruise in her attempts at toddling, Susan wondered whether Terry, or anyone, could really be giving her enough attention.

Work at least allowed Susan to forget both Lily and the search during most of the day. Her search still floated to consciousness occasionally like a maddening memory of misplaced keys or an unreturned phone call.

She got irritated with her husband, David, for not being more concerned; with her parents because she wondered if there weren't one more piece of information they might have forgotten or withheld; with Fred Kouyoumjian for, she imagined, working on other cases that progressed faster; with her birth mother and the orphanage for only thinking about placing a long ago infant and not about giving her any stories from her ancestors, any roots.

Each time Susan would realize how foolish this all was, but she also clung to her frustration as the only tangible part of her search available to her. The rest was–in Fred Kouyoumjian's hands. Not only was her biological history shaped by others, but even her search was totally beyond her own control. One time on a call to Fred she shared her frustration at not having more information to filter his search.

He replied, "Having roots is a spiritual need and at that time Thailand was a poor country. Providing for your material needs would have been everyone's sole concern, and they could not be blamed for that."

She agreed before hanging up, but a voice that had been long silenced wanted to ask why it needed to be a tradeoff. In providing materially for so-called orphans, did they really need to be stripped of everything else?

The question remained unvoiced because she was too aware of her burden of gratitude. "Have an attitude of gratitude." Wasn't that what the bumper sticker said? Most of the time it made life less bumpy for her. Where it felt like a burden was the memories of family and strangers telling her she was lucky to be adopted, that she was fortunate to have been brought to America. Most little girls and boys, she now looked back and saw, were not given those particular set of instructions. She believed in greeting the day with a sunny face, but this was something she suddenly found oppressive.

Instead she was able to persist because she was a mother. Once every week or so she'd put in a call to Fred Kouyoumjian and although he sounded engaged, she came away wondering if she sounded too aggressive or too needy. To even call this a search was off-pitch. It was more like cutting oneself adrift in a great grey sea with no seeming current or tide. She began wearing a locket with a picture of Lily in it. She touched it whenever the waiting became too much.

3 FIRST STEPS
1990

Next Saturday afternoon David watched Lily while Susan went alone to a mixed group of adult adoptees, adoptive parents and birth parents.

There were close to thirty people crowded around a conference table in the meeting room of a community center. Just inside the entrance to the room someone pointed her to a table with a donation tin, a signup sheet for a mailing list and name labels.

There were instructions near the latter two to indicate "where you are on the triad" with a key explaining which initials to use after your name. Susan skimmed her options, and then watched the tall, slim man in his early thirties ahead of her write "RA" for "reunited adoptee" and the older woman next to him who sometimes leaned on his arm for support marked hers with rapid familiarity, "AP" for "adoptive parent". Another man passed a hand dappled with liver spots over his shaved head before sighing and lowering it to write "LDA" for "late discovery adoptee".

There were large coffee makers, bottled water, and an assortment of snacks over on the meeting table; the meeting was scheduled for four hours. Susan found a chair near the onion dip and sat down.

A woman to her left turned to her and smiled. The woman had a "B" on her name label. Susan froze as she read it and then immediately hoped the kind stranger hadn't noticed her hesitation at the initial for "birth mother". It struck Susan that this place was very different from anywhere she had ever been if the woman could share via a name tag that she had given away a child.

The woman looked relaxed, which made her own burden of unease a little lighter. Susan couldn't put her finger on why, but she'd put off asking her adoptive parents for the information Fred had asked for. As she sat here she reminded herself, "It's only for medical information," even as her heart pounded.

The tall adoptee and his adoptive mother took the two seats to her right. He asked softly, "You're just starting your search, aren't you?"

"How did you know?"

"Well, hadn't seen you here before, and it's also in how you're looking around the room. You've never been to something like this.

"Yes, that's right."

Susan had never sat in a room with so many adoptees, and she didn't think she had knowingly met a birth mother before. She told him that.

He agreed, adding, "There are towns with a lot of adoptees, though. They're usually ones with communities of LGBT parents, or college campuses and older academics who put off childbearing too long. Otherwise, it's pretty unusual to see a gathering like this."

She had seen photos of fighter pilots who after they had come back from a particularly long mission bend down to touch the earth. She imagined they felt like what a part of her did now: she had found solid ground. Fighter pilots, she was sure, didn't think much about tarmacs during a sortie, just as she hadn't let herself think about what was different for those like her who lived their lives after being relinquished for adoption. It wasn't safe to dwell on it–until now.

The man was still talking, "it was great preparation for me and my adoptive family to come here together."

The woman who must have been his adoptive mother leaned forward and added, "It certainly helps parents or spouses to know how involved to be, how to support and when to step back," the woman glanced down briefly at Susan's wedding ring, "Bring your husband next time if he'll come."

"They're going to start soon," her son said.

There seemed to be a flexible protocol that depended on each person choosing a number from the tin. Those that were bursting with news–one adoptee had met her birth mother the afternoon before–tended to pick a lower number so they could speak earlier. Some others chose no number, instead offering an anecdote diffidently in response to someone else's story, and a few chose not to speak at all, just listening or witnessing the stories of others.

She realized as they went around the room to introduce themselves and give a brief background that most of the other adoptees had had sealed record domestic adoptions. The main obstacles to finding their family and medical history were US laws enacted in the twentieth century.

Susan would have extra hurdles and wondered if anyone here would be able to relate to what she was facing. She would have to confront the distance across the Pacific and either similar Thai legal prohibitions or a lack of records.

One of the first to speak, a man who was there with his fiancé, caught her off guard. He said, "I was our high school football captain, I have great adoptive parents and cousins, but I always was aware of being different. It's like I was never at home. I'd come back from camp, or later, from college on break, and it was great to see everyone again and be in my old room, but I still felt like I was an exile. I've felt displaced, or like something was absent for as long as I could put my finger on it."

He looked at his fiancé before continuing, "Jess is the greatest girl in the world, that's why I proposed, but I just feel like I need to address this before we move forward and make our own home together. If I can still feel like a stranger with her at my side, like I feel when sitting with my folks or with our friends, something is really missing and I need to get to the bottom of it."

Susan found herself quivering inside, like someone was reading her most shameful thoughts.

Despite all of her parents' love and everything they gave her, despite knowing that

David was the one, despite still having long friendships from elementary school, there were times when she felt –apart. She'd do anything for them, she loved them, but felt disloyal because she still shared that exile he described, like a sojourner among them.

When she was coming of age she'd try out different ways to explain it to herself, if not cure it. She joined the Asian Students' Association in college, took a Women's Studies class to see if race or gender or power held the key to why she felt so apart, but she couldn't relate to people raised by Asian parents, especially immigrant ones. The Women's Studies class definitely felt dated, but it was a good balance to all the male researchers and authors they read in other courses.

The Jewish Student Union had a speaker who talked about the way the one percent of the world that was Jewish like her would of course feel like strangers in a strange land because of living in a diaspora. He talked about internalizing the image of the wandering Jew, of Jewish self-hatred stemming from anti-Semitism, of the double bind that minority males often put their women in: Jewish male comedians who told Jewish Mother jokes were the counterpart of gangsta rappers who called their own women bitches and whores.

It helped to think that at some level all these different groups of humanity shared her sense of displacement. But no one had ever captured what that former football captain had just described in this fluorescent light-bathed room. He had described it better and he wasn't a minority or disempowered in any conventional sense of those words.

She might have put it a little differently, maybe because she had without realizing it, begun her search years earlier as a student when she had tried looking at power, ethnicity or being female. But sitting with any one of those groups only highlighted for her that the shadow feeling would not be shaken.

The absurdity of it! She had now finally found someone who "got it" in the form of a white, Christian male with whom she hadn't so much as exchanged a single word. She had the feeling that all the adoptees in the room might "get" this feeling, the shadow companion that she always felt. She raised her hand tentatively, catching the facilitator's eye.

She nodded and Susan looked out at the group, "I've felt that, too, that something was missing, that—" Susan paused, half expecting dismissive laughter, but when she realized everyone was waiting quietly for her to continue, she did.

"It wasn't for anyone else's lack of hospitality. It almost felt like that absence was something I was physically carrying with me. They talk of how amputees can still feel the limb they have lost, 'phantom limb pain,' and that feeling of absence has been just as palpable to me."

She stopped there. She was afraid she would dissolve in a puddle of tears if she went too far by finishing the thought. Her missing blood mother was that phantom, and her absence was the pain that Susan always carried with her. She felt so, so guilty when she thought of her beloved adoptive parents, her husband's family, their new family, her friends, all the other earnest seekers in the Asian Students' Association or the Jewish Student Union, but their presence and all the self-awareness in the world wasn't going to make her phantom limb pain go away. Maybe finding her birth mother would.

If she stripped away all the intellectual words like empowerment, disempowerment, alienation, cognitive dissonance, marginalization, what have you, she would be left with the plaintive, primal plea of "I want my mommy, I want my mommy" and that was something she wouldn't be able to voice, even here, without breaking down completely.

If Susan finally let go, she didn't know how she'd ever come back, so instead she had held it together, planned carefully, found the ways she could connect with others, but still dragged with her that phantom limb of absentness.

Susan glanced at the understanding faces around her and saw her declaration left no one perplexed. She took a drink from the water bottle in front of her and avoided raising her eyes for a while. Susan thought if she looked in another human face about now she would let out a sob. This was just so strange.

When the detective asked why she was searching, she certainly couldn't have answered with full truth. Her answer, that she wanted to give her daughter medical history, was true as far as it went. How do you say more to someone on the other side of the great divide that separated her from others who would never truly understand?

As Susan continued to listen to the conversations around the table, she began to feel well. She found herself staying the whole four hours, warmed by a kind of camaraderie.

One adopted man with salt and pepper hair and a Minnesota accent concluded the recounting of a disappointing first phone call with a sister, saying, "What I've learned over the past couple years coming here is that this group is my surrogate family during the search. My parents, may they rest in peace, aren't around anymore, and my birth mother and her husband have too much of their own baggage for us to have a relationship, so what I feel like I've wrested from this experience is the people I've met in this room."

There were murmurs of approval and another man leaned over to squeeze his shoulder. Shortly after this they broke for fifteen minutes before meeting again for another two hours.

At that point, another leader, a gray-haired birth mother with a cornflower blue wrap that set off her eyes over her pink blouse said, "Carol, maybe this is a good time for you to introduce your guest."

Everyone's attention shifted to a pair of women at the far corner of the table. The one who must have been Carol wore a soft outfit of browns and grays with perfectly coiffed hair that was now pure white and at one time must have been a dazzling blonde. Next to her sat a woman who had picked out a similar palette, and had similar hair, though looked about ten years younger. They clasped hands in a knot of knuckled skin and colorful rings. Susan guessed that they were sisters.

"We've decided we're soul sisters," they laughed together.

"Aren't you Daniel's mother?" someone asked and both women nodded.

"He's in Chicago, but I wanted to bring Cheryl this month," and then Carol introduced the younger woman with, "this is my son's birth mother."

There was an appreciative murmur that the two women received with a look of shared merriment. Then Cheryl said in an amazed voice, "I never thought I would have all this. I never thought that I would see him again in this lifetime. Carol's been able to give him so much materially with such good upbringing, I wouldn't have been able to at that time. What began with such pain, relinquishing a baby, has just turned into such a good thing because of Carol's adopting and raising him."

Carol added with a calm conviction, "Cheryl is my friend. I love her so much. I would have liked her anyway but I wouldn't have met her if it weren't for Daniel. And I think of him as the greatest gift anyone has ever given me," and they rocked their conjoined hands up slightly from the arms of the chairs they had been resting on as if to discharge some excess emotional energy.

They both laughed quietly and looked into each other's eyes. Susan struggled to pull back from their unguarded words with some internal flinch of irony or dismissiveness, but could find none. She surrendered to the wave of affection and hope she felt toward the individuals in the room, toward her parents, to her abstract birth parents even.

One burly man cleared his throat and shook his head in mock exasperation.

"Man, five years ago you couldn't have dragged me to something like this. Now there's nowhere else I'd rather be today."

The next Monday morning Susan got busy and missed calling Fred Kouyoumjian but by lunchtime he had left her a message saying, "no news is good news." Damn his cheerfulness.

~

Somehow the embrace of the group gave

Susan the courage to ask for more information, even if it meant stirring up the waters in her own familial pool. One day she did when David was away on a business trip and her mother, Masha, came for dinner with her and Lily.

Susan opened the door for her mother and noted that her hair was perfect and she was wearing some earth tone outfit that brought out the color in her cheeks. She was short with a trim figure and blonde hair that had dulled with age but not yet turned gray.

Susan thought she could never wear those warm colors; instead white, black, sapphire and bright red looked good on her. "Femme fatale from afar" is how David described his first impression of her. And before the baby she had waist length hair. Her coloring always made her feel odd girl out among her cousins.

At least now that we're all getting married, having in-laws seems to break up the club, she thought. Her sister-in-law Tracy was impossibly fair with hair and eyebrows that were almost white, and skin that burned whenever the clouds cleared. David was the first New Englander in the family with his speech that was softened by the occasional absence of r's.

"Are you still breastfeeding Lily?" her mother asked.

From behind she had the walk and the fashion sense of a younger woman but her face was unapologetic about her years. It looked well-lined, warm, and grandmotherly. Her aquiline nose was carved from between bright blue eyes and her full lips had grown slightly wrinkled around the edges–made her lipstick "feather."

"Yes, Mom."

"When you were little no one did that. We thought only cows nursed their young."

"So you've told me. Did you know that now even adoptive mothers can nurse their babies? They need to supplement with formula but if they take some lactation hormones they can really breastfeed. It's a beautiful experience."

"Unn. Have you gotten Lily to sleep through the night?"

"Sometimes yes. Sometimes no. The pediatrician says it's normal for some kids not to sleep through the night until they're two years old."

"Well, maybe if you stopped nursing completely and gave her a bottle on schedule she'd sleep better."

"Unn."

Susan at one time had tried to analyze

these annoying, recurring conversations with her mother. Was this an adoption issue, some tiresome combination of fertility envy and lactation envy (how could Freud have missed these)?

Her non-adopted friends assured her it was not.

"Don't you think Lily will get a draft if you let her play down there on the blanket on the floor? We always used to keep you in a playpen and you never complained."

"Uh-huh. Mom, I wanted to tell you something. Just before I went back to work I hired a detective—"

"You don't think David is being unfaithful, do you?"

"I don't think so... No, I mean no, that's not what this is about, Mom. I wanted to let you know that I hired a private investigator to search for my birth mother. He doesn't have anything yet. I did give him that name, and the orphanage," then Susan looked at her mother–no reaction–before going on, "and I wondered if there was any more information you had that I could give him."

"Oh, Susan, it was so long ago I really don't remember. The abbess gave us some kind of history while we were dressing you to leave, but all I wanted to do was just get out of there."

"What was it?"

"Oh, I'd have to sit down and think about it. The name of the birth mother and her home province."

"Her native province? Why didn't you ever tell me?"

"You've got to understand. At the time, your Dad and I just wanted to get out of there. We'd heard stories about girls changing their minds and coming back, and we'd been waiting so long for you."

Susan was so furious she was afraid to speak, afraid that her words would come out too jagged and wounding, afraid they would reveal how desperate she was for information.

If the adoption was so tentative that her parents felt they had to rush out the door, should it have even taken place at all? If her mother couldn't even remember basic, basic facts about that new baby's identity and roots, whose interest did her mother have at heart? Certainly not Susan's.

Mom had placed her own interests above those of her own child, Susan felt quietly lost.

Susan forced herself to speak slowly. "Mom. Mom, please, remember the name of that province. Maybe you wrote it down somewhere?"

Masha promised she would check.

That night was a night of interruptions. David got two phone calls during dinner and Lily took especially long to fall asleep. Either Lily was teething or she knew something was up. Lily howled whenever Susan put her in the crib or even just tried to cradle her face up. Instead Susan had to keep pacing, a little tummy flopped over her shoulder because that was the position that seemed to bring Lily the greatest ease.

Susan resented the monotony of a colicky baby and wished David would get off his phone calls. She wanted to sleep, she wanted to shower, she wanted a girls' night out, she wanted to be alone with her thoughts.

Exhausted, she literally said aloud in the nursery, "Why won't this baby just sleep? I'm about to face something incredible!"

Then Susan's hand brushed the locket. The baby didn't stop crying, but Susan did.

4 SECRETS
1990

She wanted to hear some news so badly that she decided to check in with Fred Kouyoumjian weekly. She was also beginning to hear about adoptees who had been swindled after paying a lot up front. They didn't even receive proof that the searchers had at least been thorough. Fred only asked for a token deposit. She almost wished he hadn't been so scrupulous so she could find fault and somehow confront him.

Instead she keyed his number every Monday morning and asked, calmly, for a status update. Her mind longed just as much for some information about her birth mother as for the next month's group session.

By the third monthly meeting, Susan realized that a few of the birth parents, adoptees or adoptive parents seemed to be veterans of other support groups, fluent in the lingo of twelve steps.

The wife of one birth father was advised by several people to "fake it until you make it," when she wasn't sure how to relate to his son from a teenage romance. The woman said she knew in her heart that she was somehow destined to be "family" to him but was still struggling with how to be with him.

One homemaker claimed to be shell shocked, and indeed she looked shaken, as she explained that she had never told her daughters that at their age she had lived for four months in an unwed mother's home before giving away a son, their brother. Her son had found her. The reunion had been going well but now he wanted to meet his sisters.

"You know the drill," said another birth mother, "keep it real." They both laughed ruefully at the AA reference.

One man who said he had been fighting demons of depression for decades explained the impact of his search and reunion. On the one hand, once he met his birth mother and a half-brother from his father's side, he felt more rooted than he had ever felt before in his life. His lifelong companion, insomnia, seemed to vanish.

On the other hand, the depression didn't completely lift. In fact, a biological aunt, his birth father's sister, had hung up the phone on him when he first contacted her, but then two years later when he reached out again welcomed him without reservation. She apologized for the earlier rebuff, explaining that she was bipolar. He could have finished her sentence when she alluded to that to explain that she "just wasn't in a good place then." The same depression that was alleviated partially by his reunion with his birth family came from their shared DNA.

At other times, members of this group really did finish each other's sentences. One adoptee described with anguish her mother's reaction to learning that she wished to search for her birth family.

Susan leaned forward as the woman said, "Once I met my birth mother and birth uncle, Mom even asked if I was still going to celebrate my birthday with her or whether I was going to celebrate it with them. Does she not want to celebrate my birthday with her own daughter anymore?"

As if on cue, five people said in unison, "Your adoptive mother is afraid of losing you." Most of the rest of the room smiled and nodded knowingly. The man to her right shook his head in mock despair at his adoptive mother.

Susan decided to go along when some of

the attendees asked her to join them as they headed over to a local pub for supper. Apparently this was part of the routine and someone had called ahead so there was already a row of tables pushed together to accommodate their number.

This was like entering a new subculture: like getting to know in-laws, or moving into a freshman dorm, or traveling overseas. She found herself alert to the unwritten rules: one woman correcting herself with "sorry, I meant to use an 'I' phrase," while a man chided another good naturedly with, "Did you really mean to give unsolicited advice?" The first one shook his head, no, and smiled with a shrug.

Her trip to East Asia was still months away but this meeting whetted her curiosity even more. First thing Monday morning she called Fred Kouyoumjian again. He counseled patience.

~

She clicked with one of the women she met, Faith, and they decided to meet over lunch later that week. Faith was an adoptee, too, but she'd "been in reunion" as the group called it, for almost eighteen years. She had waist length blonde hair and pulled it off well with shimmery earrings and trim, dark business clothes that workday.

After they had placed their orders and the waitress was walking away, Faith confessed that originally she chose not to meet her birth mother, "It's complicated. I let over three years go by before we actually met and held each other."

Susan didn't like hearing that. Had Faith been rejected by her birth mother? If her own did that, she would feel humiliated.

Faith seemed to read her mind, "Susan, we did meet and I'm glad she searched for me. The delay was because of a whole host of reasons. It's more common than you'd think. In my case, it's also that she'd married and moved to England."

Susan nodded, "I'm interested in your whole story. You'll get to that part when you get to that." It seemed like there were other parts of the search that were more important to her new friend than meeting that birth mother.

"When you're pregnant, just about everyone develops strange cravings, right? Mine were a little different from most because I didn't know any of my biological family. During my pregnancies my craving was to find out about the woman who had been pregnant with me."

Susan found herself nodding and feeling relief to hear someone say things she hadn't even been able to put a name to.

"Most states don't allow adoptees access to our original birth certificates so I couldn't find out my birth mother's name and ask her those kinds of questions."

Susan added, "Yet third parties with official titles can get access to your documents, Faith, right?"

Faith nodded, "It's creepy. They can, or at least to the non-medical records like adoption proceedings. I think with HIPAA you can't do any longer what one adoptee I met did. She used her birth name, which her adoptive parents knew and shared with her, to get the obstetric record from the maternity ward where she was born. In the end, she never met her birth mother but she at least got to read about her own birth."

Susan looked in Faith's eyes, "That's beautiful. I bet you wish you'd had that while you were pregnant. I wish I did."

"Yeah, it would have been nice to know something before my first one was born."

All this talk of records reminded Susan of her fear that a Thai nunnery might not have maintained that kind of repository. Maybe that was the reason Fred Kouyoumjian was taking so long.

Faith was spared that. "I had heard that the adoption agency that placed me with my parents kept good records and could give me more information about my first parents without giving out specific information that would identify them."

"What did you have to do to get it?" Susan asked.

"I had to send the adoption agency a written request and a fifty dollar fee to see the non-identifying information in my file. About five months later they gave me an appointment.

"Five months!" Susan gasped, "How far along were you by then?"

"Eight months. The girls kept me busy. Anyways," and she made a gesture as if waving the delay back into the past.

"That's a long time," Susan said, guessing at the reaction of her new friend. How much could she ask without sounding judgmental?

"I know," and answering the question Susan had refrained from asking, "and, no, I didn't push. That was the early days of search and reunion. I almost felt like I didn't deserve to know."

Susan nodded, "I know. I almost want to

call any delay or any lucky break 'fate' so I'm less responsible for the outcome."

"Because," Faith prompted.

"– Because, like you, I don't feel one hundred percent entitled," Susan realized they were on the same page.

Faith went back to telling her story, "I arrived at this very ornate Upper East Side entrance. I stood waiting in the front lobby for the social worker to come down. There were arches there, it was neo-gothic. Susan, I had seen these arches before when I accompanied my parents and grandmother for my sister's adoption and I still remembered them. I was only two and a half years old. It made that deep an impression."

"Gothic arches?" Susan wondered if her own senses retained memories of the sights or smells before her parents brought her home. She'd been to Thai restaurants, heard the wait staff speaking in their language, but all of it was foreign, nothing jogged lost memories.

Faith continued, "The social worker's soothing, sympathetic voice just annoyed me. That let me know I was bringing more emotion to that meeting than I wanted to." Faith laughed and Susan joined her, "Finally the social worker read me my information, and then she asked how I felt.

"I told this complete stranger that I felt like she'd just given me a wonderful Christmas present. There was so much there, facts about my biological relatives like height and hair color and similar interests, facts non-adoptees take for granted."

Susan listened and Faith continued, "It's amazing how intense it felt to have this. It was an awakening."

Susan was surprised, "Awakening? It took you by surprise?"

"Yes, there were two big surprises in the file. One was even information they kept from my adoptive parents: that my first father was part American Indian.

"Another surprise was that the social worker *thought* that *maybe* there was a recent letter from a biological relative in that file.

"'–Let me see it!!'" Faith imitated herself.

Then switching to a kind of spirit guide voice, she mimicked the social worker, "'–I'm afraid I can't, I would have to talk to the Birth Mother Department.'"

"'–Okay, I'll wait here.'"

"'–No, I can't do that now.'"

"'–But it is meant for me...'"

"'–Yes, I know that,'" the spirit guide voice continued, "'but our policy is that we do not allow adoptees to receive any correspondence from biological relatives the first time they come in here. We've decided that it's better for you to digest this initial information before you go any further.'"

"'–Then how do I get you to give me my mail?'"

"'–Well, when you're ready,'" she breathed, "'you send us a statement in writing that it's okay for you to be contacted by a birth mother.'" This, the social worker informed Faith, was to protect both her first mother's and her confidentiality.

Faith told Susan she sat back and looked at the social worker. They were about the same height, had the same level of education, even the same number of kids. They should have been equals. But the weird dynamics of the adoption system had given the social worker a power over another adult that was giddily absolute. It was fascinating in a frustrating kind of way.

Susan was still waiting to hear how Faith had pounded the table, or demanded to speak to the woman's supervisor. Faith reminded Susan that she actually took several months to digest the information from the adoption file and get back in touch with the social worker, "I now realize that the letter was mine and should have been forwarded to me, a legal adult, the day it arrived."

Susan noticed that Faith's voice seemed to waver more than her words.

Faith dropped character, and continued, "In defense of this control freak social worker," Faith paused at her own use of harsh language. Susan deliberately cocked her head to let Faith know she was there to listen through the story, no matter the pitch or color of emotions in the telling.

Faith continued, "I did find out later that this particular agency had been threatened in the past with lawsuits by adoptive parents so they have become particularly vigilant in documenting mutual consent in reunions between adult adoptees and first parents."

Faith might be getting at something more than just the professionals. Susan had never spoken about this before, but decided to try it out, "Even with the best of intentions, I think our adoptive parents, definitely my mother, are just as good at playing power games. I'm torn between feeling guilty for being curious and feeling like they're playing monkey-in-the-middle or mother-may-I when I tried to bring up the topic of adoption to try to get more information."

"But you've done it, Susan, when you pressed your mother for more information."

"I did, I guess. But it was exhausting to work up the courage."

"You just said the key word: 'courage'. Replace all those bad feelings with courage and you get what you and your family need, but you can do it with love in your heart for all the other players in adoption."

"Did you ever get the letter?"

"Yes, but it was dog eared by the time the agency forwarded it to me," Faith's voice still carried the tinges of anger and hurt they had caused her as she added, "keeping it a secret from me for five years, yet passing it around among staff social workers isn't protection of my confidentiality.

"That said, it's past. I've got it now," and Susan watched her pull an envelope out of her bag, "I deserve it. You deserve some kind of reunion, too. Having courage will make you powerful." Faith slid the letter across the table to Susan.

Susan took the delicate robin egg blue paper and saw its neat script. It occurred to her that this was a new kind of family heirloom.

Years later she wouldn't recall what either of them said during the rest of the lunch, but the letter itself with its lyrical prose was one that she would remember by heart after only one reading:

20 February 1988

Beloved Child,

I have written drafts for this letter–emotional, reasonable, doubtful. Now I shall just write to you...in the hope that there is a glimmer of desire on your part, as there is on mine, that we could meet–strangers united at some time.

I would dearly love to know who you are now....

Susan called Fred Kouyoumjian's line as soon as she got back to her office, but it went straight to voicemail.

~

At the fourth group meeting, things started out pleasantly enough. People talked about there being "good" meetings and "rough" meetings. At first this seemed like it would be a good one, several people passed old family photos around the group. Christine announced that another adoptive parents' group had joined them in lobbying the state assembly. Susan brought in a fruit loaf that everyone complimented. They finished it by the break.

After break the good meeting turned into a rough one. A man asked Susan from across the room what she expected she might find at the end of her search. At first she gave the obvious answer that she didn't know what to expect. He nodded but then persisted, asking if she had ever envisioned what her birth mother's back story—and therefore her own back story—might include.

She found herself tentatively cautioning the group that she only had a shred of the story now, so anything she might imagine was no more than just an imagining, a daydream. She was excited and her heart raced at discussing this with the circle of people who all shared a part in the tradition of adoption.

Its core was that her birth mother had stayed with nuns and the words for adoption she had picked up as a child. That's really all she had to weave from. She had never met a Buddhist nun, let alone visited a Buddhist nunnery, but in her mind's eye she transposed the Sisters of Charity retreat that one of the Christian sects maintained nearby. She also had what even strangers praised to her over the years: the generosity of birth mothers for helping childless couples, the selflessness of adoptive parents for giving a home to orphans.

She imagined a scared young girl, disappointed in love, fleeing to their comfort and charity in her hour of need. Or, she imagined before that, star crossed lovers forced apart by parents' machinations, both pledging undying love before parting at the gates of the cloister where her first mother would bear their lovechild in surroundings of kindness.

She imagined nuns attending her birth discreetly, padding along scrubbed floors carrying clean towels. She saw the decency of her birth mother and the sisters as they bathed and dressed her newborn form, and the altruism, the giving it up to God embodied in her mother's hallowed act of offering her for a childless couple. There was a basic faith in humanity behind the painful decision to relinquish her, yet to see the pregnancy through and give her life.

This is what Susan believed, although she was thoughtful enough to admit to herself and the group that reality might turn out to be different. When she finished, the circle remained silent, together reflecting on the back story she carried in her heart.

She added that she anticipated this reunion could reopen that time of grace for her birth mother, or so she hoped. It would reawaken quiet sorrow and loss for sure, but it might even lead her birth parents to reunite.

It might not, but perhaps her birth mother would somehow tell the nuns and they would reminisce together about the community of faith they had created that shepherded her into the world.

She studied the faces that looked back at her from around the group table for their reaction. Some were polite masks, but a few looked troubled.

Christine, the adoptive parent, spoke, "Susan, very often reunions don't live up to our expectations. All you can hope for is to find your truth. The truth may not turn out to be what you wanted, but at least now you will know it."

The adoptive mother who had brought her son's birth mother to the first meeting cleared her throat before adding gently, "I disagree slightly. It's good that you can put into words your hopes. I sincerely wish them for you. What you describe is truly beautiful and it's a reflection of the kind of good woman you are, and of how you choose to view people. But if the reunion with your birth mother falls short of it, at least you will be able to put into words what it is you have lost. Not just the loss of your birth family, but the loss of this specific vision of them. The vision may turn out to be true, but it may not."

Someone else interjected, "Would you be ready for that?" It was a man in his fifties who had been rejected angrily by his birth mother when he found her.

A young woman who had driven in from Paterson even reacted as though Susan had attacked her, "I feel like you didn't hear a word I said. Don't you think I'd like to be sitting here talking about grace?"

The facilitator said, "Keyshia, I don't think Susan was negating your experience."

Earlier Keyshia shared that her birth mother had probably been bipolar and living on the street. Before Keyshia got the chance to meet her, according to the police report, a drug dealer shot her birth mother in the head.

The facilitator who was an adoptee continued, "You wanted better for your birth mother, and before you searched, you were able to imagine better for her than turned out to be. I think we all need to respect where each person is on their journey. You are at a different stage than Susan is. I think what you both share is a good will toward your birth mothers."

Susan mumbled, "I'm sorry" and Keyshia shook her head, "Baby girl, you were fine. It's just all my stuff. I hope your birth mother is okay."

Susan regretted having been so open with someone like them in the room.

As she started to feel confused, Faith reached across the corner of the table and took her hand, "don't borrow tomorrow's trouble. You'll cross that bridge when you come to it. Enjoy anticipating this trip."

5 THE OTHER WOMAN
1990

By the fifth adoption triad meeting some reunion stories began to cast her fears in stark relief. There was a woman who made most people in the group uncomfortable and they all seemed to know her already. As she started to speak another woman even stood up and left, making an aside like "I can't sit through this."

Something was off about the speaker's demeanor. The woman was burly with a thick neck and high cheekbones and a heavy brow that was framed by thin gray hair pulled back severely in a bun. She wore a dark cotton shirt dress and kept beefy arms crossed across her ample middle as she began to talk in a low voice but very quickly.

Susan leaned in and noticed she wasn't the only one having trouble following the woman's monologue.

Something about "the doctor tied her

down".

Something about "the angels sawed her body in half and then Beelzebub crushed her".

She "wanted to find the missing babe that Beelzebub had stolen" before they locked her "in a tower for a hundred years until creatures rose from the ocean to draw another babe from my mouth and carry the child out to sea."

She said she "never forgot them and would have fed them tea" if only she could have kept her "babes".

The facilitator gamely asked her where the babies had been born.

She replied, "in Hades."

Okay, that wasn't going to work.

"Who brought you here today?"

The woman gave the name of a local group home and during a break it looked like the facilitator approached her to copy down additional information.

At the next session, the delusional woman was missing. One of the men asked about her anyway.

It happened that a social worker in attendance had accompanied her to a medical checkup and learned that the woman was indeed a multipara, someone who had given birth more than once. In her mental confusion, there was some truth.

She was indeed a birth mother and had carried and lost at least two children whom she still remembered in the maelstrom of her hallucinations.

Susan shuddered. How had such a woman been impregnated? Twice. Who had taken her children, where were they now?

Then another question rose from the back of her mind, leaving her physically nauseous. Was something like this waiting in the form of her own birth mother? What kind of roots would she gain if the family history included madness? How would she come home after the twenty hour flight from Thailand to tell David, and then be forced with him to wait decades to see if her tiny Lily lost her mind, too? Might her birth mother even be dangerous? There was a certain tight wound menace, barely repressed, in the racing, soft spoken rants of the amazon birth mother.

Nuns took in her unwed birth mother. Did they take in the mentally disturbed? Was the convent a kind of grassroots, faith based psychiatric facility? Her birth father, whom she had imagined as a sensitive suitor, was he instead another patient? What of that sensation she herself had of her birth family expressed as "phantom limb pain"–was that a sign of a febrile brain? She had to admit now that it did sound crazy and until coming to this group she'd never heard anyone else talk about living life as though in exile the way that football team captain had at the first meeting.

She pushed her worries to the back of her mind and listened as the next group member shared his story.

His was artisanal blonde hair cut diagonally across his forehead and he had a lean frame that one would describe as crisp for the military. He had reached out to meet his birth mother once he found out a neighbor of his adoptive grandparents had actually brokered the adoption. She had known the birth mother, a young teenager at the time. The girl had managed to keep her pregnancy a secret through the school year and then stayed indoors all vacation until he was born at home at the end of summer, the neighbor told him.

He visited the lonely neighbor a few times, using his most practiced charm. He finally persuaded her to share the name and former address of his birth mother.

It wasn't long before he located her at a

hospital where she lay with fourth stage breast cancer. He explained to the group that he felt it was fated that he located her just in time. He could thank her for giving him life. He could hold her hands, and look into her eyes.

These thoughts ran through his mind as he rode the elevator during visiting hours up to the cancer ward. He bought a bouquet of flowers for her outside the hospital gift shop, and held the elevator door open as he chivalrously allowed the other passengers to leave first. It gave him a few extra moments to compose himself before he stepped out into the hallway to meet her for the first and he told himself, depending on her condition, last time.

She recognized him immediately, he could tell by the look in her eyes. He stepped across the doorway and introduced himself, mentioning as confirmation the date of his birth.

But her eyes took on steeliness as she said, "Don't know you."

Undeterred, he extended his arm with the flowers, and then drew it back realizing she would be too weak to take it, let alone rise to place it in a vase. He laid them on a table near her bed. He repeated his birthdate and added the town where he was born.

Her face crumpled, he expected next to

see her eyes well with tears, but instead she whispered something from twisted lips.

"I-I couldn't hear you," he said softly to his birth mother.

This time she spat out the words, "I don't want to deal with this. Go away. I don't want to know you."

He rose and backed out so quickly that he bumped into a chrome rolling table on his way out. He didn't remember the walk, half sprint, back to his car in the parking garage. He told the rapt group that he had to wait many minutes before turning on the ignition because his hands were shaking.

"A week later, I finally got the courage to try one more time, but this time by phone. The hospital receptionist told me there was no patient there by that name. I guess she died. That really did turn out to be the first and last time I met my birth mother. I wasn't ready for that."

Susan now wrestled with a new thought. Instead of the wildness and tragedy of meeting a mentally ill birth parent, what if hers was simply cold? She could hire a detective, take time away from work and her family, buy an expensive plane ticket they couldn't really afford, hire an interpreter, travel by God knows what kind of transportation to the middle of who knows where, only to have a door slammed in her face.

It would hurt, it would be humiliating, and surely David or anyone else she confided in would think to themselves that she should never have gone in the first place.

Yet another phantasm entered her thoughts. She reminded herself of Keyshia. What if instead of seeing a living, breathing birth mother, even with fourth stage cancer, what if her birth mother was already dead. All that effort for nothing.

What if she, Susan, were the sorrowful secret her mother had hoped to take with her to her grave? Did she have a right to impose herself, what if her birth mother hadn't wanted prying neighbors to know? She would gain nothing, but only stir up things that that woman might have wanted to let lie. She began to doubt that she felt worthy enough to do this search, to hope for a reunion.

She wasn't thinking about laws that still prevented adults from having access to their own adoption information. In the abstract, she felt that all the decent people fighting for adoptee rights were fighting the good fight.

Her misgivings were something more

personal. When it came down not to a principle of equal rights to information for adoptees, but to she herself asking questions and upsetting her parents, possibly a family she hadn't even met in Thailand, she held her middle.

She looked gratefully at the cup of ginger ale she had poured at the opening of the meeting. It was two hours old and her mother once told her flat soda pop was the best antidote for upset stomach.

~

The night before the sixth month's group meeting, Faith and Susan spoke over the phone after dinner and Faith filled in more of her story. David put Lily to bed while Susan withdrew to his office and closed the door behind her.

"Eventually the agency reached my birth mother with my contact info and she called me," Faith explained.

Susan thought about this a minute, "I guess that's not something you expect with an international adoption. You don't expect to get a phone call and you don't expect the agency to help."

"Well, it varies from agency to agency, some are more conscientious than others. The states that let individual attorneys or ob-gyns act as adoption brokers have zip quality control on records preservation, from what I've heard."

Susan was also thinking about the phone call itself, "The nice thing about her writing you the letter, and then calling first, you know you won't get rejected."

Susan wondered again if after locating her own birth mother she just might meet a slammed door. She shook that off to refocus on Faith and asked, "What was it like getting that phone call?"

"For me, surprise or confusion. My adoptive mother actually happened to be visiting and reading to the girls. She told me once, afterward, that she had thought she was supportive of my following through and contacting my first mother. But driving home later, she felt like she'd been dropped in cement. It was the first time she'd ever really believed in such a thing as the subconscious."

Susan nodded and waited for Faith to continue.

"It was like the telephone call from my first mother reopened this dark closet of adoption. It let in a single ray of light that refracted with very different hues off my mother, my children's father, my children and me."

Susan debated telling Faith about David's

father, then decided: not yet.

"To start with, my first mother's artistic career was more of a going proposition than her own so my mother wondered if she hadn't squandered her energies by raising kids."

Susan was incredulous, "And she was cold enough to actually say that to you, her own daughter?"

"I wasn't hearing it that way, it felt like a conversation woman to woman. I don't think I'd actually say something like that to my own kids. Being a parent is a choice but I guessed it seemed to her like this first mother was having her cake and eating it, too: an artistic career, plus a daughter and grandkids.

"Did she ever deal with it?" Susan asked, wondering how Mom would react.

"I know she was moved by something my birth mother wrote to her. She sent it in a silkscreened card."

"What did she write to your mother?" Susan couldn't imagine any words or picture that a birth mother could send without scaring the b-jazzies out of her mother.

"– that no reunion would give her back the holidays, the little girl party dresses or the years together that an adoptive mother got to enjoy."

At this Susan, for the first time, began to imagine what her own birth mother would feel looking at her as an adult, with only photographs left of Susan's childhood, "You're making me want to run home to my daughter. Did you tell yours?"

"Yes, I did, in the interests of clearing away the shadows. My eldest daughter had an interesting response. She was almost six and wanted to know why her grandma couldn't have me in her tummy. My mother told her it got broken. She wanted to know why that other mommy had given me away. I told her that back then the rules were different and if you weren't married you weren't allowed to keep your baby. She wanted to know if my finding my first mother meant her grandparents couldn't be her grandparents anymore. I assured her that her grandparents were still her grandparents."

Susan laughed.

Then Faith continued more quietly, "A few times since then we've caught her threatening her younger sister with 'You're adopted,' or 'If you don't give that back I'm gonna put you up for adoption.' It was new to me, not something you say if you've grown up in a family formed by adoption."

Susan felt her heart sink. She'd been

thinking about herself and reverberations with David, and getting Lily a medical history. It hadn't occurred to her until then that a reunion might cause Lily pain someday.

Faith continued, "It honestly unnerved me but other moms told me it's a normal taunt."

Susan herself appreciated having non-adopted friends as reality checks for what was "normal"–especially last year when she was pregnant. Her non-adopted friends congratulated her on being spared their own mothers' pregnancy and labor war stories. Detailed accounts of varicose veins, swollen ankles, sciatica, preeclampsia, gestational diabetes, backache, sore gums, hair loss, weight gain, cravings, and dizzy spells.

There was a touch of wistfulness–or relief–in the way those new grandmothers, some postmenopausal, lingered lovingly over every gruesome detail. It made Susan feel a fleck of guilt toward her mother like the startling cold feel of the winter's first snowflake.

As a young woman, her mother had probably heard all these same stories from her childbearing friends, and been stung by every complaint. It was guilt, or sympathy, that allowed Susan to endure her mother's grandmotherly onslaughts.

Yet it did put Susan in mind of a scene from the summer she turned thirteen.

She had been getting dressed one morning when she saw a drop of blood on her panties. So this was it: just like the sanitary napkin movie they watched in sixth grade. It must have been the late 1970s and the homeroom teacher carefully taped construction paper over the window in the hall door so the boys couldn't peek in. Once the movie was over and the fluorescent lights came back on, the girls were still blinking as they were handed pink and blue cardboard boxes of feminine napkins.

Susan had never felt as prepared and grownup in her life as the day she pulled one of those boxes out from under her bed and ripped open the cardboard tab. After sliding the filmy paper ends of the pad into metal clips that dangled like innocent pixie tails from a white elastic belt (once self-adhesive pads were invented no one used those old metal and elastic contraptions anymore except in maternity wards). She slipped the twisty elastic belt over her knees, her thighs and finally her hips.

Supergirl.

Then she hid the box, the stained

underpants, even the coiled cardboard tab, under her bed and got a fresh pair of panties and, yes, stockings. Today was definitely a skirt day. Besides EVERYONE would know she'd gotten IT if she wore pants.

Susan remembered sitting back down on her bed to untangle her stockings and thinking: this is mine.

I'll never ever really be sad again because I'll always have this magic inside me, I'll always be able to make a period and– And the thought stopped there, victim of an ugly head on collision with a wall of guilt.

She never finished the thought until now two decades later, as the mother of Lily, "I'll always be able to make a period–and babies."

She would never take it for granted though, "I swear that I get more carried away than other mothers do about the similarity between their babies and them or their husbands or partners. They like it, sure, but they take it in stride."

"Right! Me, too," Faith exclaimed, "and," Faith leaned forward, "you know, I think I learned as much about my adoptive family as I did about my first family from Search and Reunion."

It was an observation that Susan could

completely relate to, "and pregnancy also teaches you a lot about your family, too, in that it could open up, I don't know, stuff about reproduction. I don't know."

Faith sighed with recognition, "My mom had to have a hysterectomy like yours. I think that phone call stirred up memories from that time. During her recovery, the hospital had her room with a woman who had just had a baby!"

"That's cruel," Susan responded, "that's just sick."

Faith nodded, "Back then you stayed a full week. So I imagine my mom, I never asked for details, but she must have had a full week of that new mother's parade of visitors, opening layette presents, flowers, balloons."

And it cut both ways. If her own mother had to weather a hysterectomy in silence, it broke as a storm when she discovered her daughter's blossoming.

Susan managed to keep her menstruation a secret from her mother a full three months. This was the first time her young life had taken her somewhere her beloved mother couldn't follow. She couldn't shake the feeling of possessing something magical, joyful, but deeply, skulkingly guilty.

She knew this was irrevocably true when Masha found out and confronted her. The daughter gave a confession, subdued, but inside Susan was also raging that she must be made to feel guilty, horrified that her body, something beyond her conscious control, could awaken this mystifying jealousy in her mother. For even though Masha's words were not accusatory her face, her tense torso, her tone of voice were.

That was the first time Susan realized that adults could say things they thought they meant but didn't really mean at all.

"Susan, I don't know why you couldn't have come to me. I'm always open and honest with you."

"I wasn't BEING dishonest, Mom. Why do you have to know everything?"

Her mother's voice grew higher and staccato.

"I just want you to be able to come to me with any problem."

"Nothing's wrong. You're supposed, I mean, I'm supposed to get my period."

They both let that sentence float in the air.

Her mother's hysterectomy had saved her life in the second year of her marriage, but it had also marked the end of her own menstruation. Her mother Masha turned around and walked to her own room. A few minutes later Susan heard sobbing.

"Mom?"

"It's just sad to see my little baby turn into a woman."

That wasn't it. Or at least not all of it. Mom wasn't a sentimental crier.

Later, she was dry eyed at Susan's graduation and wedding. They both must have made a silent pact that day because neither mother nor daughter brought up menstruation, ovulation, or pregnancy again. It was more taboo than sex.

It was like discussing death.

6 COMPASSION
1968

Masha drifted back to the first year of her marriage. That may have been her last simply happy year, what folklorists called an Acadian interlude because it seemed every day was summer and every sky was blue. All of the coming of age struggles, real and imagined, had been resolved with this one nuptial knot. All love songs made good sense and none were trite.

Even though Al and Masha were beyond the early intoxication of the first few months when he seemed flawless and her every gesture, every glance or phrase enthralled him, still anything the universe had forgotten now seemed spoken for and resolved.

She had fretted about whether the guests from Cleveland would attend. The rabbi assured her they would, and they did. One single girlfriend came up with an achingly complex explanation for why she cancelled last minute and even that felt like a blessing. They drifted apart eventually anyway and given that future, how much easier to have her not be in any of the wedding photographs.

Masha, in the course of scouring stores with her maid of honor for the right beads for the bridal veil, discovered and fell in love with what would become a lifelong hobby, scrapbooking.

The arts and crafts store that carried the opalescent beads they were seeking also carried all textures of paper and fabric, stickers like dollhouse accessories in their intricate detail. She bought a wedding album as well as some self-adhesive metallic paper borders for wedding photos. That wedding album would become her first scrapbook.

There were more organic discoveries: the wedding gown made her skin look contrastingly dark; a figure shaping bodice with underwire brassiere was flattering; she felt a surprising comfort when she looked at one framed picture of her own parents' wedding and realized that she had grown into her mothers' young bride's face.

Masha and Al planned to hold off on starting a family until after their first anniversary. In the second year of their marriage the unimagined began to unfold. She bled between her periods. They were delighted because she had read that this could be a sign of a fertilized embryo implanting in her uterus: she might be pregnant!

At her ob-gyn appointment the news was different.

Apparently there was something doctors and midwives looked for called Hagar's sign where the edges of the uterus soften. This wasn't happening. They scraped some cells to send to a lab and promised to call her with results. They also took a blood sample from her arm and it showed she was not pregnant.

When the sad call came from her doctor, he asked her to come in as soon as possible. The news was even worse than not having conceived. She had cancer. Even these many years later Masha could remember the conversation in his office word for word.

"What kind of cancer, Dr. Arthur?"

"Cancer of the uterus. But luckily we'll have caught it early. We won't know definitively until we go in for a look, but it probably hasn't spread to your ovaries or your abdominal cavity so we can take care of it cleanly."

"Oh, thank you," she said politely, "What does taking care of it cleanly entail?"

"We'll have to remove the diseased uterus, a hysterectomy."

He paused before continuing, "We'll follow up with radiation. If we don't need to remove your ovaries that will mean you won't suffer the effects of early menopause."

Masha, still in her twenties, wasn't sure what the effects of menopause were. She did understand that a hysterectomy meant no babies but she did have one hope if the cancer hadn't spread far.

"Dr. Arthur, can we put off the hysterectomy until after Al and I have a baby?"

He replied very slowly, "You could try and have a baby, but you won't live to raise him. He won't have a mother."

The meaning of his words seemed to spread through her physically before her mind could fully grasp them. She felt cold, terribly cold, and wished Al, or her mother, someone were here to warm her, to wake her up and tell her it was only a nightmare, it wasn't real. But his voice continued.

"I will have the nurse schedule you for the eighth and explain what you need to prepare and what your husband can bring to the recovery room. This is as soon as we can schedule the surgery and I recommend that you not delay.

Nurse Cavanaugh will be in in a minute. Is there anything else?"

She looked up at him. He seemed quite sure and final.

"No, nothing else. Thank you very much, Dr. Arthur."

The eighth was two weeks away.

~

She started crossing off each day in the calendar, to mark time until the surgery. Otherwise those two weeks were a blur. Telling Al. Telling her mother. Deciding which friends to confide in, and which friends not. She continued making Al breakfast, packing his lunch, and planning and executing a beautiful dinner each day. She herself had lost her appetite.

Oh, she was so scared, her hands shook sometimes. The restlessness she felt, it was like waiting for an execution; she dreaded the wait only slightly less than the hour itself.

To lose her womb. What else was there? It represented everything she dreamed of, save Al. She adored him. To have his child was entwined with his marriage proposal, her acceptance of it, their wedding night, their saving for a family home this past year.

She caught herself avoiding the playground when she walked back from the market. She couldn't look at those young mothers chatting happily together as they watched their children. Boys in caps. Girls in bonnets and maryjanes. Her future no longer held this.

Mostly she cried. She cried with fear, she rocked with disbelief. She cried with an inconsolable broken heart. And then when she stopped crying, it wasn't like the cleansing tears of her childhood. Even when the jag was over, the cancer was not, and the scheduled surgery was not, and the nightmare was not. There was no longer any such thing as "having a good cry".

She remembered knowing vaguely the Victorian allusions to "women's troubles". Suddenly the vagueness behind the phrase was all stripped away: women died of this! A best outcome was a bleak future with no children's laughter, no little faces to scrub at the end of the day, no one to teach prayers to.

Masha felt like the lowest wretch when she watched Al, brave Al, walk off to work each morning, back straight. He was losing all this, too, because of her. She caught herself paging frantically through cookbooks midafternoon. She might find the most delightful recipe, a soufflé, perhaps a minced meat pie so savory that somehow it would lighten the pain that he must be carrying inside, too. He carried it because of her and her failed body.

What would be the best outcome for him? If she lived, she would doom him to a childless future, too. He was meant to be a father. If she died on the operating table, at least he could have a second chance with someone else. She hated herself for allowing her thoughts to turn this dark.

The morning they were to go to the hospital, Al dressed up. That noble, gentle man. He held her close to his heart as they stood in their room, then scooped up her suitcase and deliberately made his tread light on the stairs. She hesitated so he paused at the landing and looked back up at her.

"Come on, Mash-eleh! The sooner we get you there, the sooner I get you back home where you belong!"

She couldn't help laughing through her tears. It came out sounding like a cough. They held hands walking out to the car.

~

The doctor was right, the cancer hadn't

spread beyond the surgical target. In those days many people thought cancer was a death sentence so she told herself she was quite the survivor for having lived through it.

She was alive, but as she convalesced and returned to her normal activities over the next months she had a new symptom. Masha began feeling a lump in her throat, or rather, a tight, choking sensation. Dr. Arthur could find nothing.

Finally, after six months when her final follow-up checkup for the surgery and cancer turned up nothing unusual, Nurse Cavanaugh suggested it might be due to the emotional toll of the ordeal and to go to her priest. Masha thanked her and went to her rabbi. He was the same thirtyish rabbi who had married them.

His kind eyes and the worn, but comfortable look of his book lined office made her feel like she could talk to him in a way she could not with her doctor, or even Al.

They spent an hour talking before Rabbi Safer did something unusual. He asked her to recite Psalm 126 and then to sit quietly "with" the feeling in her throat. He told her not to seek explanations or to judge what came to mind, this was not a Day of Reckoning, but just to notice with compassion for herself what emotions she felt. He looked away and somewhat shyly explained that the Hebrew root for the word compassion, *rachamim*, was the same as that for the word womb, *rechem*.

She shuddered a little. He doesn't pull any punches, she thought. Cuts right to the chase.

He glanced at her and added, "It's okay to cry."

She felt a mild confusion, she hadn't been particularly sad when she walked into his office. In fact, she'd tried to set a light tone for the whole conversation, a proactive, problem solving tone.

He explained that he was a pretty poor amateur psychotherapist and found over the years that the stories behind many of his congregants' pains, worries, hates and nightmares were too changeable, sometimes too internally contradicting for him personally to be able to interpret them. But, he leaned forward, he could still feel when pain or worry or joy were real.

He did know a counseling center he could give her the number for if she wanted a psychotherapist. She thanked the rabbi politely and left his office but felt unanswered, restless.

Later that afternoon, with some tea on the table in front of her, she did open the Hebrew Bible, the *Chumash*, and fingered through its rice paper pages until she found Psalm 126.

> *When the LORD turned against the captivity*
> *of Zion, we were like them that dream.*
> *Then was our mouth filled with laughter,*
> *and our tongue with singing: then said*
> *they among the heathen,*
> *The LORD hath done great things for them.*
> *The LORD hath done great things for us;*
> *whereof we are glad.*
> *Turn again our captivity, O LORD, as the*
> *streams in the south.*
> *They that sow in tears shall reap in joy.*
> *He that goeth forth and weepeth, bearing*
> *precious seed, shall doubtless return with*
> *rejoicing, bringing his sheaves with him.*

"They that sow in tears shall reap in joy, He that goes forth and weeps, bearing precious seed, shall doubtless come again with rejoicing," she read it first silently and then out loud without feeling much, perhaps distracted by the growing tightening in her throat.

She pushed the open book away and closed her eyes. It was hard for Masha to remember the rest of that afternoon in any kind of linear way. For a good while she sat there feeling bored and annoyed. She began to drift and daydream, of what she no longer remembered.

She saw her own long dead grandmother and felt such disappointment in herself. She would never have the chance to be the warm grandmother her beloved *bubbe* had been.

Then that story drifted away, or, she wasn't sure anymore if that was the real or the only reason she felt disappointed. Then she wasn't sure if she was the embodied object of disappointment or if she just felt sad, something having been lost. The undoubted possibilities of their first year of marriage?

She began to float into a fantasy again; she was wearing something clingy and see-through and–rain boots. Then it started to rain on and on and on. By and by each tear shaped raindrop began to seem redundant and she was losing interest in the daydream when from just the periphery of her vision she saw a wall of water coming toward her.

At first it lifted her up gently as it washed over her garden rows. She saw that the garden had been planted near a ledge and even as the dark churning water lifted her higher, it was also lifting her toward a neck breaking drop off a cliff into the ocean below. When she screamed the waves filled her mouth and an undertow seemed to clamp tight and pull down on her torso. It hurt to gasp and then she heard the thunder of the waves drowned out by an eerily human howl.

She opened her eyes and snapped her head back upright off her shoulders. She breathed, and held the edge of the table, and when she saw her drained tea cup pushed away from her place, she realized the howl was her own.

Now her shoulders were shaking and she let out a quieter sound, a sob. There was both disappointment and rage in her sob. Then something shifted and it contained sorrow, then sorrow and tenderness, then a calm longing. The sobbing faded and she let out a laugh from low in her throat.

Then she sighed and she realized the familiar tightness in her throat was gone.

She even spoke out loud, "No," with a smile when she realized it had shifted to her arms.

Maybe the tenseness in her arms came from struggling with the deluge as she dozed. Or maybe her arms ached now for any infant that needed them.

"My child," she corrected herself feeling a wave of protectiveness.

She looked over at the counter where Al

had already placed an application for an adoption agency in the city. He said it was one of the best and a week ago he'd caught the subway there from the diamond district on his lunch break. She had let the papers sit there untouched.

She scraped her chair back on the linoleum and reached over to look at the agency's brochure. Rows of metal nursery cribs, a close-up of a sleeping infant wrapped in a blue blanket and wearing a soft baseball cap. Another with laughing blue eyes and a wisp of blonde hair tied with a pink bow.

"Cute," she thought to herself. It was a playful word she hadn't let herself think for any baby in the months of recovering from her hysterectomy. She smiled quietly and repeated, "Cute."

That night they sat at the table with the adoption application. She stopped at the section where you could choose sex, preferred eye color and probable hair color. Anyone would have picked blonde and blue eyed, especially since Masha herself had that coloring. She looked across the kitchen table at Al.

"It's kind of amazing we can pick so precisely. Are there really that many babies out there?"

"It seems so. Remember they said that the state has so many, that after this one we're welcome to adopt another."

"After a reasonable time, I would imagine. I'd like them to be two years apart if we get a second one."

"Masha?"

"What, honey?"

"You know how when I was a bachelor they sent me a few times to Thailand to visit gem exporters?"

"Yes, I remember. How could I forget? I'm glad they have you back working at the 47th Street store. I missed you travelling so far, no matter how beautiful you say it is."

"Sure. Well, Masha, what with us not having a child and all, they may have me visit again before they shift to new African sources—we're developing relationships there. Wouldn't it be swell if you came along? Get you out of the house."

"Thailand?" she considered it a minute.

"Ooh, that would be fun, and," she added ruefully, "there's nothing really holding me at home."

He reached across and grabbed her hand, "Enough of that. There will be someone keeping you at home soon enough. That's part of the plan."

"Oh?"

"Masha, Thailand is a poor country, despite the gem trade. I remember hearing about an orphanage right in Bangkok. The children have big brown eyes, so friendly. Maybe we could find you your own little girl."

Masha held her breath, "You're serious? Of course, you're serious. We would be doing something fine, taking a child from an orphanage. There are plenty of other people for American babies. We could help a little Siamese orphan."

Al lowered his voice, "Here's what I've heard. There are even some of them, it's not discussed much, but there's even some who have American GIs for fathers, what with the Viet Nam war and all."

Masha knew to lower her eyes but not what to say.

He continued, "I know, it's not something you bring up but there they are. We don't need to decide now. You come with me to Bangkok, my contacts can arrange for us to visit, and once we're there we can look at all the babies."

Masha searched Al's eyes. He seemed genuinely excited talking about this. Maybe everything would be happy after all.

She began to think out loud, "I wonder if we wouldn't just know when we see the right one. I'd want a baby as young as possible, then she'd really be ours. To think, so helpless with no mother, the poor thing. Oh, Al, when can we go?"

7 COREA
1988

If Susan had hoped David would do anything more than watch Lily so she could attend the search meetings, she was bitterly disappointed. She wondered how long it would take for David to bring up his father.

David's mother had raised him alone in the fishing village of Corea, Maine, after his dad walked out. His dad had been running the family store and David's mother, Aliza, struggled to keep it going for a few years after he left. In a slow relentless process though, Aliza was forced to close it, sell it, pay off suppliers, and then find work, eventually waiting tables.

The humor and the anger from David's childhood still seemed so fresh. It felt like the ambitious, rootless pose that New Yorkers called attitude, transplanted north to the rural, salt stung coast. He could still make people laugh with his merciless reenactments of scenes where the unsuspecting person from away drove up to ask a native for directions to the village's only diner–the very one where his mom waitressed.

Tourists were always driving up, drawn by the peculiar name and by the famous sherbet colors of the fishing boats in Corea's harbor. David and the other locals used to tell them to order kimchee with the clam chowder.

David's mom could only smile and explain with mock irritation to the tourist, "Those boys have been pulling your leg, I guess. The name Corea's taken from the Korean people in the Orient wanting freedom from the Chinese and Japanese. But I don't actually think a real Korean's ever as much as set a foot in this village. Same thing with the town of Poland further aways, it's a name taken from the hymnal, 17th century England. Not a soul from Poland has ever been there either as far as anyone knows."

Then she'd bring them over some tapioca pudding with nutmeg–on the house.

David's angry stories were more begrudgingly retold. In fact, for the first couple months of courtship David seemed to Susan like a cipher. He dissolved out of reach whenever she asked about his childhood. He drifted away beyond hard walls when they started talking about the future. Though bedazzling with energy, life, passion, he was like an old time apparition. It was as if his feet never trod the earth, that he vanished too quickly, or left no reflections.

~

The first time she saw him outside of class was one Sunday in the campus student lounge. He was captain of their Division I lacrosse team.

"He's looking at you, Suzie," her roommate nudged.

"Probably one of those jocks who spends four years, or maybe the rest of their lives, being arrogant jerks," Susan decided to forget him and turned her eyes back to her Clashing Myths in German Civilization notes.

"Then he'd be taking a gut class, not," gesturing at the books and CDs on the table in front of them, "not anything that requires you to listen to all eight hours of Wagner's *Ring des Niebelungen*. Herr Hansen is a sadist."

"Please don't plant any unwanted S & M images of Professor Hansen in my mind," Susan wanted to get off this subject, "Remember for the exam the opera ends on an unresolved E minor."

"Excuse me, I'm thinking that would tie into Nietzsche's contention in 'The Tragedy of

Wagner' that Wagner was using music, in this case the unresolved E, to create longing and unrealizable expectations in his audiences." It was David himself, "Do you think that's reading too much into it?"

Susan found herself answering the jock who was now crouching down so they didn't have to strain to look up at him, "No, I think you're right. Wagner meant it to be manipulative."

David's dark red hair had a slight wave to it, and he was one of those people who had eyes that managed to pull off both intelligent and kind at the same time. But looks could be deceiving, Susan reminded herself. He seemed to sense the chill she was giving off. He turned and was now answering a question her roommate had thrown at him. As if it were the most natural thing in the world, the three of them ended up studying Clashing Myths in German Civilization together.

After a while Susan had to admit without even seeing him on the field, why he would have been chosen team captain. From his broad, relaxed shoulders to his pleasantly deep voice, there was something reassuring about being with him. He came across as book strong but not pretentious, athletic but not muscle bound. Most amazing of all, when her friend went to get a Tab to bring back to their room, David asked Susan if she would like to meet up again later for supper.

She found herself answering, "Yes."

But her handsome David only materialized for good the foggy morning they arrived in Corea to meet his mother. That village seemed truly otherworldly, perched on a crook in the rough granite coast of the western Atlantic. It took a lot of back roads to get there until the faded grey asphalt rose over a hill above the town harbor. Down below, mooring markers bounced on the waves like lost beach balls, fluorescent pinks, neon oranges, glowing yellows. The lobster boats themselves bobbed up and down behind the markers, facing upwind like stout hearted sailors as thick fog blew into the harbor from off the swells of the open ocean. Puffs of fog obscured and then unveiled the famous colors of the Corean boats: coral cabins, aqua sterns, baby blue bows, lavender rudders and turquoise helms.

David and Susan went on to the white clapboard house where his mother still lived. A clean, spare house, a clean spare woman with short silver hair. She had taken two days off from her waitressing to spend time with her son, and to get to know the exotic looking girl he had brought home with him.

~

David and Susan woke up early their first morning in Corea and went for a walk along the post road near the shore. Each clearing and each lowering of the road revealed a new scene that seemed an artful iteration of vistas they had seen only moments before. Nature was painting variations on a theme: high blue heaven above, and below that across the harbor distant dark spruce stands, and below that light green salt marsh broken with the summer-tumbles of miniature wild roses, bayberry bushes and meadowsweet, and below that glacier traced granite ledges. They had been brought from some distant lava flow far away and long ago to hem each scene along the fresh, briny foam of the Atlantic Ocean.

Seabirds crisscrossed between heaven, earth and sea stitching together these visual patches into an aural quilt. Their cries stayed in the collective memory as surely as the primeval sound of the surf: the clear throated call of seagulls, the near silent swish of circling osprey, the ululating cackles shared between bobbing loons, the languorous flap of the occasional heron as it unfolded it six foot wingspan for flight, its wake only a quiet splash in widening concentric circles on the water's surface.

Susan and David took this same walk around the cove again later at dusk. When they reached the other side of the small harbor and stood looking back across at the fishing village, the last rays of the sun played across the fishing piers. Slices of granite ledges lined the shoreline making the land look corrugated. The fading light caught the quartz, mica and feldspar in the granite as it held up the thin green coverlet of turf above the becalmed harbor. Quiet waves lapped dark or light against the pilings and ledges depending on the angle of the light.

David pointed out it was low tide. The cove encircling the harbor had emptied, and granite boulders appeared like abstract benches or chairs or tables. Each furnishing was laid with clusters of yellow and brown seaweed that were themselves set with the clinging shells of thick, white dog whelks and tinier periwinkles.

Susan noted with amusement that their spiraling shells were crosshatched with more varieties of plaid than known in the homeland of this coastline's early Scottish settlers. David, walking along beside her, laughed out loud.

And then suddenly the sky tumbled and she felt David's hands grab her back and upper arm just in time to keep her head from hitting one of those boulders. Her legs and butt were already firmly sucked into the gray clay that was the basin of the cove. She reached her hand out and got a fistful of cold, slippery rockweed. David was beginning to pull her out and as she straightened a tiny cascade of periwinkles rolled off her shoulder. She could feel the cold of the clay up the back of her T-shirt and saw both her legs sheathed in smooth gray up to her waist.

"Creature from the Corea lagoon," moaned Susan, "Thank you."

"Don't mention it. Prettiest creature this lagoon has ever seen."

"I'm checking into a hotel. I can't go back looking like this; your mom's kitchen is spotless."

"She cleaned it for your visit. Let's head home."

He was being such a gentleman. To this day, Susan didn't know what possessed her, but she took the rockweed she was still clutching in her hand and let fly. It hit him squarely in the chest with a sound like spaghetti.

"Goodness," and before he even wiped the stunned look off his face, David had expertly sailed the clump at one of her mud-encased legs.

Good game face, thought Susan. And also: he must be avoiding getting dirt on what little left of me is clean. Thoughtful reflexes.

Soon both of them were pulling fistfuls of seaweed from barnacled rocks along the low tide mark and hurling them at each other. Some missed, some made their target, each left Susan and David laughing harder than the one before. All the while the wet clay bottom forced them to lift their knees high in exaggerated steps.

When they finally clomped up to his mother's kitchen door, Aliza commanded them to stay in the yard and hose down their feet while she went to fetch clean towels. When she returned she deadpanned, "The Bible warns about creatures with feet of clay, but seeing as you seem to be scrubbing up nicely, I'll let you back in," and then held the screen door open for them.

About once a month David's relatives went to synagogue in Bangor together where the pews seemed filled with childhood Sunday school buddies, cousins, aunts and uncles. This Sabbath they stared at Susan with curiosity before remembering themselves and nodding or smiling a greeting.

Later, after he had introduced them and they were alone again she said, "David, this is wonderful. I love your family. This is what I dreamed of when I was a kid. Everyone nearby, and you all look related, and you all get together every Saturday in one place."

"Nah, it's never more than once a month because of the drive. What makes you say that?"

"You forget I grew up before multiculturalism was in. I mean, a Eurasian adoptee in an East Coast Jewish family with relatives spread around the suburbs of four different states?"

"Guess I took this for granted. So do most of us. Even if they never left, we all at least talked about wanting to get away. Everything happens somewhere else."

He looked around for an example, "You notice how many front lawns have those big parabola TV receivers? Down here we all went out and bought VCRs before the rest of the country, just to get us through those long snowed-in winters."

And where road crews weren't out laying down a shiny coat of blacktop, she had also noticed the older gray asphalt was crisscrossed with skid marks. A telltale sign of teenagers burning rubber and boredom with the same set of brakes. She knew they were there to get to know his mother. No one spoke of his father.

"Is that why your Dad left?"

"Boredom? I don't know. I was five years old then and he just kinda drove off."

Susan listened silently.

"Mama said something about his business not going well. I thought on and off he might come back. Never did. Never even called on his brothers, you know, my uncles. Just left and never came back," David said.

Susan waited to hear more but his eyes trained somewhere out in the distance.

"That's all you know?"

"A-yuh."

"If you could, aren't there questions you'd ask him?"

After thinking a long time, David answered, "I used to. When I was five I had a friend whose parents were the only divorced ones I knew. He kept asking when the divorce would be over. Finally he understood that it would never be over and he'd never have the same family back so he stopped asking. I knew from that not to ask when the disappearance would be over," he swallowed, "it never would."

"You knew not to ask. That's different from not wanting to ask. Were there questions you wanted to?"

David sighed, "When I was a little kid I

was so in love with my ma that it never occurred to me that he'd fallen out of love, but when I was a teenager it did. How do you ask that?"

She liked hearing him admit to loving his mother, she gave his hand a squeeze.

Then David said, "I wondered if he were in Heaven or still on earth. I was afraid to ask that one because I figured one of my uncles would say he ought to be in Hell."

He laughed to himself, and then added, "I questioned myself over the years about whether there were signs, something that could have given it away so I could have stopped him. Even the last day, he yelled at me to hold his hand crossing the road. How could a father like that turn his back forever?"

Just then the loud zip of a diesel motor announced the first returning lobster boat of the afternoon.

"It must be after four o'clock," David started to move, getting up from the bank where they were sitting. Almost an afterthought, he added, "It only occurred to me recently that he might have been murdered."

Susan studied his face before saying, "It's not something a son would easily imagine."

Together they watched another lobster boat come chugging noisily round the point.

Then the lobsterman cut its engine to glide the rest of the way to the mooring. She realized that David would have heard these sounds every day of his childhood–other fathers steering their boats toward home.

She startled when David seemingly read her mind and reassured her, "A-yuh. Don't think about it much."

Until now she had mentally filed away David's father the way any good adoptee files away missing parents. It occurred to her that David had, too.

~

Years ago it was David's older brother Jonathan who was the one who approached their mother for information about the father who had gone missing. They must have been about eight and twelve, the latter half of elementary school.

As David told it to Susan, his father, Abel Piper, had grown up in Corea, Maine and married Aliza Joseph after their high school graduation. Both their families were members of the nearest synagogue. It was the old one several hours away on York Street in Bangor so they would have to stay overnight with other congregants to avoid travelling back on the Sabbath.

Aliza's family, the Yosefs, had fled the tenements of the Lower East Side of New York before joining cousins up near the Canadian border in Eastport. That only lasted until Easter of their first year when some hooligans coming straight from church pulled any Jewish boys they could from their homes and bloodied their noses and smashed the windows of the rooms they were renting.

Aliza's mother told her how Aliza's grandmother explained with cheer as they packed to leave Eastport forever that it still wasn't as bad as Easter in Kishinev.

Not with a little amazed pride, Aliza's grandmother reminded her that the poem on the Statue of Liberty was written by another Jewish woman, something you would never find in the blood drenched lands of central and Eastern Europe. Although some of the few dozen Jewish immigrants to Eastport, Calais and Lubec chose to stay in those towns where the St. Croix River marked the border with Canada, the Yosefs had to acknowledge that many of their neighbors were themselves not ready to welcome the tired, the hungry, or the poor to their shores.

Aliza's grandfather took and sold the shoes of everyone in the family to buy passage down the St. Croix to another new life in a coastal town. After a few landings along the river, they were told their first docking along the coast would be for deliveries and supplies at a fishing village called Corea.

Grandfather struck up a conversation with the second mate who told them, "Its records go back to about 1700 with the earliest non-Indian settlers. One of the first was Thomas Frazer, a freeman. He and his wife sold salt to ships that passed through this western end of Frenchman Bay. "

Aliza's grandfather turned to her grandmother and asked rhetorically, "even *shwartze* can live there?"

"The town changed its name to Corea in 1896," the sailor explained proudly, "There was a whole bevy of towns renamed by the independent farmers and fisherman of Maine for colonies that had just declared their independence. Plantation One, Maine was probably the first. It changed its name to Peru in 1821 when that country declared its independence."

Aliza's grandmother whispered back to her husband, "If *shwartze* can live there, we'll be safe there, too."

The second mate continued, "Korea was different, those people were still striving to be independent but were under the yoke of the Chinese and then the Japanese."

Aliza's grandparents decided that just such a town would be the one where they would place their hopes and dreams. At some point the Yosefs changed their name to Joseph despite, or maybe because of, their relentlessly alien accents.

A generation later Abel Piper and his parents arrived, tracing a similar route down the St. Croix but coming from St. Stephen on the Canadian side. By then little Aliza worked in the store after school. Abel's parents occasionally worked in the store, occasionally resorted to digging clams, and occasionally Abel's father would disappear down the road out of town for weeks at a time, gone to sell pots, pans, sewing thread, and other items to the outlying coastal towns and island villages.

Years later Aliza was never able to tell Jonathan and David how their paternal grandparents made do. Their lives were infinitely harder, and the horrors of Europe weighed heavier. Both parents died relatively young, before either of their grandsons were born.

"They would have loved you to pieces,"

Aliza would always add.

So ingrained was this refrain that Jonathan and David remained certain of their grandparent's love even after their father, Abel, abandoned them. Aliza liked to believe it herself and while she couldn't bring herself to say a good word about Abel, she wanted each boy to feel that he had something worthy, their deceased grandparents' devotion, from that side of the family.

~

Seven years after Abel disappeared with no word, Aliza petitioned officials at the state capital in Augusta to declare him dead. She would at least be able to collect some death benefit from social security, but that was all. He had no pension, no IRA, no life insurance, certainly no 401(k). When she received confirmation in the mail a few weeks later she told the boys over dinner that night that their father was dead. They were now twelve and sixteen and neither looked like he believed her.

"What did he die of?" asked Jonathan.

"When did it happen?" asked David.

"The government didn't say in those papers, but they finally sent them to let us know he is with God now."

"How could they know and you not know?"

"Because it's just not reasonable that he would leave us and never be back in touch. This makes sense and the papers declare him dead because that's the only thing that could have happened."

Aliza sensed that her boys wanted to believe that he hadn't just abandoned them so she made her voice firmer, "Sadly, he died young just like your grandma and grandpa Piper."

Her teenage son looked at her conspiratorially and then turned to his younger brother, "They would have loved us to pieces. He did, too."

8 GHOST IN A MIRROR
1990

Just as Susan was finishing up first phase planning for the exhibit's trip to Japan, she stumbled upon news about Thailand that threatened to change everything. She had begun following news by the local press, just as she did in preparation for any overseas business trip, when she found something that hadn't been carried by any U.S. broadcasters.

"Look what's happening with the prime minister of Thailand, David," Susan held up a clipping she'd taken from the Bangkok Post, "It seems the prime minister just brokered the impossible, an alliance between the non-Khmer Rouge Cambodian government in exile–based in Tokyo–and the Hun Sen government based in Cambodia itself!"

"The Pol Pot era is really over."

"Mmm-yes, but," Susan turned back to the article, "Apparently, the prime minister took a diplomatic victory lap through Tokyo and Washington, D. C. It was the first time any leader of Thailand felt safe enough in the postwar era to leave the seat of power long enough to visit the United States.

"According to this, he miscalculated; when the prime minister returned, a general had him placed under house arrest."

"In other words, the Thai military is declaring a coup and an army general just arrested the country's first civilian prime minister?" David straightened himself up to his full height and took the news clipping. He read, "The State Department has halted most visas to Thailand."

He looked at Susan, "I'm with them. Your trip is off."

Susan had a hard time sleeping that night. The next morning she called Fred. He assured her not to worry.

He made it sound like martial law in Thailand was seasonal, "Susan, I hear this is the eighteenth coup since 1932, all relatively bloodless, no civil wars, no sectarian violence. Democracy is still 'young' there."

Fred continued with Susan's search. She pushed her misgivings aside and decided to be optimistic for the time being.

~

One morning Susan found herself laughing on the way to work after dropping Lily at Terry's home. Along with being a family caregiver, Terry did everything that Susan's mother disdained. Tupperware parties. Tarot card readings, bridge games, lottery tickets, coupon clipping, and she followed the daily horoscopes. Last night Terry had folded and baked fortune cookies with her own handwritten proverbs inside. The one she gave Susan read, "Life moves like a slinky." Terry drew her metaphors from what she knew.

In this case it fit. She felt the Tokyo half of the trip was spiraling ahead of the Thailand portion on a white wave of faxes, memos and computer printout itineraries. That evening as Susan walked through the door with her pocketbook and diaper bag over one shoulder and Lily on the opposite hip, the phone rang. Fred Kouyoumjian had news that sprung "Thailand" forward, bringing both ends of the trip together. Life moves like a slinky.

Susan put Lily in the crib as she heard Fred say, "I know it's taken a couple months, but my contact in Bangkok, Kun Sompan, just reached the right convent. One of the nuns remembers your birth mother. Her name wasn't Suwan Prichittakorn."

Susan felt confused. It seemed like at every turn, someone else got to define her history.

Fred explained, "That was the name she gave *you.*"

"I'm Suwan?" thought Susan as she let it sink in.

"We believe her name is Noklek. Noklek Prichittikorn."

"You've found her!"

"No," Fred paused, "the abbess remembered her name. Susan, this is the hard part: about a decade or so ago there was a fire at the orphanage that destroyed many of their records. Without them it's tough because she isn't listed in Bangkok. The abbess suggested Noklek may have returned to her native province, but there are seventy six provinces. They thought they gave its name to your parents."

Susan spoke quietly, Fred asked her to repeat herself.

She asked again, "So the only way to keep searching for her is to get that information from my adoptive parents?"

"Yes."

Susan sucked in her breath.

Fred repeated, "Try again. At least you've learned something about her. She gave you a name, Suwan."

Hanging up the phone, Susan found herself thinking, this is mine, this is mine, this is mine. My truth. My birthright.

Susan looked out the window at a light drizzle. The dampness made the tree trunks across the yard look darker against the yellow autumn foliage. She felt like calling David, and then realized he would have already left the office. She picked up the phone to try her mother, and then hung up.

Sitting by the phone now, Susan found herself feeling defensive.

Then, out loud, she said, "I wonder how this affected her marriage?"

Mom had always been very solicitous of Dad. Weren't most wives? That was the marriage contract back then. He brought home the pay check, she ran the home and their social lives. But was there a second pact because she was the partner who was infertile? Did she feel like she owed him extra–to be more deferential, to stay more attractive than other wives–to repay him for staying with her after the hysterectomy?

Susan got up. She could hear Lily awake and crying. Her shoulder brushed the door frame as she went out into the hall but it was still hard for her mind to focus. As she swung around the corner into the nursery, it got less hard. Her nose told her what the problem was.

"Stinky diaper. Have you been marinating in there, my little mushroom?"

Lily paused and then resumed crying.

"Okay. There we go!"

She lifted Lily out of the crib and cradled her against her shoulder as she bent to pull out a fresh diaper. She felt dampness against her shirt and forearm.

"You leaked through."

She opened a drawer and lifted out freshly washed and folded terry cloth pajamas.

After fastening Lily's clean, plump little legs into diapers with a rosebud patterned plastic covering she sprinkled some scented powder onto her baby's tummy and chest and rubbed gently. Lily cooed. Susan smiled and feather-kissed her before snapping the front of the pajamas and adjusting the collar under her double chin.

She sat down in the rocker with the

baby's downy head resting on the crook of her arm. Lily folded her fists against Susan's body as she started to nurse. She seemed to sigh and then her eyelids closed again.

As Susan rocked and held the baby, she picked up the thread of her thought.

On a weekend once, David had stood in the doorway watching her go through this same routine with Lily. After a long, comfortable silence with only the sound of the rocker brushing the rag rug, David spoke.

"I love you, Susan," pause, "thank you...for having our baby."

That moment.

That was love, spiritual, celestial, corporeal. That one tender connection in a marriage would survive untarnished come death, come divorce.

Long after they were both in the grave, they would be bound together, if not in some sort of heaven, then at least in the flesh of the child they had left behind on earth, and her children's children.

That moment.

It was the one moment in a marriage, Susan believed, that adoptive parents could never share.

To herself she admonished, "I cannot ever tell my parents that I am going to meet the woman who gave birth to me. Never.

"It's not about who are the 'real' parents. It's not about my loyalty to them. It's about breaking that unspoken pact between my mother and my father. I would be breaking their hearts."

She heard David's key turn in the lock. As he opened the door, the tiny wooden door chimes started to jingle.

She got up slowly, and carefully lay the baby down in the crib. Lily's tiny lips were still making cute sucking motions as Susan's hands slid out from under her warm body. Susan smoothed a comforter over Lily, and the baby shuddered slightly but kept her eyes closed.

Later, looking across the table at her husband as they started supper, she told him that she'd located her birth mother and that her name is Noklek Prichittakorn.

"That's great. You mentioned anything to your folks or your department yet?"

"About getting the extra days tacked on to my business trip? It won't be a problem."

He just raised his eyebrows.

Yes, it would be a problem. Could she be upfront and tell them she was adopted and was going to meet her birth mother? Nooo. She could hear that bi-atch, Yuriko, whispering to others in her office: a sign of immaturity to be looking for surrogate parents; pursuing fantasies; is Susan one of those crybabies who didn't get enough love from her adoptive parents; didn't Yuriko read somewhere that adoptees are prone to nervous disorders?

No, Susan wouldn't give that woman the satisfaction.

Tourism was big in Thailand. There were famous beaches at Pattaya, Phuket and Hua Hin. Should she say she was going there to visit the beaches at Hua Hin?

What would Terry say: a mother leaving her infant for such selfish reasons?

Later in bed she laid out each of her worries like an imaginary film negative threatening to develop into some career stopping picture. Patiently, David listened, rephrased and re-edited each spool of action until they had created an acceptable fiction.

Patience was the word here. Despite how important this was to Susan, she couldn't help picking up on a certain tone of weariness with forbearance from David, as though this were something repetitive that happened every day. David was indulging her yet again as she met her birth mother alone for the first time–ho hum–yet again.

Under the weight of his enormous tolerance she recited her fable: "My adoptive parents, who have been in touch with my birthparents all along, are urging me to go meet the couple in Thailand."

That was believable –nowadays you were hearing more and more about adoptive parents who actually knew who their child's birth mother was. No one would stop to calculate that Susan's adoption was before those days.

Since she herself felt noncommittal about the reunion, Susan would tell them, she figured she'd tack it on to the end of her Tokyo meetings rather than make a separate trip. Of course, she would pay her own airfare and take this out of her vacation time. She was doing it on the advice of her parents who thought she should do it for the sake of her daughter. Her husband was curious about it, too, otherwise she would never pursue this kind of thing.

"I feel sick."

"Susan, you feel guilty for lying. In a dog-eat-dog environment you're allowed privacy. Welcome to the world of capitalist guilt."

"Or–maybe this is ingrate adoptee guilt, or Jewish guilt?"

"All. Melting pot guilt."

"I've decided not to tell my folks about this."

"Yeah. Probably better that way."

"David."

"Mmm?'

"David, if you decided to track down your father–?"

"There's no way."

"You still see all his brothers when you're at your mom's. Maybe you all could–"

"No way."

Susan could almost picture what her father-in-law looked like, a little like David or Jonathan, but older like Uncle Todd or Uncle Ira, "If you did, would you let your mother know first?"

"She wouldn't care."

"Is that a yes or a no? Would you tell her?"

"I've put him behind me. We played catch a few times. That's all I remember."

"Your mother told me you look like him."

"Listen, I'm supporting your taking this trip. Don't drag me into this. You're looking for your heritage. I'm not. You saw Corea. The only thing it's got is heritage. My old man walked out."

"Why don't you want to know the whole story?"

"Words. He was a talker. Before he left he told my Uncle Todd that he couldn't bear to see Jonathan and me and my ma poor. So guess what? He walks away, practically ensuring we'd be poor. I'm sure I could count on some great words but the facts are that whatever the reason– he walked out. He knew I looked up to him and he just deserted us. Facts."

Their bed creaked and Susan heard David walk across the dark room to pick up his keys. She looked up just in time to see him slip on a flannel work shirt and head downstairs for the front door. Each time he did this, Susan imagined him abandoning her and never returning. She felt quiet hysteria in the silence. If it were earlier she would hide this by doing tasks, keeping busy emptying the sink or folding the laundry. She never called a girlfriend, never turned on the TV. She was aware each and every minute that she would survive should he never return, steeled herself for that.

But he always came back. One time he even turned to her and mumbled, "Twenty minutes. Tops," before leaving. It turned out to be true, he was never gone long but when he came back, smelling like the outdoors, she always thought of a John LeCarre line about "coming home from very lonely places, all of us go a little mad: whether from great personal success, or just an all-night drive, we are the sole survivors of a world no one else has ever seen."

Whoever said marriage was the joining of two souls got it wrong, thought Susan.

~

She stayed awake in bed until he came home. When he climbed into bed he kissed the back of her head and piled an extra pillow on his side, as though fortifying the trenches with sandbags against whatever it was he would face the next day. When he slid under the covers finally he pressed his back companionably against hers and she listened to his breathing. When it slowed to that of slumber her own mind relaxed. In all the emotional and aural memories of the day, one of the quietest teased itself free.

It was Fred saying "Suwan was your name."

This was hers; Susan could let herself be lulled into sleep by the rhythm of David's breathing. Tonight slumber lured Susan back to a distant land of dreams, to a particular dream of childhood. Actually it had been a recurrent nightmare. Tonight it returned, but now its message was gentle, persisting into daylight.

Years ago the dream had begun with an innocent remark. Thinking that Susan gazed at her reflection in the mirror too long, her grandmother told her one day, "Watch out or the mirror will swallow you up."

For years after that, a dream mirror on a closet door would become molten quicksilver and draw Susan into the darkness on the other side. She would feel her way blindly up wall shelves or stumble over mountains of boxes piled up in the back, searching for a secret passage.

This time when Susan looked in the mirror it was not molten and held firm and smooth and the little girl reflected on the other side spoke. She introduced herself with Susan's first name, Suwan, the name her first mother had given her and which had been hers before the relinquishment, and through the twilight until she broke day and was adopted. Susan, Suwan, had found a passage back.

9 HOLIDAY LIGHTS
1990

Susan avoided talking about the upcoming trip when her mother called about plans for the holidays. Susan knew she would see them next Friday to celebrate Sukkoth, the strangest holiday of the year. It was an ancient holiday, written about even in the Bible, to commemorate the wandering of the Hebrews in the desert for forty years after Moses led them out of Egypt, and it also marked the barley harvest in the ancient Middle East.

Susan's family put together wooden booths called *sukkahs*, each made of two by four frames with a flattop latticed roof. Once they got it assembled, it was big enough to allow a table for twelve people with one side open that kept guests from feeling hemmed in. It was supposed to emulate the makeshift booths the Hebrews lived in while crossing the Sinai desert. A whole generation lived and died wandering in the Sinai just as, the clergy liked to point out in their sermons that time of year, most of us live and die pursuing our personal Promised Lands.

Sukkoth came every harvest moon, usually October, but it varied because it was based not on the solar but the lunar calendar. Susan learned in Sunday school that while the solar calendar has a leap year every four years, lunar calendars have them about every three years when they tack on a whole extra month. Susan's mom took it a step further. Masha discovered that both the East Asian calendar and the Jewish calendar are based on the moon and Sukkoth coincides with the Asian Moon Festival two years out of every three. Her mom and dad tried to combine the two harvest moon holidays.

As kids Susan and her cousins hung colored construction paper chains and plastic fruit on the *sukkah* as decorations (real fruit attracted too many wasps) and then they'd all sit inside and eat a meal together there. It was traditional to let the *sukkah* stand for eight days. When Susan was in grade school she would have friends over to play house in it later in the week.

After work, her dad would go to the Pan-Asian grocery and buy round moon cakes. There were all different kinds. Most were pastries with cassia-leaf reliefs brightened with egg yolk glaze.

The filling was the main thing. There was sticky sweet red bean paste, coconut and almond paste, melon seed paste, crushed red candied beans, or her favorite: tawny lotus seed paste.

Susan's mom would go to the public library in preparation and borrow collections of Chinese and Yiddish ghost stories. Then after dark, under the full moon, she would take the children out to the *sukkah* in the backyard and read them. Her two favorites were the East Asian and Yiddish stories that might have been prototypes for Rip Van Winkle.

In the East Asian version, the God of Earthly Marriages plays chess with the God of Longevity. If you stop to watch a game instead of turning on your heels and running straight home, you will find that a hundred and fifty years have passed during your absence.

In the Jewish version, a bridegroom (who everyone knows is not supposed to be left alone the day before his wedding)–is left alone the day before his wedding. The ghost of his dead childhood Torah study partner appears and invites him to go study a holy text together for old times' sake.

Later, as the bridegroom hurries home before dark, he meets a young woman who takes him in because, as she says, he looks so old and confused. She turns out to be the great niece of a woman who's husband-to-be vanished the day before they were to be wed.

One year, Susan's uncle even invited a traditional Jewish scribe, a man who wore a long beard and dark yarmulke, and a Vietnamese neighbor who knew Chinese style brush painting. They were Mr. Goldberg and Mr. Nguyen. They taught the adults and teenagers calligraphy in the two languages.

The Chinese phrases were taken from poems about autumn, about the moon, about its silver reflection on a garden pond through lengthening nights. Mr. Goldberg's were short verses from psalms and prayers. Inviting these two calligraphers became a family tradition.

Her mother had even written article years ago about their combined holiday for a Jewish periodical called Instant. Masha talked about how adoptive Jewish parents should adjust to make their kid's heritage part of the family's, especially if the child was one of the many children adopted from Thailand, China, Korea or Vietnam. She explained how similar both five thousand year old harvest moon festivals were, how the Moon Festival was celebrated throughout Asia, not just China and she annotated the article with fifty eight footnotes.

The editor sent a photographer to take a picture of Susan and her cousins in a *sukkah* that the family built that year on a flat bottomed boat. Her parents had rented it and gotten permission to use it on the lake at the county park. It was supposed to be reminiscent of the floating teahouses ancient East Asian poets used for moon viewing.

Susan and her cousins had been so excited that they raced between tugging at the sleeves of the photographer and jumping up and down on the boat.

The editors cut most of the article and changed the emphasis to how unique the Jewish holiday was, how it had overcome its lunar agricultural roots by adding the ethical aspect lacking in the East Asian holiday.

"What ethical aspect? All you do is decorate the *sukkah* and then eat!" Susan's parents canceled their subscription to the magazine, but still clipped the photo of the kids in their floating *sukkah* boat.

~

This year Mr. Goldberg drove up in his old avocado-colored station wagon with Mr. Nguyen, the calligrapher, on the passenger side. The two old men were widowers who had become even more interested in their respective heritages now that their wives were gone and their children were grown.

Both were shorter than Susan and stocky, with faces so wrinkled that you noticed their eighty some years more than their ethnic features. Mr. Nguyen's eyes had single lids but Mr. Goldberg's deep set ones had grown so heavy that both men had rather narrow eyes above well rounded cheekbones. Mr. Goldberg's nose was high and Mediterranean while Mr. Nguyen's was flat but wide, set above generous lips on each man.

They walked in step towards the *sukkah* as Susan's mother ran up to greet them, "It's so good to see you. The brushes and quills are already out but first let me introduce you to two new guests this year."

Mr. Nguyen smiled. "That's right. You're a grandmother this year and I'm a great grandfather."

"Where are they, Tracy and Shoshona's little ones?" Mr. Goldberg asked, using Susan's Hebrew name.

"Here they are." Michael's wife Tracy turned a little sideways so they could see nine month old Kieran's sleeping face deeply at peace on her shoulder. Lily was awake and gave a little bounce on her mother's hip as if to get up and greet her two gentlemen callers. The two old men dropped their voices and in soft high pitches began to fuss over the babies.

Mr. Nguyen passed around a wallet picture of his four month old great grandchild, Peter. Then Masha led everyone over to a large folding table. She had blanketed it with old newspapers weighted down with rocks.

Susan thought that once everyone progressed beyond the scribble and drip phase the scripts of both languages began to look like some kind of abstract art. They used quills for writing the Hebrew calligraphy, leaning over their paper to make delicate squared shapes with a few stylistic dots and flourishes. For the Chinese characters they used broad brushes that spread the ink in strokes that varied with pressure, either generous or fine sweeps across the page.

After the calligraphy session was over they wiped up the spilt ink on the table in the *sukkah* and carefully carried the wet paper inside to dry on a worktable up in Masha's sewing room. While that was drying Susan's cousin Michael and David were in charge of decorating the *sukkah*.

Mom had popped popcorn for the womenfolk to thread into a garland.

Susan's cousin-in-law Tracy asked, "Do you think this stuff'll attract wasps?"

"Popcorn? Nah. But the cider will, but it's worth it," said Susan.

Tracy turned to Susan's mother, "Isn't there something with the cinnamon, Masha?"

"Yes, we always simmer cinnamon in the cider. When the kids were little I used to bake cinnamon cookies but Suzie never ate them."

"She means the story behind the cinnamon, Mom," Susan corrected.

"Yes, well, cinnamon is the bark from cassia trees. And cassia trees are a big motif of the Moon Festival. Like we have the man in the moon, the Chinese have a lady in the moon or a rabbit in the moon. The lady lives in a palace built from the wood of cassia trees and the rabbit pounds an Elixir of Immortality made from cassia.

"The Hebrews used cinnamon oil to anoint the tabernacle they built for carrying the Ten Commandments through the Sinai desert. And those years are the years of wandering when the Jews lived in *sukkahs*. You see, both people used that spice for what was really, underneath, the same holiday."

Susan laughed, "Which all goes to prove that they're really one of the Ten Lost Tribes of Israel."

But her mother continued, "Oh, and then last year we went to a special exhibit at the botanical gardens and the gift shop had Japanese incense. They had a blend of cinnamon with sandalwood, and cinnamon with patchouli. We bought those and they also had cinnamon with jasmine but that just didn't work, cinnamon smells like fall and jasmine smells like summer. We can light them later."

Mr. Nguyen had told them about a Japanese cult leader who built his early following from among his calligraphy students. They were now claiming to be descended from one of the biblical tribes of northern Judea that disappeared after a battle, but Israeli immigration officials patiently and repeatedly refused their requests in broken Hebrew to return to what their calligraphy master and spiritual leader had revealed to them was their ancestral home.

Masha interrupted, "Oh, I didn't mean something like that. It's just a friendly kind of coincidence. And both peoples celebrate by eating round foods, round like the moon. That's why I thought cinnamon cookies were a good idea."

"Popcorn isn't round."

"I thought about that, Susan, but...both holidays probably started as prehistoric harvest festivals, celebrating the bounty of the earth." Then she smiled and continued, "Popcorn is the only part of the bounty that doesn't attract wasps."

The three of them laughed. Tracy put Kieran on a blanket near Lily. Susan's one female cousin, Ileana, stooped down to tickle the babies by blowing on their round tummies and they laughed, too.

Ileana had broken her marriage engagement three months earlier. Susan confessed to Tracy before Ileana arrived that she felt guilty for being married around her.

"Come on," said Tracy, "why on earth should you feel guilty? You didn't have anything to do with it. She's stronger than we sometimes give her credit."

As Susan watched Ileana now she felt like that just might be true. Ileana was down on her elbows with the babies, puffing lightly on their hair. They opened their mouths in surprise and gurgled belly laughs. Their joy made the adults laugh, too.

The smell of mulled apple with cinnamon and allspice was filling the air as the popcorn cooled and its aroma receded.

"The cider must be done."

"Here, let me get the cider and you bring the garlands out to the guys."

Susan carried loops of strung popcorn over each arm. When she stood inside the *sukkah* to pass them up to Michael on the stepladder, the sun's glare caught her eye through the lattice roof as she tried to look up at him. The booth gave off a musty-woody smell. It had been in the garage now for three seasons. A last cicada's song rose and then fell in a staccato coda.

"Just in time. You always want to get garlands hung before the individual decorations. Gets less tangled."

"I never knew that, Michael."

"I learned it decorating Tracy's parents' Christmas tree."

David also stood on a stepladder a little to her left, spreading cut fir boughs across the flat trelliswork roof. Their deep woods smell would cover the mustiness coming from the walls and later that night the soft silhouettes of the needles against the moonlight would give the dinner party the feel of being held in some Acadian grotto instead of a suburban backyard.

Tracy offered the two older men seats as Michael came back out carrying silverware and plates to the *sukkah*. Now it was time to eat. There was noodle pudding, low fat cheese blintzes, baked acorn squash with butter and molasses, and steamed green beans that had been tossed in slivered almonds sautéed in curry and olive oil. Her mom loved to serve carafes of white and red wine. David and Michael were hunkered down at their end of the table with some beer steins having a private Oktoberfest.

Susan always felt relief at this point. These manufactured "traditions" were exhausting. As much as she intellectually appreciated Mr. Nguyen celebrating Sukkoth and Mr. Goldberg celebrating the Asian Moon Festival, and America being a melting pot, she had a saying she shared only with Tracy and David, "What happens at Mom's, stays at Mom's."

With their first house, she wanted to continue some but leave most of Mom's ersatz personalized rituals behind. When it came to tradition, she felt, simplicity and authenticity were easier.

She was happy that ritual objects were few in their home. Over their bed was the framed *ketubah*, the marriage contract in English and

Hebrew calligraphy illuminated with hand painted ink and acrylic. There was only one other ritual item in the house, the *mezuzah*, the tiny Jewish amulet that they nailed to the wall just inside a doorframe. It had been a housewarming gift from friends.

After about half an hour or so, the clink of silverware on porcelain was slowing, the same way, thought Susan, that the sound of popcorn popping in the microwave slows just before it's finished.

Lily and Kieran had thrown all the rattles, baby spoons, bunny faced bowls and cups from their trays and were now clamoring to join the adults around the table. Only seconds apart, she, then Tracy, pivoted in their seats to undo the highchair tray latches and scoop their babies down into their laps.

When Susan had Lily settled she caught mom looking at her evenly for a moment before speaking.

"So how long will you be in Japan for?"

"About ten days." That was too honest.

She needed to say something to explain the added days she would still be away, but in Thailand.

"That's when Waseda University has its fall festival in Tokyo. I might look up some of the alumns I met my junior year there. They close the streets and set up stages with concerts and radio shows. You can watch from the beergartens that sponsors set up–and–Miyuki told me–her old Kabuki troupe is going to perform there," Susan had to gulp air.

She wondered if her mother suspected something more behind her breathless explanation.

"That should be fun to visit your alma mater. Remind me who Miyuki is again?"

Susan liked this story. She half wondered if her mother was feigning forgetfulness so Susan could tell it to everyone. Miyuki's father had actually competed as a gymnast in the Olympics and now taught Phys. Ed. at Waseda University. Miyuki had practically grown up on campus and the story of her name was as well-known as her father was. He originally came from the tropical islands of Okinawa, but Miyuki's mother was from the north. Around the time that Miyuki was due to be born her mother followed tradition and returned to her childhood home.

Susan began the retelling, "Japanese women go back home to their parents' to have their babies and their husbands usually follow them.

"Miyuki's father had never been that far

north and the night before his daughter was born it began to snow. It snowed throughout her labor, and he literally felt awe at the newness of these ancient phenomena, the snow and the birth.

"On Miyuki's first morning of life, the way he tells it, the sun was brilliant. Snow cloaked the tree branches, the eaves of the stone lantern, the tiles of the rooftops and courtyard walls, turning every surface into a white, glittering replica of what had been there the day before."

Susan paused and found a pen to write the characters of Miyuki's name for Mr. Nguyen, "The name Miyuki is usually written with the characters for 'beautiful fortune' or 'beautiful happiness.' But this young couple, instead, chose a homonym written with the characters for 'deep snow'."

"How clever," commented Mr. Nguyen appreciatively.

"Al, did you hear?" Susan's mom turned back to Susan, "You have so much to embrace ahead of you: a job that takes you to places like Japan, a husband, a daughter. You don't need to dwell on the past."

How did she know?

Susan couldn't stop herself from saying, "The Hall of the Asian Peoples will show one thing American museums still hide."

She caught herself and slowed down before continuing to avoid sounding shrill. Susan needed to say it, "A lot of emigration from Asia to the rest of the world has been through adoption. Babies and children to meet the demand here. Losing far more than an adult immigrant. No voice in citizenship, no language left to translate. No immigrant community to share their heritage. Sometimes the only Asian in the family. Sometimes for miles."

She waited for what her mother would say.

"You were in an orphanage for chrissakes." Masha looked more stunned than angry.

The words made Susan spin sick and dizzy, almost like she would lose her balance. Then she felt David tugging at her elbow.

"Come on. I've got the baby and the diaper bag."

They started walking around to the front yard, the port-a-crib between them. Dad was clearing up dishes, his eyes studiously averted.

They all said their goodbyes awkwardly. The afternoon's breeze had blown a heavy cloud cover in and a light drizzle had begun to fall. Walking out to the car, Susan noticed a swirl of withered leaves rise up on the wind and glide up the street. Her father appeared out front and, ignoring her, addressed David.

"Drive carefully. The rain'll make the leaves slippery."

By unspoken agreement, neither Susan nor David talked until after Lily had fallen asleep in the car seat. In those few minutes it was impossible to read David's reaction.

"I'm sorry this happened at a family get-together. I didn't plan on Mom guessing, let alone bringing it up."

"I don't know that she's guessed anything specific like you going to Thailand. But she is reading things correctly with you asking for your birth information."

"Thanks, husband. It would have meant a lot to me if you could have stuck up for me. I could have used some support."

"You were holding your own."

She smiled but still felt weak.

"There wasn't a fight really, was there? But maybe I'm getting close to violating the unwritten contract. Just because Mom can't have biological descendants I'm not supposed to have biological ancestors, right?"

David peered up at a traffic light. She hoped he would have reacted.

Then she added with a half whisper, "Still I wish you would support me more. And if she's so proud of herself for telling me I'm adopted, why isn't she more forthright in giving me my information?"

"She's old. She may have honestly forgotten your info."

"Doubtful. Anyway, if that's true, why didn't she care enough to preserve it for me to start with?"

"Why do you suddenly need everyone's support? This search thing wasn't my idea. It wasn't their idea. But if you drag us into this you're trying to stir up things we just don't have the energy to deal with now. Let's have a little reality check here: you're not their first choice, they would have preferred to have their own child."

"David, why are you bringing that up? Of course I'm sorry for that."

David paused and then continued slowly this time.

"Maybe I'm being a father for the first time without a road map and I don't need to be reminded of parents who give up and walk off."

"Oh. You're not like your father. And I was always told my birth mother didn't 'give up and walk off', she only gave me away because she loved me very much. She did the right thing."

He pounded the steering wheel for emphasis, startling her. "Did you hear yourself? She gave you away because she loved you? What kind of logic is that? She gave you away because she didn't want to keep you."

"I'm sorry, David. We should be looking for your Dad—"

"–No."

"David, he's probably –"

"No. My father is irrelevant here. What we were talking about are your parents. You've got a decision to make."

"About...?"

"Where are your loyalties –"

"David!!"

"What I mean is: is your loyalty to not upsetting your parents? You kinda crossed that line–apparently–by even asking for your birth information. I'm not saying you were wrong though. Or, is your loyalty to pursuing some big T Truth?"

"Well, it's not even about me. What about it being Lily's heritage, too?"

"Let me play devil's advocate for a minute. Are you saying the only factor giving you the right to search is being a mother, having Lily? If you didn't have a child you would not have a right to search? It's disloyal to adoptive parents if a childless adoptee searches but it's not disloyal if an adoptee with a child searches? I think you're forgetting someone, Susan."

"You. I know. I'm hurting you although, yes, I know you're strong."

"No."

"But I'm hurting you by dwelling on lost parents just when you're trying to fill a role that your father abandoned when he abandoned you. Do you want me to stop this? I thought you said you would support me."

"I do. I do. But my supporting you doesn't mean I'm necessarily going to make the same choices. That's not the focus here," David paused before continuing more gently, "Realistically, how many chances are you going to have to go to Thailand? Clearly they're forcing a choice on you: you either go through with it and let them feel angry or hurt or betrayed or afraid—not that they should. Or you give up something that you've said matters to you. You need to weigh it, Susan, and choose which matters more."

"No, I don't."

He looked at her from the corner of his eye.

She continued emphasizing every word, "The search is important to my world, but the search doesn't even have to exist in theirs."

David turned on the blinker as they followed the curve into their street, the corner streetlight flashed through their windshield as they sped past it in silence. He slowed the car a little and put on the left turn signal. It and the sound of the windshield wipers were the only sound. The swing of the turn lurched her against the car door.

"Be careful, David."

~

Later that night, David, rolled over to face her in bed.

"Is it those childbirth classes last year and books that got you going? Their talking about bonding in utero and bonding after delivery?"

"Only partly. But it is a powerful feeling. A baby kicking inside. Seeing Lily the first time and watching her take her first breath. I remember thinking that her face, even scrunched up, looked familiar. Part you, part me. Can you imagine ever giving her away?"

She hoped that appealing to him through Lily would draw him out of his rationalist frame of mind. He'd already agreed once before that getting medical information about her biological family was important, important enough to spend money on Fred Kouyoumjian. But she wanted to pull him beyond that. She wanted him to understand her need to see a face like her own, to feel, deep down, like she had– it was hard to put it into words. She wanted to feel a deep down connection and she felt certain that meeting ancestors, a birth mother or a birth father would give her that connection.

They talked, their words circled, but his father still stood in the way, Susan thought. David would acknowledge no loss, no mourning, neither hers nor his own. The conversation was fading and he drew her closer, trying, she thought, to bring her back to the present.

But she persisted. "David, let's finish talking. In a way, we both lost parents. You lost the relationship you had with your Dad up until he left. I didn't lose a real relationship, but I was abandoned, too. And if a parent leaves, like yours, or dies, everyone recognizes that it's a loss. With me it had to be secret, or I would appear ungrateful to my adoptive parents. I could never ask about my adoption because I sensed it would hurt them. God, I even hid my period from Mom the first few months I got it because in some crazy way I felt guilty about being able to have babies while she couldn't."

"That was your hang up, not your mom's."

Susan thought David was crossing over to cruel when he added, "And what makes you think I could sit around chatting with Mama about Dad's walking out on me and her?"

"I'm sorry. But at least you had memories of him. And you still saw relatives from his side. When I was put up for adoption I lost all that, all the permutations of my self that most people get to see in their biological family. I lost family history, culture, even the Thai language. I'll need an interpreter to talk to my birth mother if I meet her!"

"Susan, I'm just too tired for this. It's late."

He began kissing her, and stroking her hair that gleamed faintly in the starlight on her pillow. She rolled over into his arms, excited, but also feeling like she was "surrendering" when what she really wanted was his understanding. Was this his way of drawing her away from uncomfortable words and thoughts, silencing her? Maybe, she despaired, he just couldn't handle it.

Later, after he was asleep, Susan looked out the window, bittersweetly, loving him so dearly while feeling so lonely, sure he hadn't understood her. The heavens, too, seemed especially lonely and lovely tonight. She remembered the last stanza of a Robert Frost poem "Desert Places" she hadn't read in years but still knew by heart.

> *They cannot scare me with their empty spaces*
> *Between stars—*
> *on stars where no human race is*
> *I have it in me so much nearer home*
> *To scare myself with my own desert places*

A day later Susan's father called back with the name of the province, and the name of a smaller administrative district within it.

"Hope it helps, honey."

After hanging up the phone, Susan wondered briefly why her mother hadn't been part of the conversation. Then she picked up the receiver again to dial Fred Kouyoumjian with the new information. She spelled it out for him and exhaled when she heard him say, "We may have just struck gold here."

That night Susan and David did what they had begun promising themselves: coming back together to finish any conversation that ended badly. Susan waited until it was time to slide between the sheets of their bed. She stared at David's shoulder for a minute before getting her courage up to begin, "David, I think when I visit

Thailand after my trip, I'll visit more than just the orphanage."

"Do you know more yet?" he rolled over to look at her.

"That detective Kouyoumjian sounds really hopeful. Dad called with more info, the name of a smaller administrative district in my native province. Mom and Dad knew it all along."

"Go easy on them."

"I am. But, David, why keep it from me? I have a right to know–"

"Listen, they raised you."

"Yes?"

David rolled onto his back but still refused to look at her, dropping his forearm over his eyes.

"You should appreciate what you have. You had two parents."

"Okay," Susan agreed, deciding this conversation had to be over for tonight, but not over yet.

~

That Friday after work the phone rang and Susan picked it up as she was making dinner, sautéed chicken with vegetables, baked potato and salad on the side.

It was Fred Kouyoumjian and he had more news, "Your parents' new information did help us work with the orphanage at the nunnery. Your birth mother, Noklek Prichittakorn, moved back north. She's in the same province she told the abbess. Then the district name your parents gave us narrowed it down to manageable."

Susan nodded, vindicated.

"Her village is Ban Naan, an hour away from Chiang Rai, between there and the Laotian border. She can't come to Bangkok because she has to stay on the farm. But, she says you can visit her there in the afternoon on a Saturday because her husband and two stepdaughters go to town then."

Then Susan lowered the temperature on the chicken, put down the spatula and just listened on her end of the phone as Fred rattled off the logistics.

"I have a connection stateside who sent this by diplomatic pouch to Bangkok to save time. And my subcontractor at the embassy took it from there–he's a local hire, a Thai, and he really seems to know the system. He cross-referenced the transliteration and then found that name we already have, Prichittakorn, in the district registry," Fred sounded like he must be standing up pacing with excitement on the other end, "When's your business trip?"

"Three more weeks," she answered.

"Yes, it may happen by then. If it does, maybe hire him as your interpreter, give him some extra business."

Susan struggled to believe that it was really going to happen, "Yes, yes, tell her I can come. What was the guide's name? Kun Sompan. If Kun Sompan would arrange the transportation...And–yes, please, have him come to interpret."

Susan was feeling lightheaded, "I can't tell you how wonderful this makes me feel. Is there anything I can bring you back from there? You must have seen stuff you liked there the last time."

"Actually, there is. You may not have time for it, but everywhere I went they had these really unusual birdhouses. It's so far south that that's where birds from China migrate in the fall and winter. If you can get one of them shipped back here I'd reimburse you. A Thai birdhouse."

She laughed and thanked him again, promising she'd try.

It may happen by then.

It may happen by then and she might look into the eyes of the woman who gave her life, it made her feel a pure laughingcryingscreaming JOY! An inexplicable earthly joy: like those Chinese birds, her homing instinct could sense its roost.

"Oh, she says they're tapioca farmers. She never had any children after giving you away. Her husband and stepchildren don't know about you so she said to pretend you're a development worker touring the countryside if anyone asks.

"She says she's happy you're well."

10 HALL OF THE ASIAN PEOPLES
1991

Once Susan finished her MFA research in Japan, she knew enough Japanese to stay wherever she liked. She chose to avoid the old skyscrapers of the Nishi-Shinjuku section of Tokyo whenever she came back for work. The skyscraper district seemed to be featured in every Western film made with a non-Japanese location scout.

But it just wasn't the authentic old Tokyo she and her friends knew. She preferred the quiet and traditional Japanese breakfasts she could find in the southwest part of Tokyo, still convenient to the Yamanote-sen train stops.

She was content to rise early and have the trending "Viking breakfast," Japanized Swedish for smorgasbord. She could have quality steamed rice with crisp yellow *takuon* or daikon pickles, and mouth clearing *umeboshi* or dried pickled plum alongside freshly caught and broiled fish.

Here *miso shiru* soup used fresh *kombu*, not the dried and reconstituted seaweed that was all that was available in the northeastern United States.

Afterwards she enjoyed walking along the narrow mercantile streets under the artificial snowflake sprays that festooned every lamp post in the late autumn. Tokyo was like New York in that she would always see something new when she went for a walk, and blessedly it was a walker's city. But she frequently noticed something quintessentially Tokyo that brought her back to the days when she lived here as a student.

This morning it was the semi-domesticated cats. Leave the tourist and government hubs, go to the residential neighborhoods and Tokyo must host more ownerless cats than any other place on earth. Susan's colleagues Kayoko and Hiroshi joined her one morning for breakfast and she wondered aloud about the wild cats. Susan had met Hiroshi when he worked in Boston on a fellowship. Hiroshi's eyes twinkled.

He was a bit of a wag and snickered, "The cats are reincarnations of lazy monks."

Kayoko burst out laughing.

Susan gave them both a puzzled look.

Hiroshi explained with mock indignation, "These city cats, instead of working honestly like any farm cat, they head out every morning like Buddhist monks to mewl for alms."

Now all three of them shared a quiet chuckle.

"Seriously though," Susan persisted, "I've never noticed an organized system in Tokyo, or a public will for that matter, to eliminate feral cats."

Kayoko offered, "Well, there may really be a Buddhist legacy behind that, although not Hiroshi-san's kind."

Kayoko was a fellow curator who worked at one of the more exquisite museums found on the top floor of traditional department stores here, "There is the idea of compassion. Like my mother, and my grandmother before her, I slide open my kitchen window every morning and put a mix of cat food and rice in a bowl on the sill before I catch the train. The neighborhood tabbies have known to come to this window for three generations. Everyone on our alleyway does the same."

Susan loved her work but most of all loved seeing these old friends. They were more than just work friends to her. Her visit with Miyuki was a little different from the story Susan had told for her mother back in the U.S. about visiting old college haunts. Miyuki had just had a baby and somehow Susan couldn't bring herself to tell her mother. Maybe this was overprotectiveness, maybe even paranoia, but she just didn't enjoy discussing with her mother yet another person giving birth.

Susan was able to fit in a trip out to the suburbs to see Miyuki and her son. After Miyuki had them settled with rice crackers and green tea, the baby blinked awake. He was adorable with a full head of dark hair, bright eyes and a little double chin. Miyuki let Susan hold him. This delicate human was only the length from her fingertips to the crook of her arm.

"He's so much heavier than Lily at this age, and yet he feels so light."

"She's a big girl, *neh*? Already walking, *neh*."

"Yes, I miss her so much. Ooooh, look how he's holding my finger. What a tight grip."

"Watch this," Miyuki said and put the baby down on his play mat. She covered her eyes with both hands and his face sank.

Miyuki sang, "*Inai, inai* –"

Then she removed her hands, "*Ba*!" He brightened as he saw his mother's face again.

Susan laughed, "Somebody really loves

his mommy."

Miyuki repeated the song, "*Inai, inai --
Ba!*"

Again, her baby went from content to
bereft to delighted before Susan's eyes.

"Peek a boo," Susan smiled, "Miyuki-san,
we have that, too." Susan caught the baby's eyes
and then leaned in with her palms covering her
own, "Peek a – a –"

The baby whimpered and looked away
with a pout.

"Boo!"

He looked back and gurgled.

A thought occurred to Susan but she
didn't share it with Miyuki. Much later, back in
the US, Susan would try to explain it to a friend,
Farah.

"Adoptees suck at peek-a-boo, Farah."

"Where'd that come from?" Farah would
laugh.

"Imagine your mother is your whole
world."

"I don't need to," Farah rolled her eyes,
"Trust me, moving back in with my parents, you
know, old fashioned Muslim, can get suffocating
sometimes."

"Hah. Imagine you're a *baby* and you
enjoy that your mother is your whole world."

Farah nodded, "Okay, but what is peek-a-boo? I don't know this."

Susan explained and mimicked it. Farah nodded, "We do that, too."

"Imagine the mommy covers up her eyes so she disappears for the baby."

Farah, ever the med student, nodded seriously, "Babies haven't developed object permanence yet, the sense that something or someone still exists even when not present. So, when the baby can't see Mommy, Mommy has ceased to exist, or maybe gone away forever."

"Thank you, future Dr. Farah. If the mommy disappears and really never comes back, is part of the baby stuck in a pout? Is there something jarringly wrong now in baby's universe?"

Farah quipped, "There's 'peek a' and no 'boo'. But what if a new face appears for the baby? I see where this is going. What if a new face appears for the baby, a kind, adoptive mommy face or adoptive daddy face?"

Susan sighed, "I don't know."

"On my pediatric rotation they had us attend a panel on child loss. There was a couple who had lost a child in the neonatal ward. There were parents who had lost their seventeen year old son to a drunk driver," Farah stopped.

"Are you crying? I'm sorry," Susan slid her over a pocket sized packet of tissues.

"I'm okay. Your story about Miyuki's baby reminded me of something the mothers and fathers said. They said there's no such thing as a replacement baby. People told them to have another child. Even if the grieving parents are naïve and think this will be a 'replacement baby', they find out the loss doesn't go away, Susan. It's a way to choose life, but it's no replacement. They've added more joy by choosing a new life. If there's some divine ledger out there, maybe the joy column will start to be fuller than the sorrow column, but the loss of the other child doesn't go away," said Farah.

Susan felt a darkness pulling her down, "I think I need to get onto a new subject after this. But I think I got your point. I need some time to think about it." Susan paused, surprised that she was having trouble staying dry eyed, "There's no such thing as a 'replacement first parent'. David and my adoptive parents and friends like you and I can fill the joy column, but the birth parent stays in the loss column."

"So," Farah patted her hand, "I hadn't thought of this before but maybe it's normal for adoptees to be poor performers at peek-a-boo."

Susan couldn't help laughing as she wiped

her eyes.

That was a conversation Susan would have months from now. But today, here in suburban Japan, Susan watched her old friend Miyuki lift her giggling son up in the air and then lower his round tummy to her mouth for a kiss.

Outwardly Susan remained the polite guest until it was time to leave. Inside Susan ached with homesickness, not just for her own baby but for the stranger she was about to meet in Thailand.

~

Dai Nippon Airways touched down on the tarmac of Suvarnabhumi BKK outside Bangkok after its six hour flight. Susan passed through customs to face a wall of gesturing men behind a cordon. She found out later they were cabbies calling out prices to her for a ride. A slightly taller man stepped forward and introduced himself as Kun Sompan, her guide. She let him help her get her luggage. Then he led her to a waiting car and opened the driver-side door for her.

She blanched, "Kun Sompan, I really don't know the roads–would you mind driving?"

He smiled and then she looked in and saw

that the driver's wheel was on the right-hand side, British-style. She was standing next to the passenger seat after all. She smiled now, too. It was the same in Japan, she was less surprised than sleepy. Noonday and midnight were still jumbled in her internal clock. Even so, her curiosity kept much of her jet lag at bay and she was able to learn a little about Kun Sompan's family. He'd been to Australia in his twenties once for vacation. Otherwise he had never left the country. His regular job was as an English teacher and Susan had arrived during a long weekend break.

~

He was just as curious about her.

To Kun Sompan there certainly was something Thai about her, but something inexplicably foreign. She reminded him of a disguised *bodhisattva* or ghost sent by the Buddha in some movie or TV special about the supernatural. She had thick black hair like a movie star, but when a ray of light hit it, her hair revealed reddish glints. Everyone else's would have gleamed blue-black.

Her eyes rose at the outer corners in a patrician way, but they were just a little rounder, a little deeper than normal Thais. The way her gaze looked straight at you, with no polite lowering of the eyes, was like the urgency of a messenger from the heavenly world, or the guilelessness of a child. The lower part of her mouth was not Asian at all, but quite charming. Like a picture of John F. Kennedy's wife, she had a clear firm chin that held wide lips ending at each side with an indented bracket. The curled brackets grew deeper when she smiled, which was often.

It really was a shame that Thailand had to give its children away. That, more than Susan's beautiful but unnerving appearance, was perhaps why her presence reminded him of a *bodhisattva*, a divine messenger. What was the message he was to receive? Kun Sompan looked away, a little ashamed to realize that he was inspecting a woman at such length. He felt sure there was a reason for his being asked to interpret for this otherworldly returnee, there was a *meaning* for him here. He would pray to understand the meaning that was intended for him.

~

As their car left the highway and entered

the thick of the city of Bangkok itself, it slowed as it joined the crawl through intersections. Susan noticed flashing monorails overhead. She thought she saw a canal like the ones her parents described seeing many years ago when they came to bring her back to the United States.

Kun Sompan pulled up to her hotel, and got her checked in. They must still have been making up the rooms because they took her luggage and put it by the front desk. There Susan noticed something on the wall above her bags. It was a birdhouse high on the wall, but like none she had ever seen back home.

Its sides were painted a white that gleamed with coolness and drew her eyes in the dark of the lobby. Its roof was covered with some kind of shiny orange tiles, round like ceramic fish scales, with eaves that curled up like fiddleheads. It had gilt detailed windows, wrap around veranda and door, all with mosaic trims made of colored glass. Coils of incense rose from a joss stick at its tiny entrance. Someone had laid a bracelet-sized garland of tiny white jasmine and rose buds across its miniature railings with an artful casualness.

Kun Sompan's voice broke her reverie and she followed him out to buy lunch down the street. There were more of the birdhouses. That must be what Fred Kouyoumjian had asked for. They all seemed to have scrolled eaves and instead of a bird perch, they had porch-like platforms. The little porches held small garlands of flowers or a fruit on a tiny dish.

The eatery they stopped at was almost completely open to the street on one side and small sparrows flitted between a power line that looped in front of it between poles and a soffit over the kitchen. She saw that a birdhouse was even affixed to a wall at a spot just above the heads of the patrons. She asked Kun Sompan about the birdhouses.

"You mean spirit houses, *san jao thi*? They're actually not for birds. When a family builds a house they take away the space of the spirits that already lived there. But Thais want no homeless problem like Seattle," he joked, "so we build them their own house and we feed them, brighten it sometimes with flowers."

"Have they anything to do with ancestor worship–like you burn incense in someone's memory or pray to them?"

"That's Chinese. Chinese Thais here do that with their Confucian alters, burn incense and spirit money for their own ancestors. Can do both. But spirit houses are not necessarily for ancestors, just spirits in the spirit houses.

Nature spirits, someone else's ancestors, probably no relation." Kun Sompan laughed at his own joke.

Susan took that in, "That sounds like the idea behind All Soul's Eve. I think people in northern Europe used to light fires and offer food to wandering spirits. Now it's called Halloween and it's silly, just for children who dress up in costumes."

"Spirit houses are respected, well-tended. How you treat the spirit house shows your heart connection, *namchai*, not your blood connection."

She was certain that Thais wouldn't want birds roosting in their spirit houses. Maybe she'd better not get one for Fred Kouyoumjian and just plead inconvenience.

They passed a woman on a low stool on the sidewalk behind a propane griddle. She was stir frying translucent noodles flecked with dried red pepper flakes and bits of ground meat. Kun Sompan told Susan it was called *wunsen* but kept walking. Her mouth watered.

Only a little further they passed a small storefront that had tumblers and parfait glasses of confections in a display case. Some held orange yolk colored noodles in syrup, others offered coconut milk floating with *boba* nubs.

At the restaurant a waitress used long chopsticks to filet a sautéed fish at their table. Then she gave them each a bowl of fresh white rice and gingerly ladled a green curry with pieces of meat and vegetables onto the rice and offered them utensils.

Susan had been expecting chopsticks. That's what they used in Japan or at Chinese restaurants back home so she thought that's what they used everywhere in Asia. Instead she received a fork and tablespoon. She watched Kun Sompan push rice and curry with his fork onto the spoon and then put the spoon into his mouth. Susan carefully imitated him as he and the waitress chatted.

David had suggested to Susan that she keep a journal of her visit and bought her a dainty clothbound one with handmade paper. When she got back to the hotel, she would write down her observations about Tokyo and Bangkok.

Before she left, David even managed to find a translation of the Thai novel, "Letters from Bangkok," told in the voice of a turn-of-the-century emigrant from China. She didn't have that point of view, but she certainly noticed enough that afternoon that was new compared to her second home, Japan.

Japan was a good midway point on the way to Thailand because where Thailand was exotic, Japan seemed merely different. She and Kun Sompan walked quite a bit that first evening in Bangkok, with Kun Sompan explaining what to her were strange fruits and signs.

The cooking smells pouring out of the Japanese shops were different from home and the favorite dessert, a sweet, heavy red bean paste seemed to appear in the most innocent looking confections. It was thinner than the red bean paste they used for her childhood Moon Festivals.

But in Thailand the national fruit was durian, a tough yellowy fruit that smelled like a cross between diesel exhaust and carrion. Thai meals were seasoned with pungent blends of garlic and fermented fish sauce.

In Tokyo merchants displayed their wares on the sidewalks in front of stores, even in front of pricey department stores, something she rarely saw back in the States.

Thailand took it further and seemed like there was even more going on on the sidewalks than inside the buildings. Vendors hawked their wares everywhere, squatting on street corners, walking up and down the aisles of trains.

Tokyo was crowded, but at least until

happy hour the crowds were mostly neatly dressed and sweat free. In Bangkok the crowd pressed in close with perfumed matrons, unwashed migrants from the countryside, men and women with jewels and flowing wrap skirts and they all seemed to stare at her more than the cosmopolitanites of Tokyo.

In both cities, the temperatures were extreme. Thailand had three seasons: rainy season, hot season and hotter season. She was there in October after the monsoons were supposed to have brought in the sea breezes from the Indian Ocean. The heat still felt like the kind of thing that would have inspired any self-respecting New York news station to set up a heat wave death count.

The extremes in Tokyo, on the other hand, were man made. Although the weather was temperate with four seasons comparable to those in the Carolinas, the taxi drivers seemed to only set their heaters and air conditioners full blast.

Fine in torrid August or frigid January, but it being October the cabbies had been unable to reach the consensus Japanese were supposed to be so famous for. Thus whenever she hailed a cab she never knew whether she would be stepping inside the simulated climate of

Antarctica or the blasting dry winds of the Sahara. Back in her Tokyo hotel, the heating and ventilation of all the rooms were centrally controlled by the management, who had the same temperature sensibilities as the cabbies.

She was relieved to find that temperature wise her small room here in Bangkok was pleasant. Its walls barely filtered any of the cacophony of the *tuk-tuks*, in fact the room fan and air conditioning provided an interesting bass line.

She could take anything with cheer knowing it was only one night. She flopped down on her bed, already composing her journal entries. She had three or so hours until Kun Sompan returned for a dinner foray.

11 SPIRIT HOUSE
1991

The disorienting walk back from dinner through the Bangkok lights, the drive north, and the sight of the tapioca fire were behind them. Just moments ago they had climbed the ladder Noklek lowered for them. She was really here.

They took off their dusty shoes as Susan's birth mother greeted Kun Sompan with smiles in a slow sing-song voice that was still girlish. The woman nodded and stared as Susan climbed to the platform. Susan's birth mother grabbed her arm and helped her up the final rungs. The sudden physical contact startled Susan and she gave a quiet cry.

Now she was gazing in her mother's face for the first time, a woman a little shorter than herself, a stranger who felt completely familiar. Noklek hadn't loosened her gentle grip yet, her hand was warm, and her eyes were happy and loving. Susan grabbed her mother's other hand.

They stood, two thirsty souls, letting each other drink until the moment broke. Then they both turned their eyes elsewhere.

Susan saw they were on a wooden verandah with three single story structures. One was small and enclosed like a cabana or a tool shed, another was open. From it poured the same scent of fermented fish sauce and steamed rice she had encountered in Bangkok. Her mother, Noklek, led them past it as she and the interpreter exchanged pleasantries in Thai. Inside Susan could see a deep metal pan and a wok and assorted ladles and a long wooden spatula hanging on the wall above a small portable stove.

Then they turned at the largest building. Susan's birth mother slid open the door.

It was dark and cooler inside and at first Susan couldn't see, only aware of the woody smell that came from the hand woven walls. They walked directly into what must be a sitting area with no foyer and sat down on cushions on a cool, polished wooden floor. It was worn but appeared to glow red-brown from the teak so common in the countryside. The woman left them and then returned with earthenware dishes of food. Susan watched Noklek serve them herself using the same long serving chopsticks she had seen in Bangkok.

Finally, Noklek pointed to the photo album Susan had brought with her. Susan was happy to have something to show her. Relying on an interpreter was more unnerving than she had expected.

Noklek spent a long time looking at a picture of Susan with her parents in front of their house. It was taken one winter years ago after they had built a snowman. Their white colonial house, with snow on the roof and smoke pouring out of the brick chimney looked as unlike Noklek's woven home on stilts as anything Susan could have deliberately conjured.

Noklek was curious about snow. She explained to Susan that they had no refrigeration in the village but she had seen freezers and ice in Bangkok. Noklek aaahed over a few pictures of David and Susan's wedding. She thought the wedding gown Susan had worn was opulent but wondered if she couldn't have worn something with more color. Noklek's own workaday skirt was a fuchsia print under a lime colored blouse.

When Noklek came to recent pictures of Susan with Lily, she looked startled and then began speaking to Kun Sompan as she thumbed through them.

During the rest of the meal Susan noticed

that the woman did not eat and would sometimes pause and stare at her kindly. The woman did have a long neck, her hair was cut short and there was something similar around the eyes and highly placed eyebrows. How to talk to her?

Susan had the urge to ask, bluntly, "Are you really my mother?" The conversation seemed maddeningly superficial. Susan remembered a children's book someone had bought Lily about a baby bird that fell out of the nest and went around asking insects, trucks, and dogs, "Are you my mother?"

That's how stupid and silly she felt as she awkwardly shoveled rice from her fork into her tablespoon. She had gone from being a professional the day before in Tokyo–to this.

Then she felt a stabbing pain in her throat.

It felt like acid was burning the inside of her mouth. This evil woman had poisoned her! She was coughing and crying and out of the corner of her eye she saw the woman run out of the room.

That woman hadn't been concerned about me all these years, she only agreed to meet me now to take final revenge. Did she hate my birth father that much? I was only an innocent baby.

There's probably not a hospital for miles. David will never know exactly how I died. Why didn't she kill me then, why wait until I have Lily to take care of? I'm dying. This is a delayed infanticide. She doesn't have the right. I want to live. I can't breathe. I'm dying.

Kun Sompan leaned over concerned and a little amused, "You bit a hot pepper. She's getting you some more rice."

"Water!! Water!!"

"No, water will just spread the pepper oils, rice will dull it."

Now the woman was back, sitting very near her and holding her chin with one hand and spoon feeding her warm rice with the other. With tears of pain still streaming down her face, she accepted the food open-mouthed, now really like that baby bird in the children's story.

The woman put her hand between Susan's shoulder blades and the young woman found herself crying into the shoulder of the older woman. Susan could tell from the gentle shaking of her shoulders that Noklek was crying, too. They stayed like that for a long time, kneeling near each other on the cushions, one leaning over the one leaning down.

"Mai rong hai, Suwan. Mai rong hai, chai yen-yen." Don't cry, Suwan. Please don't cry, just

be calm.

This woman knew the name Suwan. This is the woman.

"*Kun-mae*?" Mother?

"*Chai. Mae kon Suwan.*" Yes, I am your mother, Suwan.

Somewhere behind them Kun Sompan shifted on his cushion. *Kun-mae* straightened herself but still held Susan's hand. She began talking softly in Thai and he repeated her words to Susan in English, softly.

"Perhaps you have already heard it, but this is the story. I went to work to support my parents from the age of fourteen, far from home. Around the age of twenty I got in trouble, I had to stay an entire hot season through the rainy season at the Buddhist temple where the nuns took in unmarried girls. The nuns let me work in the garden until the baby came," *Kun-mae* paused as though done telling her entire story. Susan prompted her with, "What did you think about when you were pregnant?"

Kun-mae looked at her long, proudly, as if to let her know she had asked the right question.

"There were no men to look at me," she resumed.

"I tried to imagine how the nuns or how the other girls looked at me. But for the first time in a very long time, by carrying a child within, I could begin to see my self again, to think from my self again. Often my thoughts were a conversation with your spirit, this other being: 'I know it will hurt to have a baby but I know we, you and I, have an agreement: because I didn't kill you, you won't kill me.'

"This is what I told myself. I actually spoke these words to you before you were born. I don't remember the labor clearly but I do remember that two nuns stayed with me and after you were born they fed me a special broth to make the milk come in. I nursed you for one full month."

Noklek paused, and then looked away, "But I had to go back to work so I gave you to the nuns. They are clean and pure-hearted and dear to the Buddha so I knew it was a better place for a child. I came back to see you once, but you were gone. I didn't know foreigners took babies. I returned to my old job and I worked for another eight years. Then I returned north."

"Didn't they explain that you would lose me when you signed the relinquishment papers?" asked Susan.

There was a pause in Kun Sompan's interpreting as her mother pressed her lips together. Susan wanted to ask Noklek another particular question. It begged asking, but she worried that it would be thoughtless to ask something so direct again just yet. Somehow later today she would have to ask it.

It was clear to Susan that her birth mother was taking the conversation in a new direction when Noklek finally answered, "I'm not saying I'm disappointed, because America is a rich country and houses are big, but now look. I can't talk to you in *Phasa Thai*, in the Thai language."

Susan looked at Kun Sompan.

"No," he anticipated her thought, "she didn't answer your question about signing papers. I believe she did understand it."

Hadn't *Kun-mae* had to sign papers in order for her parents to adopt her? Or, had the woman abandoned her there, no papers, no planning? The alternative would be a possibility that Suwan dismissed as soon as it occurred to her: that the nuns engaged in black market adoptions–that her own parents had bought her from baby sellers.

"By and by, I left Bangkok and my older brother arranged for me to marry this widower, only second generation Thai from China. He is my second husband. I had another husband first who was also Chinese Thai. A man who made

Canadian passports for Fujian Chinese found me as a bride for that man."

A man who made, who forged, Canadian passports? How did Noklek know these kinds of people? Susan wondered but she let Noklek continue.

"But he divorced me because I couldn't give him children," Noklek paused looking down, "Perhaps there is a lesson in this because I gave away a child."

Susan leaned forward to touch Noklek's arm gently. She wanted her to feel loved and forgiven for the hard decision she had had to make many years ago. Her poor mother.

Suwan didn't know which was crueler: what her mother back home had suffered in finding out she needed a hysterectomy so young, or what this somehow familiar stranger had endured, a failed romance that led to her being forced to give away a child, only to face infertility and rejection.

She thought about her parents' marriage. She may have misjudged them.

Despite any fights or any emotional debt her mother might have felt toward Dad, there was never really any doubt he would always be with Mom.

At least Noklek had born a child and they

were meeting again today. All these years of feeling welcome in her adoptive family made Suwan compassionate now, feeling even keeled, and now her birth mother's vulnerability flooded her with a sense of beneficent strength.

She relaxed at being able to touch her birth mother and offer her solace. Her friends in the group were right, searching and truth were empowering.

Yet nothing prepared her for the revelation that came next. Noklek added matter-of-factly, "Many of the girls in the life, even after they leave the life, their insides are ruined and they can never have babies like other women."

The life?

Suwan's heart lurched and sank, but Noklek didn't pause.

"This man is good. He married me quickly after his wife died because his daughters were only two and three years old. I was thirty-four. He couldn't afford more children and he was very progressive about not desiring sons. He says we can just adopt one of our sons-in-law when the girls marry."

The life.

Susan turned the idea over in her mind.

"I am their only mother," Noklek added.

"My two girls were like two birds at first. I had to be very calm-hearted and clever to win their trust. The youngest, in the beginning, was terrible and used to bite me, and the older would ignore me. Yes, I was very calm-hearted because I truly felt sorry for them, and, because I could see that their father had only married me for their sake. All the neighbors could tell from my northern dialect that I was born around here but they knew I had worked in Bangkok. The women watched to see if I would flirt with the men or pinch my little girls or hoard food when visitors came."

Noklek seemed like she was trying to convince Susan as much as she had once tried to convince the villagers, "Then people began to see that I was not wanton or cruel or miserly or haughty and now this is my home."

Susan shook her head involuntarily. The life.

"It took several years," Noklek was trying to distract Suwan back to the present.

"No one knows about the times when I used to go to the lily pond to sit and cry. I was too ashamed to visit much with my own family," Noklek was already holding Suwan's hand but now reached for it with her other hand as well.

"The women here, I harbor no bitterness

and will not speak ill of anyone in particular, but there is pity for a woman who is not fully a woman. And there is pity for a woman who has to earn her place in a home like this one here where the children are already at home. If my husband's children knew and if the women in the village knew that I, too, had born a child, I would be free of their pity. But I would earn their curiosity and their scorn."

Noklek looked at her, "You are my secret, beautiful mouse: I, too, had a child."

Susan smiled a little uncertainly at her mother.

"My life has been hard but I am not bitter for my life or when I see newborn babies, because I had a child, too, who grew up rich in America."

Kun-mae began to collect dishes, but with a slight hesitation each time she reached out a slender arm toward a bowl, before placing it back on a lacquer tray. Finally, she paused and rocked back on her heels and said something to Kun Sompan.

"Please come back in two days," she said. Then she added something to Kun Sompan that he didn't translate.

She placed the serving tray, now full of dishes, back down on the floor where they were sitting. The woman seemed like she might continue speaking but instead she pressed her lips together, closed her eyes, and nodded her head, as if to affirm that that was enough.

As her shoulders started to shake, it was Susan's turn to comfort her. This wasn't what Susan had imagined.

She didn't know what she had expected, maybe more questions about her adoptive parents or her education or a comparing of noses and toes, and she hadn't in fact imagined what it would mean to this mother.

She didn't expect to be the witness to Noklek's deep grief. Silence and an embrace seemed the only reply.

Susan held her birth mother for a long time.

But as the shadows shifted slightly in the room, *Kun-mae* backed away and rose, a sign, Kun Sompan explained, that it was really time to go.

Before they left, Suwan handed her camera to Kun Sompan and posed next to *Kun-mae.* He snapped pictures, the flashes lighting up every corner of the dark woven hut.

Then reluctantly Susan backed down the ladder to the ground. She noticed the spirit house, *san jao thi,* across the compound.

It stood on a pole halfway between the ladder and the lily pond where her birth mother said she used to weep. It was made of weathered gray wood with gracefully curved eaves over a tiny ornately carved door sill.

Self-consciously, while her birth mother watched from above, Suwan-Susan walked over to the lily pond. She leaned down and picked a miniature blue water lily no bigger than a buttercup and walked back to reach up and lay it in the doorway of the spirit house.

She imagined that it was spiritual graffiti saying, "I was here," left behind as a reminder that, "somehow even now I heard you when you cried alone here. I know your tears fell and gave birth to concentric circles that lifted and rocked these delicate water lilies."

Suwan looked up at *Kun-mae*'s face just in time to see the same pressed lip, eyes closed nod. As they drove off, Suwan waved, *Kun-mae* kneeling, nodding, but now following them with her eyes.

~

The tapioca fires had been put out and dusk had obscured the smoke though the smell still hung in the bowl of the valley. As the car rose over the ridge and then began its gradual descent past the same rice paddies and hamlets they had seen earlier, Susan watched everything through the intense azure of evening.

The loveliness of the strange tapioca fires without and the loneliness within of the woman in the shadows of the wood scented sitting room filled her with an ache.

Suwan wanted to hold the images like amulets against her heart and sat through the long ride back to the nearest district town in a fugue of emotions and remembered sensations: the angry red embers in a blackened field; the curry on warm rice; the rawness that lingered in her mouth from the acidic pepper oils; the incomprehensible but beautiful, youthful voice of Noklek Prichittakorn; traces of incense on her birth mother's hair and shoulder and clothes; the blue of the water lily petals like the inner blue of a flame against the soft gray of the spirit house; the spring green of the rice seedlings in the silvery paddies; the men and women with dark hair like her own, in sandals, holding blue plastic pails.

Eventually they pulled up behind a small family owned hotel. She wasn't completely over jet lag, but was able to walk with Kun Sompan to a small night market strung with electric lights where they found a noodle stand.

They smiled at each other the first time she gamely tried to slurp the noodles only to have them slither back down into the soup, splashing her shirt. The second try she succeeded. It was perfect, the saltiness of the broth, the few pieces of pickled mushrooms and vegetables that floated in the freshly made noodles.

As they walked back to the hotel through the night market, she was relieved that there were no ugly surprises like the little boy they had encountered in Bangkok. Here nightlife belonged to the merchants and their families.

She found religious stalls for incense and *bodhisattva* icons, sandal and clothing stores, a corner stall with cages of live chickens, another with bolts of fabric and a case of gold necklaces. There were at least half a dozen more noodle shops and one confection stand like the one in the city with turmeric colored candied egg yolk balls. The tapioca bubble tea was local.

They stopped at a shop that sold crafts from the hill tribes north of this area. She bought pillow covers that were the strangest patchwork quilts she had ever seen, nothing like the New England bridal quilt she and David used on their bed. These covers had blocks of light blue on dark blue batik as complicated as Celtic knots, overlaid with fine applique spirals in red or black, with seemingly random bands of cross stitching.

She reflexively picked out two more for her mother, before remembering and putting them back. She would bring her adoptive mother presents from Japan only to keep *this* trip a secret.

That night the owner of the little motel, who was apparently the mother of the family that lived behind the check in lobby on the first floor, knocked and began to explain discreetly how to use the sparkling chrome and tile bathroom. It was appointed with inexplicable, but cheery pink, orange, blue and green buckets that the woman seemed very proud of.

On a dais raised about a foot up, and also completely covered in tile like the floor, was a porcelain toilet bowl that, the innkeeper explained with gestures, Susan was to squat over. One shined lever was to be turned for a small rush of water, the other lever for a larger cascade of water.

Susan smiled, nodding, "Squat, then small flush for number one, large flush for number two," to the agreeable but uncomprehending hostess.

Stepping backward, the lady pointed to one of the buckets and pantomimed that Susan was then to fill the bucket to wash her privates with water from a faucet in the wall only two feet from the ground. There was not a roll of toilet paper in sight.

Pointing to a pair of buckets near a cistern, the lady gave Susan to understand that one was for bathing her lower body, but not for washing after relieving herself, and the other was to be used as a basin only for her face, shoulders and hair. There were two separate towels. One was to be used for just her face, shoulders and hair, while the other was only for her feet and lower body.

Holding up three and then two fingers, Susan tried to confirm, "Three buckets to wash with, two towels to dry with?"

The woman nodded vigorously, and patiently pantomimed the taboo against mixing upper body bucket with lower body bucket, or upper body towel with lower body towel.

This seemed in keeping with how Susan noticed people carried themselves as they moved around the shops here and in Bangkok. Even though furniture was often low to the ground, and wares might be displayed right on the earth, people didn't point with their feet at them, but instead squatted down to gesture at a low object, or move a low piece of furniture with their hands.

The soap was scented and smelled like cantaloupe, or that's what was pictured on its pale orange and cream rice paper wrapper. Susan actually felt a little thrill to realize that the room spray near the door smelled like honeysuckle. This demonstrated what her friend Kayoko in Japan had taught her two years ago when they worked on a spice and aromatherapy exhibit. People whose cuisines were heavy on poultry or wheat tended to prefer pungent lemon and traditional potpourri scents. Those whose diets were heavy with soy and rice tended to gravitate toward slightly milder scents that they blended better with, like honeysuckle or cantaloupe. Honeysuckle was the most common cleaning product scent in East and Southeast Asia, while European descendants in either the New World or the Old World bought citruses like bergamot and lemon, or herbals like lavender.

In her room later that night, she had planned to call David but decided against it. She finally understood what he meant when he told her he didn't want to talk about his feelings or the particular events of the day because he simply didn't know what his feelings were and didn't know what he wanted to say.

She hoped he remembered this if he was waiting for her to check in with a description of her day and their daughter's birth grandmother. She pulled the covers up around her and felt the starched sheets scratch her cheeks. She smiled. Tapioca starch?

~

That night's dreams quilted together images. Rectangles of weathered gray Thai homes on stilts faded into frames of grey-stained New England lobster sheds. Squares of green and silver rice paddy stitched together and then swirled away until she was not looking at Southeast Asian terracing but looking down from a jet plane at New England farmland in pale greens and browns and yellows from fields of soy, fields of corn, fields of wheat, and fields of clover. It produced a vertigo that wakened her in the small hours to the hum of the motel air conditioner.

Traffic had fallen still in the street below and she slept again. Suwan saw her birth mother kneeling before a pot of broth with lemongrass in the kitchen area. This time she noticed intensely how *Kun-mae*'s brow flattened between her eyes then sloped gracefully to a small, wide nose. It wasn't exactly like Susan's own but it was close enough to what made Susan unique in her own adoptive family.

12 SOJOURNING
1991

The next day Susan was up early. She found herself, as she usually did after flying eastward, dressed and fresh and stepping out onto the street well before many shopkeepers began sleepily unlocking and raising the security grill in front of their stores and then sweeping or hosing the sidewalk of the previous evening's detritus.

She knew to enjoy while she could the lightness of waking up curious and rested so soon after dawn. By midafternoon the leaden exhaustion of jet lag would belie the brightness of the noonday sun, felling her into the time zone back home that was deepening into the wee hours of the morning.

Kun Sompan gave her another reason. He suspected she would wake and leave the motel before he could stop her so he had advised, "Get out, if you must, while there's still a breeze up. It will be beaten down by the scorching heat of midmorning. It will come."

She remembered the other advice Kun Sompan gave her before last night: don't drink any beverage from the open air tea houses that lined many side streets. Traveling alone she could easily be drugged. So her first stop was at a convenience store where she bought precooked rice and egg in a package, along with a bottle of something labeled "healthy water".

After she paid for them with *baht* she slid the change inside the traveler's pouch she wore on a strap that slung down over one shoulder, crossed her chest and wrapped around her opposite waist. She carried both plastic containers to a round table out front and sat down on a stool.

Just then, a monk in a saffron robe rounded the corner directly across the street. His head was completely shaved and he walked sandal-less on the uneven concrete teeth that glinted in the rays of the low morning sun, rows that lined the upper and lower jaw of the avenue embedded in the red earth here. She watched the middle aged monk with the curiosity of an archeologist, having made a find.

The monk trailed behind him three or four dozen elementary school boys, the younger ones in front, with a pair of teenagers sweeping up the stragglers. The teenaged assistants and their soft faced charges wore matching saffron robes, the ends of each one's cloth tossed over their shoulders, much like David and Jonathan and the other men at the synagogue deftly draped the extra folds of their prayer shawls over their own shoulders as they rocked in concentration.

She noticed that each boy carried a bowl made from unstained wood. At the first storefront nearest the corner, a woman came out. She clearly expected them. She held the handle of a metal bucket in one hand and a small yellowish bamboo paddle for scooping out plain white rice into each of the bowls.

At one point one of the smaller boys climbed up onto a folding chair meant for patrons. It earned him an animated, breathy scolding from the troop leader. Susan couldn't make out a word he was saying, but he seemed to apologize and thank the woman in a quietly theatrical way that drew the attention of the line of little brown eyes away from the rogue and back toward their benefactress.

Each child, imitating him, thanked her and recited a set phrase. An incantation? A blessing? Then, single file, the procession moved on, visiting most doors on the block.

Kun Sompan had explained that most non-Muslim Thai men ducked in and out of membership in the monkhood for multiple reasons during childhood and adulthood. There were farmers who joined a Buddhist retreat during the rainy season when they couldn't work their fields anyway. Many bachelors, in the month before their wedding, would temporarily take vows. They were giving the life of the monastery one last chance before making the decision for matrimony. They would also accrue merit during that month that would bring the blessings of good karma to themselves and their bride.

As society changed, more children joined the orders. Families left the cycle of tilling, planting, tending and harvesting that used to force schools in Thailand, in fact in every country, to close during the warm months so children could join their families in the fields. The schools continued to close, but now children in the towns attended camps at their municipal convent or cloister, becoming the juvenile nuns and monks that tourists found so photogenic. Susan remembered how in early spring most of the churches and temples back home unfurled banners on their lawns advertising summer

Bible camps.

Susan pushed the stool back and got up. She planned to meet Kun Sompan in the late morning. He had arranged a trip to an elephant park for them. Before that she wanted to walk toward the paddies she saw just a few hundred yards beyond the end of the town proper. She went back into the shop and the shopkeeper looked up from the red and green inked headlines of a newspaper she was reading behind the counter. The lady said something incomprehensible before Susan held up the packaging from her meal and pointed to it. The woman understood and took it, still talking in the best of spirits. Susan did her best to smile enthusiastically and say,

"*Khopkun ka.*" Thank you.

Then Susan turned and headed up the street toward the open fields. Before her departure for Thailand, Fred Kouyoumjian warned her about scorpions, red ants, and snakes so she had overdressed in thick socks and hiking boots. As the sun rose, the air was dry and clear but must have already hit a hundred degrees, and Susan realized her footgear was more suitable for temperate Lyme tick woods.

She only had about two or three blocks to go before the dentures of sidewalk gave way to a banked road that threaded through alternating fields of rice and mullet on its way through the long plain.

A few meters along, she saw a low, baby blue cinderblock building set back from the road at the far end of a packed dirt courtyard. Mounded plants with blue-green heads of saw tooth spears lined the edges of the playground and either side of the cement walkway to the schoolhouse door. They reached just below her knees and when she stooped down to look more closely, she saw that these spiny blades rose from the tops of tiny pineapples. She had never realized that pineapples grew low to the ground.

This might be the place that, when it was in session, those little monks were enrolled. She noticed two or three mangoes rocking gently from a tree near the curb and she could imagine the boys in the neat black shorts and crisp white short sleeved shirts of their Thai school uniforms reaching for these fruits during recess, inching up the smooth trunk with their knees and elbows.

She was enjoying the town buildings in the near horizon and their Thai kitchen smells–boiled and steamed rice, stir fry with the ubiquitous pungency of *nam pla*, fish sauce, and *prik*, small hot peppers, or the citric aromas of cilantro and lemon grass.

Another ten minutes of walking and she found her rhythm.

She felt buoyed by her own cadence here six hours north of *Krung Thep*, Bangkok, seventeen hours from Anchorage or L.A., and over twenty hours from Toronto, New York, Washington or Atlanta. Every detail of what might have been her homeland turned out to feel foreign.

Yet this was hers.

Groundedness now came with the rhythm of her hiking boots on the earth, the swing of her arms, and the stroke of her breath as her heart beat evenly.

Now, after days in taxis, airplanes, trains and *tuk-tuks*, she had found her footing by meeting the woman at the top of the ladder, but also by realizing she carried it with her.

She passed dry tilled fields and flooded paddies that were occasionally punctuated by a single tree left to grow where it stood in the middle of rows of cultivation. Rough emerald and cobalt mountains rose in the distance. The outlines of corrugated metal roofed homes and lean-tos threaded between the paved road she was traveling and the base of the foothills. Raised dirt trails crisscrossed the fields of the valley up to the horizon.

Her thoughts drifted to something she was seeing clearly but had only glimpsed through a dozen panes of glass in the past two days. Travel guides and coffee table books had prepared her for the glossy leafed tropical trees and *louche* jungle birds, but no atlas mapped the fearsomely tall heavens that towered over the horizon in front of her.

Cumulus clouds rose higher than the fiercest dark thunderheads of North America while gleaming as white as the greatest ocean crossing four masters from the Age of Exploration. A fleet of these equatorial clouds floated high in the skyscape, reaching stories taller. Sunlight streamed above and below them and sunbeams passed between their breathtaking girths to the fields below.

There was not a dark hint or scent–yet–of a storm but Susan decided to head back to the little hotel. She turned around but kept up the cadence, swinging her arms, striding lightly but quickly.

She cut across to walk back on the opposite side and was rewarded with a strange encounter. Susan spotted a long, gravel driveway that passed through a stand of palms to a yard planted with topiaries.

Its gravel driveway and sculpted evergreens would have already been distinctive back home but here they were discordant. She could hear the hum of an electric trimmer.

A pair of children, a Eurasian boy and girl, perhaps seven and eight, appeared from behind a giant tiger topiary. Susan smiled, waved and called out, "Hello, *sawas dee ka*," and suddenly the buzz of the hedge clipper stopped and she heard it drop.

From behind a giant topiary tortoise she saw the sunburned back of a heavy, shirtless Caucasian man in putty colored safari shorts and Birkenstocks running for the front steps of the veranda. He jiggled as he seemed to take the staircase in two bounds. He never paused as he waved her away angrily while keeping his face averted before disappearing inside. A minute later a Thai woman appeared from inside the house and called sharply to the boy and girl.

Susan smiled at her and walked toward her but the woman called out, "Go, stop. *Yung!* You, go!"

The woman called out the words again before Susan could believe what she was hearing. She felt herself flush at having been yelled at. Her excitement at seeing the Eurasian children withered and she left their grounds–but slowly and with shoulders thrown back.

Later that day, as Susan rode with Kun Sompan, he mused, "Some expatriates come here with secrets to hide. There are almost no *farang,* Caucasians, here yet clearly they were not happy to see another one. Very expensive house, *nah*?"

"Bought with embezzled money?"

She remembered hearing that some corners of Thailand were treated like the Wild West. Now she was seeing it.

"Or, maybe a fugitive. You can also earn good money once you're here, even in this countryside, if you speak English."

~

At the elephant park, Susan and Kun Sompan sat in back of a jeep. A driver sped them along the paved road to the grounds that seemed divided into a military checkpoint and barracks, a wooded elephant yard, and a well-watered garden with a broad thatch roofed pavilion where a bartender was mixing drinks in a metal shaker.

There were Thai families there on holiday and about two dozen pale skinned Chinese tourists being shepherded by a tour guide. When Suwan's turn on line came, the ticket taker spoke directly to her, looking puzzled. Kun Sompan leaned in and cleared up whatever the issue was.

Smiling, the ticket taker now tried out his English, "*Sawas dee klap*. Good day. Ride okay," and he put his palms together in a *wai* greeting.

"*Sawas dee ka*," Susan replied in the feminine, returning his *wai*, "*khopkun ka*," thanking him. She realized it felt good to try on her lost mother tongue.

Kun Sompan would ride the elephant behind her. At the command of the trainer, her elephant kneeled on his front legs and they helped her up a three stepped mount from which she swung one leg over the tasseled saddle and blanket. She held on to the upholstered horn of the saddle as the elephant rocked upward and she found herself eye level with the fringes of the forest canopy.

She was rocked in the cradle of the saddle and after about a half hour of this, the undertow she had already begun to feel from jetlag strengthened and gripped her. Susan would have to ask Noklek tomorrow if any of her ancestors drove elephants in the northern lumbering operations. Other than that thought tying her forward to the second visit with her birth mother tomorrow, she spent the rest of her mental energy trying to fight being lulled into sleep and losing her grip on this lurching pachyderm.

At one point the trail descended and both elephants stopped at the bank of a muddy river.

The trainer led Kun Sompan's elephant across first and then his assistant tapped her elephant with his crop and she found herself startled awake as her feet held on to the hide of her elephant, just a few inches above the murky river eddies. But by the time they were back at the pavilion at the garden's edge, she was so sleepy she asked Kun Sompan to bring her back to the motel and take the rest of the afternoon off.

13 TRAFFICKING
1991

The next day Kun Sompan met her at the hotel with suggestions for a new itinerary. She could only extend her overall stay by one more day so she would shorten a layover she had planned in Bangkok. Then she and Kun Sompan drove out to the village again. The husband and stepdaughters had gone for the day to the next valley.

This time when Kun Sompan and Suwan climbed the ladder up to the platform of *Kun-mae*'s home, they met a smiling, slightly darker woman who appeared from behind *Kun-mae*'s shoulder. Kun Sompan introduced her as a girlhood friend of Noklek's who had eventually married into this village, too. Her name was Tuptim, which meant Ruby, they told her. It was clear that Tuptim had been invited specifically for this second visit between mother and daughter.

Before Noklek began speaking through Kun Sompan, she gave Suwan something the length of her arm.

"For you and Lily."

As Susan took it from her she saw that it was a bolt of silk. It was a nubby vermillion woven through with gold threads. Susan held it at the ends, as though her skin might stain it, and she laid it next to her as she sat with them on the gleaming wood floor so she could feel it at her side through the afternoon. This was the first gift she had received from her biological mother.

Now Noklek settled in to begin telling Suwan more of their story. Tuptim had left the room and Suwan could hear her in the cooking building.

"Mother believed that Father hid money, actual *baht*, somewhere at the edge of the jungle. Even though we were cassava root farmers like all our neighbors in the hamlet, Father often seemed to be dreaming up one side business after another. This never seemed to ease the hard summer rainy season or the heavy heat of April for the rest of the family. Instead these schemes only took too much time away from work that actually had merit, or at least that's how it seemed to my mother and me."

As children, Noklek and the others sometimes found Father's schemes inspired, or, at least funny.

They often involved a pushcart he would set up at the crossroads just outside their village where the road divided and could take you either across the valley plain between planted fields to the next hamlet or up over the low mountains that ringed her horizon.

The first road took you to the market during the two harvest seasons. The second road took you to the train that would travel all day and all night before reaching Chiang Mai or even *Krung Thep*, Bangkok.

"It was at the crossroad that Father tried selling various wares from his pushcart: Bollywood magazines, cricket cages he had learned to make by hand as a boy, batteries, sweets and shoes for trips beyond the village along either byway. When a rumor spread through the village that he was also selling condoms, the grannies put a stop to his venture."

Noklek heard that a group of about a dozen women in their sixties or so dissuaded him, perhaps violently, from carrying such wanton wares.

Noklek overheard the mothers say that, "what the grannies really feared was that selling condoms would bring venereal diseases and pimps to the village. Didn't all three travel together just like the monkey king, the abbot and the dragon prince?"

They were the three characters from the Chinese opera "Journey to the West" which traveling shadow puppeteers performed after every harvest.

"Whether Father abandoned an old scheme or initiated a new one, Mother seemed resigned. He always did sell out his wares but not before too much time had been spent away from the fields for the cash to improve the condition of the family.

"Auntie joked to Mother, looking at Noklek's ten siblings, 'that using rather than selling the condoms might have offered more promise.'"

Susan was growing very uncomfortable. She wasn't a prude but the way all three people sitting with her in Noklek's home held themselves at the discussion of condoms troubled her. Condoms seemed to be a prelude to what they already sensed was coming next.

But Noklek continued, "in the year I

turned fourteen and became one of his schemes myself, from then on I could never remember any of his side businesses with the same amusement or innocence. Not even Mother, while she was still alive, let herself understand the depth of my bitterness.

"Older girls had started to go work in mills in the provincial capital. One day some men from the south, maybe Bangkok, came to town. Somehow they met Father and after a night of drinking and gambling had convinced Father to entrust me to them. They promised to find me work in Bangkok that paid better.

"Another girl," Noklek looked toward her friend, "Tuptim, was about two years or so older than me. She left that same day and we rode together on the back of the men's truck. Tuptim told me she heard her own parents fighting because in her case, her father had indentured her to the men to pay off a gambling debt. He accrued it that same night.

"We made a stop for snacks and petrol. The men came to the back of the truck and explained to me and Tuptim that we would be helping our families immensely. Indeed, Father had made me promise before I left to send back part of my wages every month to the family.

These men would show me how to set up remittances through a bank. I was to have a bank account!

"Shooing away the younger children," Noklek pantomimed with her hands, "he said that and many things, first to my mother, then to me."

What happened next, once they got to Chiang Rai, was something even now Noklek found–"not painful- but something I never could match with what I had known, or thought I knew, about the nature of people and their limits. There was haggling over my virginity."

Then Susan wanted to cry out, why are you telling me all this? But she was also fascinated.

Kun-mae continued, "For quite a few months after it was sold and lost I was moved from town to town so my keepers could present me anew as a virgin. Then the haggling would begin again."

Susan remembered yesterday–the steady pace of walking through the fields, feeling rooted even in this strange soil. Now she was aware of its opposite: floating. She floated on a plane to get here. She was sitting several feet above the earth on a platform on stilts, as though floating.

The Japanese once called red light districts "floating worlds." The brightly lit district she had seen on her first night in Bangkok lacked the rhythm of dawn mornings on the farm, or seasonal tapioca fires like the ground of this valley.

In the early days Noklek sat and waited on a bed in some house. At first the new cities and towns, the unbelievable crowds of people and *tuk-tuks* on the roads outside made a part of Noklek awaken, even as the liquor, the nauseating smell of strangers' sweat and the overwhelming boredom of waiting and the monotony of servicing seemed to numb each of her senses.

Tuptim put her hand on Noklek's arm and interrupted, "It wasn't just boredom, it was boredom soothing rage. Or, boredom soothing terror."

Kun Sompan looked uncomfortable. Susan briefly wished she had a female interpreter, until she recognized that he was clearly moved. His dutiful interpreting had deepened from a monotone and carried notes of true feeling and pain.

Noklek continued, "You have to

understand, Suwan, we were so young. In *Krung Thep* they used to say how much younger we country girls looked than the city girls. Even the city girls look younger than the *farang* and Japanese girls. Maybe two, four years younger, our periods start later because not much food in the north back then."

Noklek leaned in and added quietly, "At fourteen, I hadn't even had my period yet. I didn't even know what it was when I left home. I learned that at the first house we stayed in where they trained us. There was a woman there and her grown daughter. They took money from the men and trained us: *ab ob nuat,* bath and massage, with all that comes after that."

Tuptim spoke, "Noklek was a child. She was two years younger than me and I was still young, too. Imagine what kind of men would sell her. What kind of men would buy her?"

Tuptim waited for an answer that Susan couldn't give before continuing, "perverts. The strange ones who didn't like grown women. Look how petite she is even now," her tone was intense, pained. "she was still growing, she was only a child."

Noklek nodded. Susan wished David or Faith were with her now.

Noklek spoke, "Sometimes men would

open the door and see me in my camisole and be shocked. They would get angry at the keepers, who would chatter and rush to find a grown woman.

"But the ones who stayed liked it when I showed fear. They were satisfied when I wept, especially if I bled. When I didn't, there were some who would pinch the skin on the insides of my arms or face and twist it to make me cry...."

"You could hear them with her, it wasn't about 'sexy lady,'" Tuptim added the English feelingly as though better to reach Susan, "they wanted to hurt children."

After *Kun-mae* had been in the life about two years or so and she had lost much of her girlishness, she was sold south to new handlers who no longer passed her off as a virgin.

It was a border town near Malaysia with a tiny brothel. She would wait with the other girls in a window they called a fishbowl. A john, after scanning them all, might return his eyes to her and call out the number on the card pinned to her dress. That was the *ab ob nuat*, "bath and massage", frequented mostly by local men and East Asian sex tourists.

The fishbowl in the south was so poor it didn't actually have a glass window. Noklek and Tuptim laughed that it at least allowed a breeze in the heavy heat.

Kun Sompan mopped beads from his brow self-consciously.

Mostly though, it meant the keepers no longer feared that she might run away. Somehow the keepers could tell that she had changed completely from being a daughter who saw outward from her own eyes to seeing herself as others saw her. It was safe to let her work outside in this southern province; she couldn't read and had no other skills. In fact, Noklek now would have to go out and bring in business. They called it luring.

The bordello owner liked to dress her and the other girls in gem colored satin shirts with crisp short sleeves and ironed collars that closed with cloth covered buttons right up to the neck. A group of little boys once saw them leaning languidly by an open air bar during the hot season and called out "dragonflies." Noklek couldn't help smiling: clustered around the bar, their untied hair was black like the wings of dragonflies and their thin bodies were sheathed in topaz, emerald, amethyst, or ruby. She and the other girls waved the boys away and then went back to sipping their drinks and chatting with whatever man was sitting at the bar.

Sometimes looking only from others' eyes

made it easier to understand coldness and cruelty. Eventually this new perspective became the only one and her own senses continued to fade. The men became odorless, or at least no worse than the overused sleeping pallets.

She began to carry a small bottle of clear liquor with her that dulled the noise of the town and the voices of the rude keepers. The lights and ever changing faces of girls, johns and passersby lost their brightness.

Piped in music, and the thump of pop tunes through the walls was so ambient that it became only vibrations to her, while the touch of skin against hers or another's body part moving within her own insides seemed something impersonal, far away, only observed.

Her sense of taste left her but hunger never did. "It was that hunger that made me want better. The best I could imagine while luring was being a 'short-term girlfriend'. You travel a little, get room service, maybe even show vacationing *farangs* from Europe and the Americas around."

Suwan was excited. So her birth father wasn't just any john, "You traveled? You were a girlfriend?"

Noklek shrugged, "I did this when I could for a few years. You usually never see them again but it's better than the regulars at the fishbowl. One got me into trouble."

Suwan sat up straighter. The phrase "got me into trouble" didn't match the tone of romance Susan hoped to hear. Even two days ago when *Kun-mae* first mentioned having been in "the life," Susan still clung to the idea of ill-fated lovers who had met in the floating world. Interpreting was tricky and perhaps, Susan hoped, Kun Sompan had gotten the nuance wrong.

Then Susan's *Kun-mae* turned to Kun Sompan to explain that, "most *farang* prefer to meet their short-term girlfriends at the bars. Even the servicemen preferred that if they were here for a week from Vietnam. He didn't like bars."

But Susan's birth father was unusual. Susan was relieved that she was about to hear something special about him, about them. Noklek gestured to show how the *farang* chose her from among the girls sitting in the fishbowl. After what seemed like an interminable bout of haggling between the *farang* and one of the keepers she was allowed to leave with him.

Later the *farang* would tell Noklek that he wanted to visit the island of Phuket. In broken

Thai he explained they were going to cross the bay. She laughed out of habit, but an old part of her really was interested. Sarasin Bridge just opened and she had never visited the sea. Noklek clung obligingly to his arm during the day when he decided to take in the sights.

Another small part of her mind fleetingly wondered if perhaps this foreign soldier was going to sell her to the deep sea fishing boats. She'd heard of boys from Chiang Rai which was nowhere near the ocean being pirated away and sold to shrimpers. But that was boys, she'd never heard of that for girls, only prostitution and indentured service.

After the week in Phuket, Noklek and the *farang* checked back into his hotel on the mainland. He took her one last time on his hotel bed, not even bothering to pull back the covers. Then one of her keepers knocked on the door to bring her back to the brothel and the relentless boredom of the fast life Father had found for her. She hadn't made the *farang* wear a condom.

"When did you see him next?" Susan asked.

Noklek looked at her coolly, "I think he went back to his unit in Vietnam. I don't know which one. He was a nice man but I never saw him again."

Did that mean Noklek was hurt? Had they fallen in love during that short time? Suwan couldn't tell. Noklek just continued her narrative.

For the next couple weeks Noklek was always sick and haggard but didn't stop working. She would try to coax johns into hand jobs as much as possible because the assault of their stench when they insisted on oral, or even intercourse, was overwhelming. Noklek would spit them out or leave to wash right away. She didn't care that she was bringing in less money.

"But finally I was so big that the men couldn't mount me. One john was so disgusted that he beat me, but at least not on the stomach. I kept crying for him to not hit my stomach so he kicked me in the legs and slapped me in the face and then I really couldn't work so they sent me up to Bangkok again."

Noklek paused to let Kun Sompan's interpreting catch up, "They sent me to some place, I don't remember the name, where nuns let me work in the garden until the baby came."

Susan almost startled. That was her.

Somehow with Noklek and Tuptim talking about "the life" it seemed like some other person's story until now. It was so far removed from her own middle class home life that she could almost forget it was her back story, too.

Noklek, seeming to read her mind, and clarified, "– the baby, who is now you!"

There it was again, thought Susan, that ability Noklek had to switch between the distanced coldness of this narrative to the more appealing sweetness Susan had first seen two days earlier.

She wanted to clear up for herself the growing dissonance between Noklek's demure demeanor and the flicker of another quality, deeper, that Suwan had picked up on.

Suwan decided to ask the question she had been saving, "What if you had kept me? What if—"

Nokek stunned Susan with the swift assuredness of her reply, "—you would have been a prostitute."

Kun Sompan cleared his throat uncomfortably. Tuptim went to get him some water.

Just as Suwan suspected, the ignorance that Noklek professed at their first meeting– about not knowing that Suwan would be adopted–was probably a screen.

The enormity of the gulf between the romance that Susan once imagined for her birth parents, and the reality of the anonymous john and this, this calculating former hooker, made her ears ring.

And then just as suddenly it didn't.

Susan wasn't sure what she would say before she said it, but tried this out, "The other day you said you didn't know that foreigners adopted babies from the nunnery. I think you did. I imagine it's very hard for a young country girl, who would later become a devoted stepmother, to choose between two hard futures."

Susan's voice broke and she felt a tear slide down her cheek. She wanted to sound fair but felt little girl jealousy toward her *Kun-mae*'s stepdaughters.

Noklek sighed, "There were other girls in the life who had babies, too. I saw what became of them. I watched pimps force mothers into having their boys or girls enter the life even younger than I did. That was how some mothers were able to keep their children."

By now Noklek and Suwan both were crying, "I wanted to keep you, and I am sorry, truly sorry. I have carried the guilt for you every day of my life, just like an infant tied to my back."

Tuptim surprised Suwan by interjecting,

"I have watched you look at us like we're cunning."

Susan began to protest.

"The truth is that we are cunning," continued Tuptim, "We have lied, we have flirted, we have made plans that we kept close to our chest. That is how we were able to save money and escape."

Tuptim gestured to the walls of the narrow room, "Do you see what we have done with our cunning? Noklek marries a tapioca farmer. I raise pigs. We are faithful to our husbands, we are generous with our neighbors in the village, we –," and Tuptim held her uplifted palm toward Susan, "saved you from a terrible life. We could do that because we were cunning."

There was nothing Susan could say.

They were right.

When they parted that evening they made a pact that Suwan could write not to Noklek directly but to Tuptim and her husband Durek who lived with no children at home. Tuptim would serve as courier for Suwan's letters to Noklek because Noklek didn't want to explain them. Either side would write Kun Sompan. He in turn would slip in a handwritten translation for a fee that Susan and David would pay.

14 THE ORPHANAGE
1991

"Susan," Kun Sompan said to her later, "I wish for you to understand the history of farming valleys like Ban Naan. Noklek's husband, Jugo, must be aware that girls from poor families have been leaving for generations to join the life in Bangkok.

"Sometimes these daughters make this sacrifice knowingly and with great devotion send money back to their parents.

"Sometimes they or their parents are tricked. Some girls have been drugged and kidnapped.

"Sometimes their fathers are desperate or venal, or so impoverished that they sell their daughters–like your grandfather did."

"You're trying to say this is common?"

"Not common, but, not rare."

"Is that why you took me past those places my first night in Bangkok?"

He seemed hurt, "No, no, I would never do that. I deliberately steered you away from the main red light districts. But this you would find at night in the cities."

He continued, "However they end up in Bangkok or Pattaya or elsewhere, that work they can only do so long. The sooner they get out, the better. Luckier ones manage to return to valleys like this to marry. This cycle everyone knows here."

"So you're saying her husband probably knows about her being in 'the life'?"

"Almost certainly he knows. He knows and doesn't know."

"You mean she needs to keep me a secret even though there are other women like her and Tuptim living right there?"

"Please understand," sighed Kun Sompan, "it's not about you. That there is such a pattern as this–it would show that the parents and the village elders–whom we are all raised to venerate–have failed women like Noklek and Tuptim."

Susan started to say something, not realizing Kun Sompan wasn't finished.

"Susan, when these girls return they are sadder, faded beyond their time. I sense it. You can tell who they are. They have an air that could be interpreted by one beholder as defeat or by another as relief."

Susan nodded with resignation, "He would know it, but there is no need for his daughters to know it."

Kun Sompan pressed his lips together. He seemed to want to correct something, "I am making it sound like it is only the elders of Ban Naan. Does America send its children to other countries to be adopted?"

"No, there's actually a shortage of healthy newborns in the U.S.," she hated the term shortage in the context of adoption. Wasn't it good that children weren't being relinquished?

"I think it is a national tragedy for *Muang Thai*, the community of Thailand. Your *Kun-mae* was able to meet you and cry. We call ourselves the Land of Smiles, but there are a thousand un-cried tears in *Muang Thai*. Perhaps it is the best way to manage once a decision is made."

He sighed, "*mai ben rai*," which seemed to indicate some heavy resignation.

"There was a time in *Muang USA*," she heard him laugh at her new phrase, "when many more children were placed for adoption,'"

Susan paused when he shuddered.

"Go on."

"I don't know the history of Thailand

really. I will read up on it. But there must have been many decisions made by many people before the girls or their parents or the elders came to this. I don't believe it was always '*mai ben rai,*'" she said, "There must have been a point where a different decision could have been made."

"I agree, I don't know where it was," and he seemed to think of something pleasing before going on, "It's no longer such a situation in your–*Muang USA*?"

"Yes, it's no longer the situation in the USA."

"Do you know the dharma?"

"I don't know the dharma. I know they're from Buddhism." She resolved to listen hard to what Kun Sompan was about to teach her.

"One idea is that all is illusion. This is just such a case. It seems inevitable that girls must leave Ban Naan and villages like it and the elders can't prevent it. It seems like this cannot change. Also, when a child like you is taken away from a mother to live in a foreign land, it would be impossible to meet in this life. Both things are illusions. One teaching of the dharma is that we must fight illusions," Kun Sompan looked at her expectantly as though her one opinion was terribly important.

International adoption had only grown exponentially since the late nineteen sixties when her parents visited here. But somehow he looked at her as though –

"Kun Sompan. I am not the Buddha," she laughed.

"Uh-uh," he laughed, too, "a *bodhisattva*," but sobered as he continued, "someone who returns to us to remind us to fight worlds of illusion." He put his palms together in a *wai* and bowed his head as he had taught her to do before shrines. He was only half joking.

This was too serious. Susan had encountered this before back home: both Caucasians and Asians project all sorts of meanings on to her because of her looks, her back story.

She waved her hand as though brushing the topic away, "tomorrow we go to the orphanage. I bet they've seen returnees like me."

"No," he countered, "the news that you are visiting created quite a stir. The abbess had special recitations of sutras in your honor."

"I'd heard that many East Asian adoptees only visit the orphanage. They rarely find their mothers."

"I don't know if that's true with the new state funded orphanages. The sisters created a home for unwed mothers that you and your mother stayed at long before there was a state system. When they could, the sisters helped the mothers find peaceful jobs so they could keep their babies. The nuns were not always successful. Perhaps most left as your mother did. So either the mothers and children were never parted or the children never had–perhaps the courage?–to come back."

"There are so many more of us now. I think there will be more like me calling on them."

"Perhaps."

They drove on a little in silence before Kun Sompan added, "I don't know much about this convent other than the abbess saying this over the phone. I never visited one before."

"Have you been to a monastery?"

"Oh, yes. Like most men I took vows before my wedding. But in Thailand and Sri Lankan Theravada, nuns often work without ordination. If it's possible," he was telling a joke now–Susan seemed to always fail at the jokes with Buddhist overtones–"nuns are more humble than monks."

Susan laughed politely, bewildered.

"Seriously, though, the government supports the monasteries. They had monks come to our classrooms to teach the dharma and meditation. Before Songkran, the spring New Year, or other holidays our whole class would go on a field trip to the monastery. We never visited a convent."

As they drove, Kun Sompan went on to tell her more about his month in the monastery. She asked him what school and university was like. The camaraderie and the stories made the next six hours back to Bangkok pass happily.

~

During a lull in the conversation, Susan remembered Faith's telling her she recognized the gothic arches of the adoption agency that Faith had last seen at age two and a half. Susan had raked her own memory, half hoping she would experience that same déjà vu, half hoping she would not. It would seem somehow unhealthy to uncover at this mature age a memory you had somehow "repressed." Nothing she had encountered in Thailand–so far–carried that double burden of strangeness mixed with familiarity.

"What I struggle with," she found herself confiding in Kun Sompan, "is that I wish I had memories of this place. My parents described it to me, and I'd asked them about it over and over so many times that I don't know if I imagined it from what they told me, or if I actually remember it."

Kun Sompan laughed, "Aren't many family stories like that? I heard some stories about my Aunt Nawarat so many times that I think I was there. Yet some of them happened before I was born."

"Are there many children there?"

"There are only about fifty at any time, and only from an infant to age six."

"What happens to the children after age six?" she asked.

"Then if their parents don't come back or they don't get adopted, they go to a larger state-run facility with an educational program until they are sixteen. This orphanage is unusual because it is run by nuns. In the past two decades, I guess, the King has established orphanages throughout the country and those government-run ones are more common."

She remembered something from her parents, "The nuns gave shelter to unwed mothers, and ran a small orphanage–both. Right?"

"Now it's just the orphanage," Kun Sompan answered, "As you learned, Thailand is slow to fully ordain nuns so it's harder for them to get state funding. I suppose it limits the size of their ventures compared to the monasteries. Yet," he added as a sign of their robustness, "even they give alms to the monks."

What Susan thought she did remember was lying on some kind of white mat or mattress: the weave of the sheets, and that they were printed with blue and pink shapes. She couldn't see far. Beyond these sheets what she could make out was blurry. There might have been slats. She remembered tan arms lifting her up and also placing her down. She thought she remembered being aware of other babies, a row of them lying on either side of her.

She would never know if this was a memory, a remembered dream or, as Kun Sompan said, one of those oft repeated tales that become such a part of the family that they *should* be memories.

The orphanage stood at the end of one of the long, residential alleys that crisscrossed Bangkok. A low wooden fence wrapped around a dirt yard. At its heart was a cluster of multicolored painted traditional buildings, perhaps a little idiosyncratic for sprawling Bangkok, *Krung Thep*, she thought. By traditional, she meant they were supported on low stilts, circled and joined by a dark wooden veranda.

One of the nuns, kneeling with her robes tied up around her knees, was scrubbing it with a large sponge and pail. Susan thought she saw glimpses of a garden at the rear of the compound.

Another nun, wrapped in white long-sleeved, floor-length robes under a gray smock, came out to meet them. She seemed polite but more comfortable facing Kun Sompan than Susan. She led them to the main office where the abbess was seated on a cushion on the floor, emanating regal cheerfulness.

After exchanging pleasantries, the abbess switched to a purposeful tone, "Just last year a lot of processes for adoption matured. Thailand now has an expanding system of state-supported orphanages. It wasn't like that when you and your mother stayed here."

"My mother," thought Susan. Even having just met her–to hear another person acknowledge her own connection to Noklek–it was strange and new and wonderful.

"Under Article 7(1) of the UN Convention on the Rights of the Child, they've built a vaster system than the sisters and I were able to maintain years ago. I believe it is well-monitored by the Child Adoption Center of Thailand."

Her parents never mentioned it, yes, it must be more recent.

The abbess continued, "That wasn't our goal. They don't provide care and training for birth mothers, and I suspect that may contribute to the large number of infants available for adoption. I remain neutral on this. I was unable to maintain our own support of birth mothers. But in the days when Noklek stayed with us, it seems more mothers were able to keep their infants."

Then she added, "at least until they left here."

Susan suspected that the abbess was more careful than neutral.

Another thought: Had the abbess also heard what *Kun-mae* and Tuptim hinted befell some of the children who returned with their mothers in the life? She couldn't bring herself to ask.

"That doesn't mean our record keeping was lacking. Often mothers who were unwed gave false names in ungentle situations. Deception happened here, too, I suppose. But I feel that most girls prefer to be truthful when they are treated with compassion. Your mother was here for several months."

An acolyte with shaved head entered the

room and walked toward them with a tray carrying cool drinks in perspiring ceramic cups. Unlike the rest of Bangkok, this convent seemed to have no air conditioning. The architecture was traditional with sliding doors that opened wide onto the cool polished verandas.

"We kept records that," she looked over at Kun Sompan, "we shared when given the proper written permission. The fire changed that, destroyed many records. We hope to get them online someday and avoid that ever happening again."

It sounded like the abbess remembered her mother in particular. Was this just–just merciful graciousness toward Suwan?

"What, if anything, do you remember of Noklek?" Suwan asked.

"She was neither old nor young, compared to the others then. She was one of the few who stayed to nurse you a full month before leaving you."

Susan nodded; this matched what Noklek had said about the timing.

"Did she sign relinquishment papers?" Susan half wished she hadn't asked. Did it matter anymore? It was certainly something that Noklek had been vague about.

"Most adoption agencies call it 'make a

plan for adoption,'" the abbess said with a mirthless laugh that seemed to broach no sugarcoating, "yes, she did sign the legal papers. Your parents struck me as the kind of couple who would have left empty handed rather than accept in the name of expediency what might have been a questionable transaction."

Susan gasped. This clever old woman seemed to know Susan's mind better than she did herself. The abbess' eyes twinkled when she said, "You came here to learn about your first mother, but you are also learning something about the quality of your parents."

"Yes, I guess I am relieved that everything was done–as best as possible."

The abbess nodded, "As I said earlier, even though ultimately she gave you away, your birth mother nursed you for a month," and then feelingly, her swathed forearms lifted as though cradling an infant, "holding you at her own breast."

Susan gulped and fought back tears. She didn't know when she would see *Kun-mae* again. She missed Lily, too. How could this celibate nun paint such a clear picture of their physical bond?

Susan asked, "What do you know about my birth father?"

"I believe he was a US serviceman. That's what Noklek thought."

She looked at the abbess, wondering if there was anything to press for about him.

The abbess met her eyes, "We don't know if he survived the war. No more information."

Susan took this in. He could have been her age or younger. He might have died before she was born. Then again he could have returned home and she might have half brothers and sisters she would never meet.

She decided to stop these thoughts for now and asked her next question, "Do any of the mothers come back after they sign papers?"

The abbess shook her head, "Rarely, and the ones who did encountered no happy coincidences."

Susan said aloud the obvious, "Their babies were already gone?" The hall seemed to echo with her question.

"I think some waited quite a while before returning. In one case I know she was relieved to find that her son was no longer in an orphanage. She came back, I suspect, just to follow up, not to reclaim."

"Oh. I see," Susan felt a little awkward.

Then the abbess decided to fill the silence with general information, "We have had other adult adoptees or young adoptees with their adoptive parents visit since the UN Act. For most this is the final visit on their journey because there are not enough records. If a child was abandoned and then brought here, there is no possibility of them finding where they came from. If they were left by an unwed mother, only a few like you meet their families again. The best results are in the case of a married couple who are forced to relinquish due to poverty or incarceration."

After a few moments, the acolyte who had been hovering said something to the abbess who dismissed her with a nod.

"I will show you the nurseries myself, if you would like."

"Oh, yes," said Susan, surprised by how high and eager her own voice sounded to herself.

There were about a half dozen rooms, three in each of two buildings. The floors were linoleum, cool underfoot in the tropical heat. It was naptime in the four rooms with the youngest children. Some of the toddlers had wiggled off their nap cots onto the clean floor to be more comfortable.

The colors in these two buildings were white or pastel with plenty of sunshine. Somewhere a Thai folksong warbled from a radio and the air wafted with the faint smell of honeysuckle.

Susan caught herself looking for Eurasian faces in the last two rooms where the older children were playing. Kun Sompan must have read her mind because he pointed out two boys who might have been mixed race in the five year old room, and a little girl in the six year old room.

The abbess noticed Susan looking and said, "Her name is Yien. She was brought here by neighbors when she was three. Her father is gone. Her mother was released last month from serving her sentence for selling pills. We are holding Yien, hoping the mother will come. Otherwise, she must go to the state orphanage in a few months. Her mother is probably trying to secure a job and a stable place. I am sure of it."

Little Yien was sitting quietly on the floor, legs crossed under a picture book. She wore the same crisp pinafore that all two dozen children in the room wore. Someone had gathered her hair in a ponytail that sprayed from the top of her head. Susan watched as the little girl tried to sound out words in the curly alphabet. Yien moved rosebud lips and her voice was a tiny clear bell. Her fingernails were pink shells and when she lifted her eyes for a moment to inspect the visitors, Susan could see they were beautiful deep almonds.

Yien seemed the embodiment of solitude and concentration as she turned the pages with plump arms that were still babyish. For a brief moment Susan imagined calling David to say she wanted to adopt the little girl. Then she guiltily offered a prayer that the mother would return soon.

The Abbess led them outside the room. They were on a veranda that faced the front gate of the grounds. This must be the end of the tour and now the Abbess was saying something to Kun Sompan. He was listing other charitable projects the nuns were leading. Susan understood and decided to slip all the *baht* she had in her purse to the Abbess. They could stop at a bank later or have her travelers' checks exchanged at the hotel for more *baht*.

"*Khopkun ka*, Thank you, *sawasdee ka,* goodbye then," said the Abbess, but seeming in no hurry.

Immediately Kun Sompan made a *wai* and bowed deferentially answering in the masculine, "*Khopkun klap.*"

Susan echoed, not quite like a native, "*Khopkun ka. Sawasdee ka.*"

As they left, Susan debated: the rooms may have matched the vision–or dream–or memory–she had of the orphanage. But, she realized, this was all of it and there was no seizure of recognition, none of Faith's gothic arches.

~

As Kun Sompan drove her to the airport she wondered what, if anything, he had thought about all this. She had grown fond of him. Somehow letting go of her birth mother so casually made letting go of anyone, even a paid interpreter, seem unbearable.

She wondered if she would see Kun Sompan again. Susan offered to show him around if he ever came to New York. He lamented that she couldn't stay long enough to really see Bangkok and then asked her to visit again.

As Susan scribbled down her address to give him, she thought she saw a group of about nine teenage girls being led through the terminal by two older men. They didn't seem like a family; in fact the two leaders had the unsavory look of Japanese yakuza. Susan guiltily averted her eyes.

Kun Sompan noticed the group, too, and said hopefully, "maybe they'll be stopped at the gate."

They didn't say much after that. He reminded her not to use *Kun-mae*'s address and pointed her to security.

He lingered politely so she smiled from the other side of the metal detector and waved him away. When he still paused, she placed her carry on down and matched her palms together in a farewell *wai.*

She wasn't sure if her accompanying bow was too formal, but he returned her *wai* and smiled. Perhaps he was amused at her awkwardness, but she guessed that he understood her sincerity, too.

He waited as his *bodhisattva* turned to walk toward her gate.

SUZANNE GILBERT

~ PART II ~

"Be kind, for everyone you meet is fighting a hard battle."

~ Philo Judaeus of Alexandria, born 20 BCE

SUZANNE GILBERT

15 THE SCRAPBOOK
1991

Susan made out David's face in the shifting arcade of faces waiting to greet disembarking passengers. She ran to him and he hugged her before holding her away from him. Behind his smile she saw that he was waiting to tell her something.

"What is it?"

"Do you have anything checked? Let's just get out of here and I'll tell you. Your mother's been taken to the hospital."

During the long moments at the baggage carousel, she found out that something so urgent had happened that David had asked Terry to take Lily overnight and Terry had readily agreed. The original plan had been that David would bring Lily to the bustling international terminal because the long separation from her mother had been hard. Given the nature of the reunion that Susan herself was returning from, it seemed especially important to be able to hold her own child.

But instead of re-embracing mommy-hood, and her sweet-smelling little girl, she found herself playing daughter again, this time to her adoptive mother.

"Apparently it's something your Mom and Dad learned about the week before your trip but didn't want to tell you before you left. They didn't think things would take a turn for the worse like this."

"What's going on?" she asked.

"Your mom started getting some kind of stomach discomfort. They thought it was intestinal so they cleaned her out, but it continued. Next they had a colonoscopy done but it showed no cancer. It did turn up open diverticula which should have been no real problem, they said. Then a CAT scan revealed ovarian cancer throughout the abdomen. The prognosis with surgery, chemo and radiation is for a few extra months of life."

"No! No!"

"Your Mom said, 'Forget it. I don't need to go through treatment to gain so little.' The staff will be able to keep her basically pain free, but she'll only be able to be at home for a little longer. Your Dad has been coordinating that."

They let each other drive on together in silence. It was too late to call her parents.

~

The next day when Susan arrived at the hospital, it was almost as if the ethyl alcohol and disinfectant smell of the corridors awakened the spirit of her inner child. She felt that same brave mix of having half convinced herself that she was untroubled by her surroundings while also knowing that she was paying extra attention to the muscles that made her face and shoulders appear relaxed.

Her mother was lying up in bed with a clear intravenous in one arm. Dad was already there. She brightened when she saw Susan.

"Mom, I'm here. I came straight from the airport, Mom."

Susan took the second chair in the room and all three of them sat in silence for a moment. Then Al gave her an explanation like the one David had repeated the night before.

At the end of it her mother added, ever the hostess, "I'm still thinking things through. Passover is in six months. I'm not sure I'll want to sit through a whole *Seder* meal, but I'd like to celebrate it in some way."

Al handed his wife a drink he had poured from their old thermos brought from home. Susan recognized it as one of their favorite concoctions, Darjeeling tea made with boiled milk and a little sugar and cardamom. Her mom held a spoon that was monogrammed ornately; it had been a wedding present from Al's parents.

"You know this is yours after I'm gone."

Susan was silent, not knowing if the kinder thing was to demure, implying her mother's departure was not imminent, or to accept the heirloom as an appreciative daughter.

Susan rejoined brightly, "Maybe I should start hosting Passover this year. You already do all the other holidays," and then stopped, realizing that who hosted what holidays after these few remaining weeks was mute. Mom wouldn't be alive to see them. She took her mom's hand in both of hers and noticed how the texture had changed in only the past few weeks. The skin felt more like a delicate casing.

"Mom."

"Don't worry. We've pretty much worked out all the arrangements."

"No. No, that's not what I was going to ask about. I love you so much. I wish I hadn't gone away, I feel so bad that I wasn't here, I –"

Susan realized that she would not tell her

mother about finding Noklek. She and mom had shared enough over the years and there was enough to say without bringing up that other world. Maybe it would have to be Susan's world alone–just like David suggested–and not one her mother would have time left to share with her.

Susan had a thought she could not utter aloud: that not only her search and reunion but everything of the living would cease to be something her mother could share with her. The next thing Susan heard herself say was,

"Let me have your recipes, Mom."

Her mom laughed and then sighed.

"I've never really said this before, Susan, but I think in adoptive families those things like family recipes, or the silver, or our particular interpretation of holidays, take on more meaning. It's all we've got to pass on. I don't have your biological history to give you."

"No, mom, it's okay." She wanted to make this whole hospital scene disappear.

"At this point, Susan, I'm glad of it. Your uncle had cancer, now I will die of it. There must be something genetic about it and I wouldn't want you to have this. I'm glad you didn't inherit this."

Her mother had Susan's stunned attention. Her mom reached across the hospital tray and took Susan's hand before continuing. She had rehearsed the words. She knew Susan would be surprised to hear her bring this up, "I can never erase the fact that your birth mother, whatever her reasons, gave you away. And you, precious, precious daughter, can never carry on my DNA for me, or erase the fact that your father and I could never have biological children."

~

One afternoon when Masha was discharged from the hospital, she thought she might do what it sounded like all who were given time to do it should: "put her personal effects in order". She and Al already had a will, and as he was very much alive, she couldn't see disposing of much, other than to Susan.

That left the sewing room closet.

Al had looked at it once before quickly closing the door again, "Do you think the archeologists got it wrong by looking at the Neanderthals' cave floor core samplings and assuming by the depth and the amount of debris that they lived forty thousand years? Maybe they just never cleaned up."

She rolled her eyes at her husband but let him amuse himself.

"If they took a sampling of this closet, I wonder how long they'd think you had lived" and Al's over-explanation faltered. Instead he turned back to her and reached out and held her.

Masha knew then that the thing she would miss the most would come from breaking up their entity "Al-and-Masha." Whether or not there was a Heaven, she would miss Al-and-Masha.

She did feel some guilt at this closet. Al would have no idea what to do with the bolts of fabric, the spools and the balls of yarn that she hadn't used, would never, in fact, use. That afternoon she worked on the closet and the rest of the sewing room until past the time she should have taken her pain medication. Feeling weary and cramping, she decided the sewing room was enough.

Al could throw out the rest of it, and everything else for that matter, but she was not going to waste another blue sky day sorting things. She made her way down to the kitchen and shook the pills from their amber vial into her palm.

She was pleasantly surprised really at how easy it was one moment to accept that it might all get thrown away once she was gone. Then the next moment to ache with a sweet fondness and affection for all the things she was saying goodbye to.

Masha had done a lot of gazing out windows. The season had grown too cold for her to want to do much walking, but she wished to at least see every breeze she could that moved the trees. She wanted to hold each and every dear face she saw, every visitor, but most of all Al and Lily and Susan and her son-in-law, to hold them long and hard and close but somehow not to smother or frighten them with her intensity.

She turned her attention to the manila envelope she had carried downstairs with her from the back of the closet. It contained what she thought of as heirlooms from Susan's adoption. She and Al had already given their daughter what they could of her adoption and Thai papers, Masha thought, but this would be more personal.

It would not give Susan any keys to the past. It probably wouldn't 'empower' her daughter. She had read in a piece by one adult adoptee that seeing her original birth certificate or name would. Masha knew that what she could give her daughter wouldn't erase any loss whatsoever. It was just part of "putting things in order".

When Susan was a teenager their family looked into one of those "Family Heritage Tours" where an international adoptive family visits their kid's country of origin. But Susan wasn't interested. She even seemed to resent the multiculti of family Sukkah parties until she was well out of college and on her own.

Despite what the literature said, Masha's daughter had never seemed to like the idea of looking at her Thai culture or bringing it into their family life. Masha now thought she understood why.

Adoption, or more correctly, being surrendered for adoption, was a little death. You lost your first mother, your first father, first relatives. You lost your culture, yes, and maybe it seemed to Susan, Masha imagined, that the rest were only pale imitations. Learning Thai dances with your white mother or even going to tourist attractions in your country of origin could become a way of avoiding something deeper and simpler: loss.

Some losses are for keeps.

Thai dance class wouldn't have been wrong by any means (although it was a two hour commute each way to the only place in Queens that offered it when Suzie was little). Masha hoped that Suzie would still somehow stay in touch with Mr. Goldberg and Mr. Nguyen, but it wasn't an urgent hope. Both old men carried their art, their calligraphy, with them into their respective diasporas, Jewish and Vietnamese, just as firmly as the remembrance of not being in their native lands clung to them, of always being a stranger in a strange land.

Perhaps Susan intuited that pre-war Vietnam for Mr. Nguyen and inter-war Europe for Mr. Goldberg were as surely dead as Susan's own possibility of a sense of home and belonging in Thailand.

This, Masha now guessed, was the reason Susan hadn't wanted to visit Thailand. Perhaps Suzie was already acknowledging that international adoption had taken Thai home, Thai family, Thai language and culture away from her. What they could give her in diaspora, what they could give her as adoptive parents, was like a pale ghost of the real, a doppelganger. Masha, too, might well know soon what it was to lose everything, every familiar sight and smell and sound.

Acknowledging that, Masha was not particularly enthusiastic about the prospect of Heaven, if it existed. How could it supplant the real and the good that is right here on Earth? She looked out the pantry window and breathed deeply of her garden's hyacinths. She had transplanted them just below the sill and she tested out saying, tenderly, "Goodbye."

~

On Susan's next visit, her mother wanted to say something about this: about all of life's vibrancy being interspersed with little deaths, of adoptions, of diasporas and of migrations that could be sweetened with Family Heritage tours, or traditions, or rituals.

Susan's mother was searching for the words to explain this and began with, "I have what one can only call homesickness for everything near at hand. Sometimes," her mother laughed, "I even say 'goodbye' to a familiar building, to my kitchen, to the formal china, to that one wooden floor plank in the dining room that always creaks."

Susan knew what she meant. "Yes, especially if you step on it alone at night."

Masha looked at Susan for a long moment before saying, "But I don't think either of us can stand this much emotion."

Mother passed daughter a scrapbook. Susan had never seen it before. She opened it and took in what she could before becoming distracted by her mother still being here now.

The scrapbook wasn't very old; there were plenty of trendy foam adhesive boarders on some of the photographs and poems, along with opalescent pages that had been bought at extra cost and added in. Many of the framed pieces of better fiber paper bore handwritten notes and were clearly far older.

Its cuteness seemed out of place with the quiet in the hospital room.

"The scrapbook is new, but the poems and quotes are from when I was waiting for you."

"To come back from Thailand?"

"Both. The actual scrapbook I did start putting together while you were–away. But the contents–those were from when we were trying to adopt."

Susan leaned closer with a mix of awkwardness and excitement. Her mother showed her already familiar baby pictures, and pictures at the shore, then abruptly closed the scrapbook, suddenly looking pale.

"Mom?"

"I'd like to rest now. You can look at the rest at home. It's yours. I love you, sweetheart."

~

Later that night, when the house was

quiet, Susan took out the scrapbook. They had put Lily to bed and David turned in alone. She thumbed through the first pages of photographs her mother had shown her that afternoon.

Then she found a booklet in what she recognized as her mother's handwriting from stronger days, and realized it was a kind of *Haggadah*, a Hebrew booklet that first recounts a story, then poses questions to expand its theme and then answers them.

Her mother's note conscientiously explained, "Some say that these *haggadot* are the intellectual heirs of the Greek symposium. They are also the distant cousins of Italian Renaissance 'dinner pieces.' They were preciously bound and illuminated booklets that enlivened and mapped the after dinner discourses at banquets among nobles and the intellectuals at court."

Susan noticed a note that stuck out from the front of this *Haggadah* written with the more spidery penmanship of her mother's final illness. She opened it.

"Beloved daughter," it began.

"I could not give you my hair or my eyes but I hope I have given you enough love, and memories to pass on to your own daughter. I also want to give you this story. It's the story of

Passover, of Moses leading the Hebrews out of Egypt, but it's told with a twist to reflect our story, yours and mine. This version is not well known, but it is authentic, woven from the Bible and from stories in the Talmud."

Then, as though a scholar writing to a forgetful pupil, her mother noted for Susan that "the Talmud was also known as the Oral Torah, the Jewish 'new testament' of parables, explications and questions compiled across north Africa, Europe, Byzantium, Arabia and Persia. The Talmud is the canon that completes what Christians called the Old Testament or the five books of Moses, the books of the prophets, and the more lyrical psalms, proverbs, Song of Solomon and what you know from Pete Seeger, Ecclesiastes."

Susan recognized her mother's pedantic tone with fondness instead of the usual exasperation.

She continued reading, "Everyone knows the story of how Pharaoh's daughter rescued the baby Moses from the bulrushes–how his Hebrew first mother set him adrift in a little ark because all the midwives had been ordered by Pharaoh to kill newborn Hebrew males. Did you ever wonder why Pharaoh's own daughter saved a Hebrew baby? I found something once by the historian Josephus in his Antiqui, and I saved it:

"'...on account of her childlessness she was always depressed and sad. In an attack of melancholy, Pharaoh's daughter left her house to seek solace in Nature for her aching heart. She betook herself to the river where she found the infant Moses.'

"This reminds me of the beautiful canals we saw throughout Bangkok when we went to adopt you. I've heard they've started filling them in for dry roadways. When we visited Thailand all those years ago, there was one that I sometimes visited to just sit when it wasn't clear at all that we'd be able to take you back with us. Only a dozen or so orphans were adopted from Thailand in any given year. It was near your orphanage. The situation filled me with such pain all over again, the same pain I felt when I learned I wouldn't be able to bear a child.

"Here's a very roundabout way of explaining your mom's feelings at that time when we were waiting to adopt you, Suzie. Do you remember how God sends Ten Plagues to convince the Pharaoh to let Moses and the Hebrew slaves go? It reminded me of the 'Ten Plagues of Adoption' I had to endure years ago.

"Just as a side note, honey, there were sweet writings I discovered at the time that I wrote these. Those quotes, from Shakespeare and the like, are paraphrased on other scraps in this envelope. I'd always intended to put them into some kind of album but the world will go on whether I do or not.

"I'm sending you my list of imaginary plagues, based on the ones you already know that we recite at Passover: Blood; Frogs; Lice; Untamed Beasts; Disease; Boils; Hail; Locusts; Darkness; Death of the Firstborn."

Susan checked her watch and shifted in the sofa where she was sitting. Then she continued.

"Now here's my adaptation, sweetheart. These are the sad, funny plagues that I carried with me:

1. Blood = Waiting for the results of blood and other tests. Waiting for a biological child. Then waiting for an adoptable child.
2. Frogs = Dealing with the sad, angry behavior of a cute little girl who has been hopped away from home.
3. Lice = Jealousy like irritating lice.

Jealousy of others' fertility. Jealousy of any attention paid to a birth mother.

4. Untamed Beasts = Invasion by untamed experts. Supercilious, duplicitous, invasive and evasive but omnipotent, unfortunately.

5. Disease = Infertility that can feel like a disease on one's femininity or masculinity.

6. Boils = Fear that bursts forth like boils. Fear of never becoming a parent. Then fear of losing their child to a birth mother after a reunion.

7. Hail = Something as uncommon as what those social workers told us, that   if we only loved you, you would never be curious about your own origins.

8. Locusts = Fees (oh, those fees) that eat up "green" like locusts

9. Darkness = The darkness of (well-intentioned) secrecy and deceit surrounding adoption that I fear may have harmed our relationship, Susan.

10. Death of the Firstborn = Death of the hope for a biological child."

To the darkness, Susan said aloud, "I don't think I ever completely imagined what Mom and

Dad went through. I saw only some."

Susan looked back at the scrapbook and went back to reading silently, "At one point, honey, according to some story in the Talmud, Pharaoh's daughter scolds Moses for bringing these plagues down upon his Egyptian adoptive family and I must admit there were times when I wondered what my flesh and blood child might have looked like and even, misguidedly, resented you, or fate, a little. It was unfair of me and I think sometimes I might have been too hard on you. Well, in the rest of that story, Moses stood up to his mother in a way you never would have. He tells her not to blame him, that the Plagues came from God. (Your mom sometimes thinks God deserves a kick in the derriere.)

"Do you know what happens in the end? When Moses leaves Egypt, not just the Hebrew slaves follow him. So do many Egyptians who realize that things haven't been fair there, like adoption hasn't always been pain free for adoptees. One of the people who follows Moses is his adoptive mother, Pharaoh's daughter. You see, we adoptive parents can change and grow with our children.

"Susan, there's another line from one of my favorite psalms, it's part of the Hallel prayer we say at Passover, Psalm 113:

*'God raiseth the poor from the dust, and
      lifteth the needy from the dunghill;
To assign him a seat amongst princes,
Even with the princes of His people.
He setteth up the barren woman to dwell in
   the house as a joyful mother of children;
Hallelujah!'*

"You see, each and every year when I celebrated Passover at our house or at anyone else's, embedded in it, for me, was my story about adopting you. Every time we sing the Hallel in the prayer book, no matter how many other people were at services with us, I was thanking God privately for taking you out of that orphanage to set you up 'with the princes of His people', and for blessing me, 'the barren woman,' with you."

Susan put the letter down and began to weep softly. For her mother. For her mothers. But most of all with relief that her mother did understand her need to return and search, even if her mom did not actually know that Susan had visited that other mother.

Susan reached over and turned off the reading lamp next to the sofa and leaned back. The tears rolled down her cheeks undammed, undamned. The blackness around her was soft and quiet and only the hum of the refrigerator over in the kitchen accompanied the slow, rolling sobs that rocked her into a quiet peace.

She eventually fell asleep like that, with a black and red afghan wrapped around her shoulders and her cheek leaning against the arm of the sofa. When she woke there were purple and yellow finches chirping outside the window.

Without even looking in a mirror she knew her eyes looked puffy. She shivered a sigh and pressed her chin deeper into the woolen patterns her mother-in-law had crocheted one winter. She thought of each one in turn: her mother-in-law, her mother, her first mother, her own new competence as a mother, she felt she had been cosseted by a coven of mothers.

But Masha, wife and mother, died in the early spring.

16 MINT JELLY AND FIDDLEHEADS
1991

Susan and the rest of the family plunged into a timeless chaos during *aninut*, the twenty four hours following a death, within which arrangements were to be made and a funeral held. Friends, cousins, the rabbi, the funeral director, pointed her to vaguely familiar traditions as though hands were reaching out through the darkness. Unlike her mother's quirky traditions, these were shared with the larger community. Rather than conjuring a specific person's will, these traditions were like railings up out of the dark, back to light.

Among the gracious chorus, the people who moved her most and also spooked her with their unflinching ability to stare down the minutiae of Death were the *chevra kadisha.* They were a corps of burial volunteers from her parents' congregation who washed and dressed the body.

Together they recited the ancient Hebrew blessings over her mother and made sure that there was someone to "guard" the body around the clock until the funeral.

Susan ducked in to thank them and noticed a custom she had never seen before. The *chevra kadisha* were winding a simple white shroud across her mother's chest in the shape of the Hebrew letter "shin". She noticed one of her mother's dearest friends from girlhood, Rachel. Rachel explained the tradition to create a "shin" because "shin" was the first letter in a name of God used in several psalms.

Absently, Susan remembered that the *mezuzah* just inside their front doorframe was marked with a *shin*. Rachel hadn't mentioned that connection, Susan didn't ask more. The familiarity of Rachel's always kind face made her feel her mother was in good hands. She thanked Rachel and the others in the *chevra kadisha*, turned and was about to go back to Lily, David and her father when Rachel stopped her. Rachel pulled her down and gave her a hug.

~

A few weeks after *shloshim*, the first thirty

days of mourning when no one feels like celebrating holidays, the extended family began to talk about making plans for Passover. It had been her mother's favorite holiday and biggest project. Susan and David considered using the "adoption" *Haggadah* she had found with her mother's scrapbook. They rejected it given the mix of kids and personalities that would be gathering.

Instead, they all made the trek up to Corea to gather at David's mother's. Al, Susan's dad, drove up in his own car, alone. He insisted it was better to have two cars with them. Susan imagined that he wanted a solitary road trip. Even Tracy and Michael made the trip up to Aliza's, bringing two jars of mini-gefilte fish and an extra *Seder* plate.

Susan and David made a low fat potato pudding from cottage cheese instead of sour cream in Aliza's kitchen. Al, as he had for the past twenty-odd years, tossed a salad with lemon and parsley dressing.

Then he and David, just as they did every year, sat down at a coffee table to horse-trade over which passages of the *Haggadah* to keep in and which to keep out. They had even clocked it once–a full read would otherwise have taken four hours not even counting the meal and dessert.

On the afternoon before the *Seder,* the holiday meal, Susan turned back the quilt on the spool bed in the guest room, intending just to lie down for a minute, but it was much later when the sound of cousins arriving downstairs woke her.

The men were tall and broad-shouldered with deep set features like Dave. They didn't gesture when they talked, in fact they were quite taciturn just like the stereotype of Maine downeasters. It was the wives and women cousins who carried the conversation and the serving dishes. The lamb chops had white and blue paper tasseled leggings. A bright green jar in the middle of the table caught Susan's eye.

"Is that the mint jelly we made last summer?"

"Ayuh, and the mint's growing like weeds again out back of the porch."

"Many fiddlehead ferns this spring?" Susan asked.

Aliza shook her head, "Ned Eaton's been clearing the woods out where I usually go to pick them." She passed a china serving bowl of the pale green fiddleheads to Susan.

She enjoyed watching what was transpiring near the high chairs. David was sitting with Lily and Kieran explaining the cup of Prophet Elijah, named for the prophet whose final resting place is unknown.

The Bible holds no record of Elijah's death so a legend grew through the Middle Ages that the prophet still lived. He wandered, from exile community to exile community across Europe, North Africa, the Middle East and Asia, disguised as a beggar, visiting the poorest Jews and asking for a meal or a place to rest. Prophet Elijah's humble hosts would give unstintingly, the tales went, and once the mysterious guest vanished, they would find in his place a barn full of gold, or the new cow that they desperately needed to survive the winter. Susan's favorite version had the wandering prophet leave behind a golden samovar which when rubbed provided food for any neighbor in need. From there the tradition grew.

David explained to the toddlers, "We are to set a cup for Elijah every year and children are to leave the table at one point during the Seder to welcome Elijah at the door."

Susan smiled, not sure how much they understood yet. She wished her mother were here to see this.

She smiled to keep from tearing up. The result may have looked more like a grimace.

Michael was now at her side, "Remember when all us cousins got back to the table and the grownups would tell us Elijah had already come and gone–came in by the other door?"

Susan nodded.

Most of the grandparents were gone by now, but her mother was the first of that generation to be gone. They would show Susan, Michael and the other children that the cup had indeed been drained, proof that the sojourner who brings solace had been there.

David's mother pulled Susan from her reverie into the kitchen and started talking about something to do with *matzo brei*. She abruptly pointed to a glazed jelly roll on the counter, "I always thicken the jelly with tapioca starch because it freezes better than potato starch."

Susan had just enough time to realize that this would really be about *Kun-mae*. Aliza must have heard from David that Noklek lived in tapioca fields.

Susan's mother-in-law came to the main point "Your mother–your real mother–and I talked before she passed, and we both agreed we'd share you with that woman, but we won't share Lily. A little girl would get confused with more than two grandmothers."

Susan was tempted either to laugh or

make some logical objection on the grounds that many children have more than two sets of grandparents because of divorce. She could also have pointed out that *Kun-mae* couldn't even speak English to Lily, let alone come visit. Susan might have been within her rights if she had explained that it was Susan's decision, not theirs. Instead, she just smiled indulgently and nodded.

Later, after the dishes had been washed and put on the rack, Susan went to look for David who stood talking out back with two of his cousins.

"Hi, guys," Susan said.

"David's been telling us about that 'Hall of the Asian Peoples' exhibit," said Cousin Ron, "Nikko, Japan? I never knew that's where the three monkeys come from."

"Yeah, 'see no evil, hear no evil, speak no evil,' the monkeys are carved just below the eaves of a building where the Tokugawa shoguns rest," nodded Susan.

"Tokugawa like the movie, 'Shogun'?"

"Right."

Cousin Ron had been leaning on the railing and now took the cig from his lips as he pulled himself up, "David ever tell you about Corea and the Berlin Olympics?"

She shuddered, "You mean when Hitler

watched Jesse Owens take the gold for the USA?"

Cousin Bill laughed, "We showed him and all his master race!"

"Sounds like you haven't heard the Corea history then," Cousin Ron looked delighted, an opportunity to tell the story.

Susan sat on the steps.

"What with your 'Hall of the Asian Peoples' I guess you know what happened in 1910."

Her mind raced. A lot happened in 1910. European royalty was lining itself up for a war that would wipe out much of its own nobility. Japan had already won the Russo-Japanese War over who would carve up the East Asian mainland and the US, while still appearing to support Korea, gave Japan the nod through the Taft-Katsura memorandum and the Treaty of Portsmouth.

She boiled it down, "Japan annexed Korea. The US let it happen despite promising Korea to be allies."

"That was the federal government," Cousin Ron said emphatically, "Here's what happened during 1936 at the Olympics. It was the editor of the Frenchman's Bay Weekly who spotted what they were doing to the Korean athletes. Suzie, did you ever wonder why we spell it Corea with a C?"

"Yes," she leaned back on her elbows against the step behind her.

"That's the way it was spelled for centuries. But at these games, the Japanese decided it wasn't enough to annex an ancient country. The editor noticed in a photo of the opening games that the Japanese, letter J, were marching directly ahead of the Coreans, letter C."

"They march in alphabetically, don't they," agreed Susan.

Cousin Ron nodded, "Except that Japanese Olympic officials had insisted to their own government and to the committee that everyone now spell it with a K, so Korea'd march behind the Japanese athletes."

Bill snorted, "Ignorant."

Cousin Ron now stood his feet apart, gesturing, "This editor, one of the Billings' family, got men and women who barely picked up a pen and paper normally to do just that. The paper had a whole big campaign going to get readers to write to their legislators. Urged them to have the federal government keep the spelling of free Corea. Well, apparently there was some conversation up there on Capitol Hill but the U.S. Foreign Service ignored its own values and adopted the name 'Korea' with a K. Corea, Maine never forgot."

He took another drag, slow this time.

Everyone was still savoring the story when Cousin Bill added, "*'Je me souviens'* like the tourists with the Quebec license plates, 'I will remember'."

"Ayuh."

"That's a good one. Wish I'd heard of it before we put together the exhibit," Susan smiled at her cousins-in-law.

Cousin Ron looked pleased.

Susan turned and tilted her head. "David, wanna go for a walk up the road? Your mother wants to give Lily a bottle herself."

His mouth spread into a slow grin as he answered, "Sure, sugar."

The two others nodded as he took her hand.

The edges of the blacktop crumbled into white gravel at the shoulders on the road they were walking up. Falling away at either side were three foot deep gullies with banks carpeted in tangles of wild strawberry and blackberry creepers. The strawberry vines were still covered with small white star-shaped flowers and the blackberries wouldn't bloom for another month yet.

Susan caught David looking over his shoulder at her and she found herself smiling back up at him when he told her, "We're almost at the clearing where the old settlers' cemetery is."

And then there it was. The cemetery hugged the side of the road and the low metal fence around it was just that side of the gully. It sloped leisurely up to a stand of darkling spruce. Dave bent down to unlatch the metal fence that had been carefully oiled so it swung open silently into the well-clipped grass.

Susan asked him, "Where does the road go?" It was little more than two deep sandy ruts with an aisle of grass between them. It meandered along the gravestones and out of sight among the shadows under the tree trunks.

"Don't know. Shed or something."

Susan walked on the gravel of one side and Dave walked on the other as though they were following two separate but parallel paths. She let him clasp her hand in his–and she could tell he was rubbing the now familiar smoothness of her wedding band. Her fingertips rested on the orange hairs of the back of his hands. They always felt warm.

The newer stones were thick polished

slabs of pink granite from a quarry up in Oceanville. Back at the hem of the graveyard were the older ones. They were thinner and smaller but of pure white marble. Green and orange lichen laced their flanges. Some had nosegays or tall ships chiseled in them.

"Those were the ones that died at sea. Think of all the sailors that came from these parts and it makes you realize men growing up and leaving this town isn't all that new after all."

Susan wasn't looking at David.

"What do you suppose funerals are like in Thailand?"

His exasperated sigh made her wish momentarily that she hadn't opened that topic up again. But then she continued on stubbornly anyway, driven by the longing for some kind of closure. She kept her eyes on the crushed quartz of the cemetery road.

"I guess I'll never be invited to my mother's funeral. The way she's so secretive, no one will want me there. I guess I know what it really feels like to be a bastard," she glanced sideways at him.

She usually didn't use that language in front of him. "Noklek is a pretty, sweet woman and it choked her up to see me again, Dave, but deep down the fact is that I'm not part of the family."

"You're right."

Susan looked at him.

Then he put on his aw-shucks face, "But, heck, you should meet some of our vendors if you want to see some real bastards."

They both smiled. He stood with his knee resting against the inside of her thigh.

"This is awful. I'm laughing but the truth is terrible. When she was carrying me, my first experience in life, it was all about not being wanted. My mother didn't want me."

"Or it feels that way," he said as he shifted her around, "but that's not what she told you. And, Suze, I want you. I want you."

She nudged his knee away and continued uphill until they were at the top of the cemetery. The road continued on into the dark woods but she had lost interest in following it to its end.

She turned instead to look down over the rows of white and pink stones. Then beyond them you could just see, above the tips of spruce, the light blue of the spring sky curving down to meet the darker blue of the ocean. A breeze from below mingled its briny coolness with the warm woodsy smell of the deep green spruce needles. It smelled like anything but death here this spring morning.

Dave stepped onto the little grass meridian and stood close behind her. She put her palms over his as he clasped her in his arms. They talked about the Passover *Seder* and she laughed at his imitations of some of the family.

David and Susan were sitting on the earth now face to face, his bent legs forming bridges over hers. She reached up, still laughing, to kiss him on the lips and then rested her cheek on the smooth space of his open collar so she heard the rumble in his throat when he spoke.

And Susan closed her eyes as her lips met his and their legs entwined. Their lovemaking started out slow and hand-made, heart-made, but the rocking of the two lostlings rocked the earth, the trees flailed in abandon against the wind, and the sea and the sky embraced as though never to be parted. When they finally drew apart, legs weak and lips still warm with blood, they were amazed to see that the tombstones still stood in even rows, stark and unmoved.

"It didn't seem wrong to do it here this time."

"The dearly departed know I love you, Susan. Forever."

Susan didn't take her eyes off him as she felt for the shell buttons on her dress, pulling them through the buttonholes up to her pink cotton collar.   David dragged his shirt off a marble headstone and put it on as he stood up. He pulled her to her feet and they started back down the slope together. His footsteps matched hers. He finished buttoning his shirt by the time they reached the little silent gate and he unlatched it for her.

17 PLANTATION SIX
1974

Russet pine needles clung to his palms. The sun had already risen high enough in the sky to shine above the tops of the spruce trees. He was sitting in a clearing. Or rather, he was sitting on a smooth pink stone ledge that prevented the trees from growing in this particular patch of forest. He could not for the life of him remember how he'd got here, nor see any road out. There was no rifle near him so he couldn't have been hunting. He had no tent, no wallet, and no keys with him.

The cry of a cicada rose and fell and he realized that the back of his head was throbbing. He felt the back of his hair. It was clumped and sticky and when he drew his hands back in front of him he saw they were smudged with coagulating blood. Enough panic hit him to send him to his feet and in a vaguely downhill direction.

He stumbled over the pine-needled floor. It was an effort just to lift one work boot and set it down in front of the other for a couple hundred yards until he saw a swirl of smoke that rose up, blending to the eye with the beginnings of morning light.

Below the smoke was a log cabin and a few hundred yards below the cabin were the rooftops of a small village. He waved and tried to cry out but his tongue seemed bloated and it strangled his voice before it could leave his throat. Just as a chestnut-haired, middle-aged woman appeared in the widening crack behind the door sill of the cabin, the ground lurched and the carpet of pine needles suddenly heaved upward and met his face.

He awoke to stare into the two fluorescent tubes of a ceiling light. There was a distracting whirring sound in the background. His muscles ached and there were wires and IVs stuck in both arms. He caught the smell of ethyl alcohol in the air.

Eventually a nurse came in and called a doctor and then more nurses and more doctors. They wanted to know what his name was. Where was he from? What was he doing in the woods above Plantation Six? They looked very cynical when he said he'd like to know all that, too.

"What is 'Plantation Six?'" he asked.

They said it was the name of the logging village near where he came stumbling out of the forest. The paper company owned all the forests from here to Canada and the villages at the edge of their lands were given numbers like Plantation Six, or Camp Nine. They were full of loggers, an occasional Bible-quoting survivalist, and veterans who had returned from Vietnam, or more distantly Korea but who just couldn't seem to return completely.

"Are you a veteran, Sir?"

"No."

"He sounds like he's from around here. This is the Ashkenuck Hospital in Ashkenuck, Maine. Where you from? What were you doing up there?"

"Please, stop talking so loud, I can hear you all right I guess. I don't know where I was. I honestly can't remember anything."

The doctors, the nurses and the air floated away and then the two fluorescent lights floated away and it was dark. Days passed through the yellow humming light of day and the blue distant lights of night. Doctors ran tests.

Those cynical looks stopped and some young doctor named Gideon Ames who talked softly like a librarian started meeting with him every day after breakfast to ask questions. One day the patient asked him a question and it led to an answer.

"Why is it, Dr. Ames, that I can't remember my kin or the company I musta worked for but I can remember other things like how to tie shoes and brush my teeth?"

"Well I guess that even with this amnesia, you never really forget what you know. Learn to ride a bicycle, learn to handle a chainsaw, a catheter and it never leaves you. It sinks in 'til your body remembers, no matter what they bonk you on the head with...But memories, feelings, relations, they're harder for the mind to hang on to. Nope, but I guess that you can really say that a man never forgets what he knows."

"A man never forgets what he knows."

"Yep, even if he does forget who he is," nodded Dr. Ames.

As the weather got warmer they started taking him into town. The best was the hardware store. It seemed like he'd pick up a hammer and his arm would remember just the right arc it needed to drive a nail through a pine board. He also still had just the right feel for the leverage it would take to use a crowbar.

"You're pretty strong," said Dr. Ames, standing back by a bin of nails.

"I can take care of myself."

Dr. Ames seemed about to answer and then the man thought to answer for him.

"You're thinking that I really can take care of myself. There's no real reason to keep me in your hospital. You give me a name and maybe send me back up to that plantation and I can start a life. I could put up with one of the loggers 'til I get my own place. You give me a name and I can take care of myself."

"You should give yourself a name for now. I'll discharge you if you let me take you to Boston first. The hospital's bigger and I'm going to a meeting there in a week and a half."

"Alrighty. You scratch my back and I'll scratch yours. And I already got a name that'll suit me. Paul Bunyan."

"Paul Bunyan?!" Dr. Ames laughed, "Fine name for a Maine lumberman but it's already taken. In fact I'll bring you a book on him from the library for our meeting tomorrow."

The next morning Dr. Gideon Ames arrived with a children's book under his arm with the name "Paul Bunyan" written across the top.

"Actually," began Dr. Ames, "the name you picked fits quite well with your new choice of career."

"Yeah, yeah. It came back to me. He leaves everyone behind because that's the only way to go on being a lumberjack. Except, Dr. Ames, I don't know who I'm leaving behind. Just before I fell to sleep last night a name came to me. Then I woke up this morning and it was still with me. Piper."

A slow smile spread across Gideon Ames thin lips.

"Peter Piper?"

Now Piper got that, too. But a man doesn't forget what he knows and Piper was beginning to realize that if he weren't his amnesia patient, that thin-limbed little Dr. Ames wouldn't have the courage to sit across a table from Piper.

"Pied Piper?"

"No," Piper said, finally letting his irritation show, "Joseph Piper. You can look it up in your fancy files when you're up to Boston since I'm probably the most interesting case you've ever had. But, sorry, I'm not going with you. I'm tired of books and questions, that's your line. I'm going back to that Plantation Six to sign on some work papers. You come call when you find anything in Boston. I'm not going with you. I don't need to. I'll check myself out of the hospital soon enough."

Dr. Ames had a sour look when he said, "You're making a mistake."

Piper's hunch was right–they couldn't keep him there–but he almost showed too much glee when he repeated, "I'll check myself out of the hospital anyways. Joseph Piper's the name you're looking for."

The next day, seeing that Piper was bound and determined to check himself out of there, Dr. Ames came up to him sheepishly with a glass in his hand. Another doctor he'd never seen on the floor before started talking. More to Dr. Ames than to Piper.

~

"If he's really going up to one of the Plantations he's the best choice. With all the testing you've done on him we know he'll provide good specimen."

"Good specimen?" Piper asked, suspiciously.

"There's a couple who have been trying

for seven years to conceive and they have finally come in for testing. It's the husband who is sterile. Probably due to an adolescent case of measles. If you agree to cooperate then they won't have to adopt. We've all decided that the child will never be told about his true paternity, that way everyone will adjust better. They've seen you and they approve."

~

Joseph took the cup. Three quarters of an hour later Joseph was back in the exam room and handed Dr. Benjamin the cup. Wonder if he'll look like me–that's what he thought as he watched the doctor leave the room.

As the weeks wore on, Dr. Ames ran through the causes for what Joseph was overhearing him call retrograde amnesia. Despite all the blood he'd discovered when he came to on the overlook above Plantation Six they ruled out blunt trauma brain injury. They called it a surface wound. Apparently the head had so many arteries and capillaries near the surface that just a cut he sustained in a fall was enough to create a gory clot.

The staff also ruled out a dissociative amnesia because his memory loss didn't seem due to any other underlying medical condition or neurological disorder. He seemed still at home in his own skin so they ruled out depersonalization disorder. Dr. Ames had narrowed it to either dissociative fugue or dissociative identity disorder.

The doctor even read him a list of common symptoms about each dissociative disorder that went something like this:

Memory loss (*amnesia*) of certain time periods and people

A sense of detachment from yourself (*depersonalization*)

A perception of the people and things around you as distorted and unreal (*derealization*)

A blurred sense of identity

Joseph said, "I find the list pretty insulting."

"Well," said Ames, "hold on. I think you'll find this interesting:

'A Dissociative Fugue occurs with an unexpected and sudden abandonment of the place where the individual normally resides, together with amnesia. The patient presents confusion concerning his or her identity and may assume a new one, starting a new life in the true sense. Episodes of Dissociative Fugue generally occur following a traumatic or stressful event or period,'

"It's something to think about. Here's what you might expect, 'They are characterized by variable duration, ranging from a geographically and temporally limited move to a more substantial abandonment of the individual's habitual place of residence (and this is the case in which a new identity is assumed). The recovery of memory is generally complete, although the time of recovery will vary quite considerably.'"

Joseph felt uneasy. There was something Dr. Ames didn't know, but he let the doctor go on reading.

"'Dissociative Identity Disorder. In this disorder an individual assumes at least two distinct identities. Each with its own persistent manner of perceiving, relating and thinking about itself and in relation to the environment. They emerge and become manifest, recurrently assuming control of the individual at different times, and it often occurs that one identity has no recollection of the other, is unaware of the existence of the other personality and can preserve no memory of it at all,'"

Dr. Ames took a breath and looked at him

before resuming, "'However, the primary identity–like the other secondary identities–will be aware of having gaps in its memory and will occasionally have a hunch that the other personality exists. This condition, formerly known as multiple personality disorder, is characterized by "switching" to alternate identities when you're under stress.'"

What they didn't know was that one day, after they had decided to give him back his clothes, sealed in a plastic bag, things shifted as he was handling his work boots. It was almost like being handed an old toolkit after a period of disuse. It was as though he had opened it and suddenly remembered the use and meaning of each thing he saw in each compartment.

In fact, it was less like having forgotten his boys, wife, home and store and more like merely having set them aside, lost them as a frame of reference. The questions the doctor asked about them were perplexing because they were gone outside that frame.

He didn't feel relief at recalling his old life, he hadn't been struggling to reclaim it at all, and decided against telling Dr. Ames or the staff when the memories started coming back. Now, as though feeling tool handles in his palm, he was weighing each missing memory to judge its worth.

One, when he reached for it, made him laugh out loud. Oh, the irony! There had been one afternoon when he tinkered with–no, longed for–an escape from his life in–it was on the tip of his tongue–Corea.

He remembered the feel of running his fingertips across a cool axe blade late last autumn before hoisting its weight above his shoulder and bringing it down to perfectly crack apart a log in their backyard.

He remembered thinking then that his wife and her parents had shouldered the preparations before each change of season matter-of-factly. But he struggled, not physically for survival as his immigrant parents had, but with the same sickening dread at the relentlessness of obligations. He would chop the firewood to feed the Franklin stove through the winter, but he did it as if waiting for salvation from it.

Aliza–that was his wife's name–seemed to face the yearly round meditatively.

Close of summer was time to pick and wash the late vegetables. Chop, pickle or boil, then can and put them up through the cold months. Aliza sang while she lifted blankets from chests in the attic and brought them down.

The first good thaw was time to air those same blankets on the line strung from the back of the house to the tree. It meant spring cleaning kitchen cabinet shelves and what Aliza playfully called "outings" to gather fiddleheads. In the fall Aliza would go down to the ocean at low tide and gather seaweed to spread as fertilizer over the vegetable garden for the winter.

Inevitably, in the spring she would turn the same bed, raking down the half-rotted rockweed. Aliza and the rest of their families had grafted themselves onto this land through this coastal hamlet. As spring advanced they hoed, planted, thinned, weeded, harvested, preserved and traded the excess to each other in seasonal cadence.

He took over running his father-in-law's dry goods store. In the beginning he took to it with gusto, even weighing whether there was enough cash flow to open a store further inland. There wasn't. He tried to think up new customers by seeing if the local boatyard might buy directly from him. They placed a few orders but generally seemed content to order directly or let the men buy on their own or do without.

He tried placing ads in the area weekly papers in summer, not so much for the locals as to attract people from away, the New York and

Massachusetts vacationers. In summer he set up side walk sales to catch the tourists as they walked up the pier into town from visiting schooners.

But the way the business was structured, checks had to go out every month to family members who held equity stakes. Some did come work in the store, but whether they did or not he had to write those checks.

Technically, he was no more than an employee of this group, albeit the one with the largest salary. The salary rose in summer and then drained like neap tide in winter, leaving a coldness in the pit of his stomach.

He found himself cursing this store he'd been given to run, but not to own. He couldn't even sell it off and start fresh. He understood that Aliza's family had built up customer good will from nothing. He understood that he was luckier–in their eyes–than the European immigrant generation that came with nothing.

Oh, they must congratulate themselves; yet it was he who kept something going that wasn't entirely his. It was something so woven into family life that he couldn't walk away like an employee. He felt strangled by this debt of gratitude.

They recognized that he worked hard, but

not that he worked without hope. After about a decade it was becoming clear that the store wouldn't grow. In fact, orders from the regulars were slipping and Abel–that had been his name, Abel–could see clearly in the eyes of the regulars that they didn't hold him in the same regard as Aliza's family.

Everyone knew his father had been shiftless, and he found himself wondering what it must have been like for his father to be able to slip away from the town and his family to be a traveling tinker. He wouldn't have to see those expectant faces every morning and every evening, demanding he earn their food and clothes.

His father earned what he could to maintain himself and brought the extra home, arriving to bestow bounty like the prophet Elijah. Abel was poorer as a child no doubt than his boys, Johnny and Davie, but he appreciated his father more, for the irregularity of his homecomings.

By deep winter the wood piles were low and he wished he could be forgiven if he joined the winter drunks. They were the men who didn't work most of the dark months, but sobered up by springtime to mend their nets and rejoin the daily pre-dawn ritual of turning their engines, steering the boats off their moorings and pointing them out toward the channel.

He could not do that with this store. Instead day in, day out he opened the empty store, sat alone most of a wintry day until he could flip the sign that hung on the front storm door from "open" to "close" and head home with his thermos and lunch bag, and a despair that his tea-totaling nature couldn't lift.

In those winter hours he began to work out how he might leave and not be found. Then the isolation that winter imposed would become an ally. He raised and rejected the thought of returning up the St. Croix to Canada. There really was no trade for tinkers like his father anymore, he concluded.

He thought about becoming a trucker. Maybe it was the closest thing to that same freedom. The very afternoon he hit on this–he wouldn't call it a plan yet–notion, he caught himself responding to a customer's "good-bye" with "ten-four". The man turned around to look at him as though he were a little off, before continuing the motion of pushing open the door and leaving. A tinkle of bells hung in the air after he left.

Abel grabbed one of the fishery magazines that his brother-in-law left the day before and flipped to the back. There he found two black-and-white ads for truck driving schools. He ripped them out carefully and folded them into his back pockets.

He froze for a minute. Would it be worse for his brother-in-law to find the torn pages or for him right now to throw out the entire issue? He hadn't finished reading it but he rolled up the magazine and let it drop with a thud that reverberated in the metal trash can. It was already getting dark out. Time to lock up. He had taken the car today instead of walking because Aliza had wanted him to pick up some fresh halibut.

The fishermen's co-op would be closed by now but given the season he knew "the Italian" would still be open. Mario Fifield ran a grocery. Though it was only a great-grandfather named Mario on his mother's side who came over from Italy as a stone carver, that and his first name were enough to earn him the sobriquet.

Sure enough the Italian was still there under the yellow fluorescent lights of the butcher counter, and greeted Abel with a gruff but familiar "hello." As was his habit for locals, Mario asked if he'd like the halibut wrapped with ice shavings. Abel nodded yes and in the back of his mind noted that the ice would keep fish better should he take a drive on the way home.

Mario reached up for twine dangling from a spool on the ceiling, pulled it down around a sheet of wax paper at the same time that he used his other hand to roll the wax paper around the filet and ice shavings, all in one practiced motion. Mario handed the package across the glass butcher case to Abel.

The drive found him crossing the causeway out of town. By now it was dark and he had to avert his eyes from oncoming headlights. He decided to steer north, not sure why. It was a decision that turned Mario into the last person to see "Abel Piper" alive.

To this day "Joseph Piper" couldn't remember the events that happened next. But he did resent Dr. Ames' insinuations. He had only gone for a drive with the halibut on the seat next to him, as promised for Aliza and his boys waiting at home. But for that halibut he would have walked home that night, and walked back to the store in the morning.

It had been entirely fortuitous, thought Abel, this new life through the gift of amnesia. It was like finding a full wallet in the street, it was a second chance. Just as it was different from committing a crime to steal that hypothetical wallet, this new life had befallen him and he had not knowingly left his family.

It was too late now with him sitting across from this doctor in Piscataquis County. He had no explanations for him or them, but they would be in good hands with Aliza, and they had that damned store.

18 RAMONA'S PAST
1981

Dr. Ames did help Abel get his papers straightened away and drove him back to Plantation Six. Everyone had heard of him, seemed concerned. After Dr. Ames drove away, the former patient introduced himself as Joseph Piper.

The foreman was the kind who agreed now and then to pay men under the table. He'd justify it with the savings on payroll tax.

Down the road that would mean Joseph might miss out on Social Security and Medicare, but down the road was years away and who knew if those payments were even going to be around then. Joseph figured that what he was saving on withholding and income tax would make up for it.

His needs were few and for a solid year he never felt sad, never felt particularly worried or angry.

Finally he understood what clergy meant by living in a state of grace. That was the first year.

There at Plantation Six is where he lived ever since and only came into Ashkenuck for provisions. He didn't miss what he'd left behind.

He was already at home with the smell of spruce in the air that mixed with the diesel fumes from their chainsaws. The men he was with worked hard mostly. Eventually he saved from renting to owning his own house built like others by the paper company. He never replaced the wood stove it came with.

By the third year he had saved himself enough to buy a pick-up, without having to go through the paperwork and credit check of a loan.

That fourth year he caught himself feeling slightly restless. The doctor with the probing questions was long behind him. Joseph's life was easier, what with the foreman making the decisions and the freedom from dependents. Joseph'd settle for hours of ennui now and then.

He started going down to a tavern with the rest of the crew on an occasional weekend. It was there one night that a Passamaquoddy pulled her car in and ordered food from the kitchen behind the bar.

That night Joseph was feeling lonely, itchy and brave. He found himself sliding over next to her and offering to buy her a beer. She demurred, but just as he turned away he thought she said something softly.

He leaned in, "What's that?"

"Maybe a ginger ale would be nice," she repeated.

He laughed and ordered her one. Her hair smelled like someone who'd been driving with the window rolled down for quite a long way. He felt obliged to ask why a woman was out alone driving to a place like this. When she averted her eyes and stayed silent, he wasn't disappointed. Her ginger ale arrived and as she peeled back the wrapper on the straw he tried, "Mind if I finish up my beer here?"

She looked, not displeased, but bashful and nodded. She added, as though to make up for her silence a moment ago that she had been driving for a few hours.

Reflexively, Joseph asked, "Where from? Where to?"

No answer. Instead of answering she asked, "Is there a place to stay near here?"

The night was damp with fog. There really was nowhere to drive this late.

Half an hour later as her car climbed the road behind his pick-up, his heart raced with both anticipation and fear. What kind of woman would stop at a lumberjack's bar, but order ginger ale? Why would she follow him so far from anywhere with streetlights? As they left the tavern he made sure she knew the guys knew she was following him, a precaution he took just in case she was a psychopath. At that she tucked her chin in modestly and looked down but didn't slow the pace of her footsteps to her own car.

When he stopped his car outside his cabin, he realized he'd left no lights on. He would be able to make his way by the dim light of stars.

He walked back to where she sat after turning off the ignition and leaned down to pull open her car door. He felt joy when she held out one hand for him to pull her out of the bucket seat.

Her palm was perspiring and he couldn't suppress a chuckle. He heard her breathing change–was it alarm or something else?

He explained, "I haven't done this in a while." It was almost four years.

They walked up the slope to his door in silence. He pushed it open, never bothered to lock it. She waited as he walked across the one room to the nightstand and turned on the lamp.

Then she came slowly to him.

The next morning he looked over to see her stirring, too. He asked, "What's your name?"

"Ramona," she answered simply. He was relieved that she didn't respond with a question of her own, yet there was nothing aloof about either of their warm bodies.

~

Joseph Piper married Ramona Graves five years later. Ramona was quiet and seemed relieved he didn't ask about her past. They often held hands.

I'm quite good at being married, mused Joseph the first summer after their marriage license. A man never forgets what he knows after all. There were a few irregularities in the provisioning of the marriage license. It served the interests of love and, an added benefit to "Joseph Piper", buried "Abel" forever.

He knew that doctors say they are supposed to come back to you eventually, those memories, and Dr. Ames and company were growing suspicious because of something Joseph refused to do. Dr. Ames was unable for a good long time to track down anyone by the name of Joseph Piper serving in the armed services, registering to vote, applying for a social security card, marrying or dying.

When that day came, though, Dr. Ames drove up the dirt road below Joseph and Ramona's cabin. Ramona preferred to stay inside but Joseph came out to greet him. Ramona poured the doctor water from the kettle that was almost always warming on the wood stove this time of year. Dr. Ames came in and settled in a platform rocker. He warmed the inside of his cold knuckles around the mug of instant coffee.

"This has turned out to be more complex than even our last foray, Joseph. Quite."

"What's got you all sour, Dr. Ames?"

"Well, I found an Abel Piper who was reported missing seven years ago. Then I traced your parents Charles and Shirley Piper to a Bangor cemetery."

"Well, that's the end of it then."

"Oh-oh. Not. At. All. It seems that you ran off and left behind a wife, Aliza, and two small sons named Jonathan and David."

Joseph took a sip from his coffee cup but Gideon held his own mug motionless in mid-air and just looked at Joseph.

Joseph avoided his gaze.

Instead Joseph looked for some time in the direction of the lamp in the corner, under it a rocking chair, and in the rocking chair, bent over some darning, Ramona. It was so quiet he could hear her rocking back and forth, back and forth across the polished plank floor.

Her hands were steady, one holding in her lap a torn shoulder seam, the other rising and falling in a steady motion as she pushed a threaded needle up through the cloth, then from the other side, pinching the sharp tip to continue drawing it up halfway to her chin before she changed direction with a deft flick of the wrist and aimed the needle down until its crimson thread silently pierced his shirt.

Every bone in her birdlike frame was tuned to this conversation, he knew, listening for what he would say next. And it would only be left to him, Joseph, to speak next.

As if his words were the tiny glass beads Ramona used to embroider the purses she sold at the general merchandise store, he strung each one together slowly, awkwardly, saying, "I think I know that what you are saying is true. I may have had a wife, but I'm sure I left her long before the amnesia, I–"

"–have children and you must do right by them," Gideon was indignant.

Gideon was stunned by what came next. Abel's thick accent and his gait, which was literally lumbering, belied a quick mind. Joseph looked at Dr. Ames evenly. "Which ones?"

Dr. Ames glanced nervously at Ramona, remembering the favor they did for the obstetrician-gynecologist.

"Maybe we should go outside."

Joseph was ahead of him out the door. Gideon continued angrily, but in a hushed tone, in case neighbors were about.

"Those are two completely different cases."

"I reckon so, I reckon so. One child I have out there, you wanted me to leave and forget to another man. The others I'm supposed to leave Ramona for. What happens if they've got a stepfather? I'd just be in the way there, too, and I don't honestly see the difference."

The doctor tried not to show his own confusion, "It's a matter of holy matrimony. In the former case it was another man's wife, in the latter you were the one who was married."

"I'm married now, too. And," Joseph stammered out, "I'm no bigamist!"

"Well, I guess you are now, too," Gideon paused, "Every man has to live with his own conscience, Abel. I won't call on them, but, I'm leaving you the address of your wife and your boys. I won't intervene but you've got to come to some decision on your own."

Gideon handed him a sheet of yellow paper torn from a legal pad which Joseph took, folded and stuffed into the rear pocket of his corduroy trousers. Then he turned back to the house before Dr. Ames had even reached his car.

When he opened the cabin door it took a few seconds for his eyes to adjust to the darkness again and find Ramona who had left off darning to put some folded wash away in the chest of drawers. She stood just beyond the crack of light that fell from the front door.

The light wavered as he thought to open the door wider and come in, but instead he called to her, "Nothing's changed, wife, I'll be out the side chopping some firewood," and with that the arrow of light disappeared.

Soon she could hear the thud-crack, thud-crack of the axe.

~

He'd thought this through once before, when his memories had righted themselves. He needed now to–damned Dr. Ames–think it through again. He would, Joseph told himself, but only this once.

The early orange sunsets and late dawns

of autumn held the least foreboding in his youth. While he had nothing against summer and being able to strip down to his shorts to swing from a rope into the water as it rose to 60 degrees or more in the cove, cold weather suited him best.

Even when he had lived on the coast in Corea, finding himself with a wife and two young boys and no other family, he had not been one of those people that took to the bottle during the wintry scallop season. If you liked categories, there were maybe three, he reasoned. The lobstermen who were most resourceful went and refitted their boats with nets to drag for scallops. The miserable repaired their traps and dug clams in the icy mud until spring. The most miserable drank.

But for him, winter's clean dryness seemed to make every sensation clearer. Even through his work boots he could feel the contours of frozen tire tracks or the smooth slickness of an ice-glazed puddle more surely than he could feel the cloying of mud beneath his feet in springtime. What would only be an abrasion in summer broke skin in winter.

After shoveling out on a frosty morning, he enjoyed stepping back inside and slapping heat back into his thighs and arms as he peeled off the frozen shells of pants and jacket. When he was old enough to grow a beard, he appreciated the way his breath crystallized in its strands. He didn't mind how in winter a night's sky seemed spread across a higher dome, still brilliant but more aloof than the nearer stars of summer.

This might be why when even old Canadians headed to Deerfield Beach and other warmer enclaves of Florida, he had headed to the northern woods for his escape. His amnesia was real enough, whether induced by a miraculously mild stroke, a blow to the head (they were never able to determine whether the lump he sustained happened before or after his fall), or something else.

Even before his past was fortuitously but ephemerally erased, his intention was to head to one of the plantations. There were still about twenty-six plantations then in Maine, semi-incorporated villages drawn for logging and paper. He had never been deliberate enough to pick this one, yet here he was in one of the plantations.

The cold emptiness was exactly what he had sought. The silent cold was sharper than any sound in his ears. His nostrils burned as he inhaled and lifted the axe high above his head for the first hard swing. Crystals formed all the way down to the stubble disappearing into his collar.

He had sometimes hated the inevitable tug to chop firewood before the October frosts became constant in Corea. He would line up each whole log grudgingly and then moved down the row, splitting each log one by one, pausing only to revisit the larger logs that needed a second axe-blow for quartering.

Now his knees and shoulders got into the swing of the axe in air, and hummed from the reverberation of the blade through the handle as it sunk into each log. He felt like he had found where he always needed to be. He marveled that without meaning to he had accomplished what the summerfolk called "following your bliss".

The first time he heard that term was years ago when Aliza and he were courting. They went to the Elk Hall to hear a lecturer from away. The speaker called himself a Christian Buddhist or Buddhist Christian and claimed that one religion "completed" the other. Abel didn't recall which was supposed to be completed by which but they had laughed because like all Jews, they were used to being told how Christianity or Buddhism or Hare Krishna completed them.

If he and Aliza had known the topic ahead of time they wouldn't have come here. On the other hand, they didn't leave early when a half dozen other people did, offended by some sectarian volley, and he did come away from the evening with a story that stuck with him.

The speaker called it the lesson of the *bodhisattva* to the woodcutter. A *bodhisattva*, the lecturer explained, is an enlightened being who foregoes enlightenment, or his own reward, in order to save others. A woodcutter asked the *bodhisattva* what he should do until he, too, attained enlightenment. The *Bodhi* replied to the woodcutter that he should chop wood. Then the woodcutter asked him what he should do after he attained enlightenment. The answer at first astonished the poor woodcutter, but he finally understood the nature of enlightenment when the *bodhisattva* explained that he should continue to chop wood.

Joseph set up and swung the axe more easily than he had ever done in his old life to the south.

Aliza, he mused, was truly an excellent lady and people would ask how he could have done this: left her and their sons. He, too, had joined in when others wondered aloud at the occasional story about a loving divorced father who stopped showing up for visitation. But Joseph hadn't planned to divorce Aliza.

He had also sat in judgment of the story of an uncle or great-grandfather known to have abandoned his wife and children during the Great Immigration. It really wasn't the woe of bills that had driven Joseph away. He wouldn't even call it being driven away, it was a going toward something else.

If for one instant he had had any doubt that Aliza wouldn't somehow always find a way to make things work, to make ends meet, he would never have left. She was solid, an excellent lady, who would do right by his sons. They, like many great men throughout history who had lost a father, would do fine. They would even be stronger for having to be the little men of the house once Abel left, decided Joseph.

He almost visibly shook his head at the thought of being categorized with the unprincipled ne'er-do-wells who left a struggling wife to feed young mouths alone. Aliza had a business acumen that you couldn't get from books. They were so young then, but he could feel already that his wife was growing beyond where he could ever lead her.

She didn't realize it but he saw through her false deference to him, something she had been raised with. She might even soar now that she was free of it. Even with her lowered eyes and soft voice, he felt insubstantial next to her strength and good sense. You could rely on her;

she was an excellent woman.

As for Johnny and Davie, if someone had asked Joseph to lay down his own life for his sons, as though one life outside of a movie plot could actually be called upon to stand in for another, he would have done it in a heartbeat. After he left them he even caught himself once or twice in daydreams where he pulled them out of a sinking dinghy, or ran into a burning school, pulled them coughing from some debris and carried them out like little cubs one under each arm.

Deadbeats walked away when families were struggling–something that was against his deepest principles. He hadn't abandoned his own principles or fled to avoid seeing his loved ones suffer. They wouldn't suffer and he had a right to feel, finally, like his own man.

As if in punctuation, his axe blade split another round log leaving one half teetering but still upright while the other half fell down and rocked against the frozen turf.

~

"Nothing's changed," he'd said, but everything had. Ramona had married him out of relief, as a simple man who never cared to ask too much about her people. He had given her a home and by being just her husband he let her hope that she could be just his wife.

"Well," Ramona, thought to herself, "the Lord always makes it trickier than that. Now it'd turned out he'd a past, as have I, and it might eventually lead him to see right through me," to see her as more than just a wife. She was bound and determined to never let that happen, for them to go on being just husband and wife with no stories to tell beyond that. From that day the quiet Ramona became more resolved still.

19 SPRING TURNED BACK TO WINTER
2007

Even before Susan and David opened their car doors and swung their feet down to the ground, the couple saw that something powerful had burned and matted down the trees as though they were only so much thinning black hair blown flat against an aging skull of a mountain.

Where she would expect to see the pale green buds of spring on the conifers and shoots pushing their way up from the forest floor, all she saw was a white and gray blanket thick as any snowfall on the trees and yards around them. It wasn't quite right to call them trees, they were darkened spars.

About two hundred yards to her left she saw a line of prison inmates in yellow jackets and helmets aiming hoses to knock down smoldering underbrush.

Another crew worked shoulder to

shoulder facing up the mountain while cutting a line through tree roots and unburned brush just in front of the road ahead. They seemed to be hollowing out a trench below a finished berm of heaped soil. Susan noticed they hacked at the ground and fallen timber with short-handled tools with the head of an ax on one side and the head of a hoe on the other.

Their trench succeeded in catching two new firebrands that sparked and then rolled downhill even as she watched.

All along the hill were the charred foundations of a dozen homes, a few empty white plastic water jugs the firefighters had discarded, and about a half dozen pickups with U.S. Forest Service or Maine Hotshot brigade insignia on their doors.

A puff of smoke and ash a few feet taller than their heads rose just a little uphill from what had once been a homestead. With it came a stench like nothing she had smelled before. It wasn't the nostalgic smell of a wood fire. It carried an acrid hint of seared rubber, scorched rock and the ominous sting of an electric fire. With horror, Susan realized she also smelled something like meat kept too long.

Large ugly tire treads that had gnashed up the side of the hill and on into the dark of the logging trails offered the silent explanation for the loud rumblings Susan heard. They were the pumpers still feeding the hoses for mop-up.

The burnt gashes of the hill oozed dozens of white rivulets formed by the run off of water from the pumpers, carrying the forest fire's aftermath down to the gullies on either side of the road. In the gullies white ashes mixed with the pink slurry that had been dropped as fire retardant from the fuselage of Forest Service planes.

In an hour, satellite transmissions to broadband would report that over seven hundred acres of timberland had been destroyed and that mop-up continued over an area twice that size. Names of the missing and dead had not yet been released, out of respect, until families could be notified.

Her brother-in-law Jonathan and her David had gotten calls early that morning from the state police and driven in separate cars to this place where neither had ever been. Jonathan had arrived a little earlier and walked toward Susan and David once they called up the slope to him

"The warden located us so quick because of a death notification website. Our Dad musta gone in at some point and had us listed as next of kin," Jonathan said.

"He didn't do it in any way that we could have found him while he was alive. If it hadn't been for that, we never would have found out," David said.

The officials could have no idea that neither son would have been able to identify the father they had not seen in over thirty years. That wasn't something either Jonathan or David, it turned out, would need to worry about. All human and animal remains of Plantation Six had been burned beyond recognition.

David and Susan followed the officer up the hill to the blackened logs of the little house. They stepped into what was now only a charred rectangle on the forest floor. Together they walked over to where Jonathan had been standing.

Even David recoiled.

Susan saw an outline of ashes where what the authorities described as two figures must have been. They looked smaller than adults. One of the forensic investigators explained to them that carbon frames had been made to appear shorter and thinner due to desiccation from the inferno. The silhouette of one–they said it was the woman–lay on the floor among what must have been the remains of the bed frame and a quilt. Nearby on the floor was the stain left by the man, a two-dimensional ebony mannequin toppled over sideways, knees drawn up, and around them were objects–tools–perhaps housewares whose original forms were no longer certain.

Even without actual corpses, Susan found herself covering her mouth and nose with her sleeve. Susan saw that David watched her eyes tearing, while he himself was working hard to stay composed. He came closer to her, his back toward the officer.

He was always her strong, solid husband so what he said next startled her, "Susan, stay near me here. I just don't want to lose it in front of these guys."

Between the U.S. Forest Service rangers and the Maine Hotshots, there had to be a couple dozen husky men around them, geared up and self-assured. They had a deft urgency to their movements, the shared purpose kept everyone on this charnel landscape moving and calm. She knew David didn't want to break that. She stayed within arm's reach of David near one of the corners of what had been the log cabin.

She noticed and then nudged a strange blue and brown glob with her foot. Nearby that she also saw what looked like a charred metallic handbag clasp. On closer inspection, the glob turned out to be melted glass, perhaps a container of beads that melted and then flowed together into a mass. The person they referred to as Ramona must have been a beader.

They hadn't been able to identify, let alone locate any next of kin. Susan thought it curious. She saw other people at each of the burned out foundations of the homes around Plantation Six, a small group of family members like themselves, or sometimes just a solitary figure poking through the debris. There was no one for this Ramona.

Jonathan came walking back toward them and spoke first, "I think it's a good thing we found him. Whatever he was, it's a good thing to finally know where he is."

She watched David slowly shake his head, "Don't really know anything about him."

"At least we know he's not just out there," Jonathan insisted.

Now leaning next to David, she could feel his body was taught, "Have you told Mama?"

"No, I thought I'd wait until we knew for sure," Jonathan straightened a little and raising his chin, said, "There's nothing here I'd really bring back. I thought there might be something. I didn't give a shit about him anyway."

"He remarried," David said without any inflection.

Jonathan nodded, "He went and remarried. He and Mama never even got a divorce."

"At least he thought to have you listed as next of kin," Susan added and then decided to stay silent or the two brothers would probably not talk.

"Yes," but then Jonathan assented to what her husband had said earlier, "If it weren't for the fire, we would never have found him up somewhere like this."

The three of them lapsed back into silence.

The pain hung so heavy in the air, that she felt tears beginning to roll down her own cheeks. She couldn't decide which was thicker, the sorrow for a father being dead and forever lost to her husband and brother-in-law now, or the sorrow of that father not having died sooner. Instead, he had moved on to build a new life without these sons and their mother.

Just then the ache in the air was broken by a woman in a scarf and boots calling up to them from one of the other charred homes. She climbed up the dirt road toward them, stepping over another cluster of white plastic water jugs. Neither brother seemed much prepared to return her anticipated greeting so Susan took a few steps downslope to intercept her visit.

The woman was from further east in Piscataquis County and had come up because her cousin had lived here. He was among the dead.

She seemed to know much more than they did about the fire and held the screen of her device toward Susan, saying, "They're already reporting a cause online."

David and Jonathan were at her side immediately, leaning in to read from the stranger's palm. The newness of her gadget and the escape of reading about the event in third-person revived them from the stupor they inhabited only seconds ago at the outline of where their father had lain.

Somehow they, in their two cars and a pick-up, found their way to a diner just before the highway ramp a few miles away. At a booth together, the newly close stranger seemed to bubble with attention from David and Jonathan, especially from unattached, tall and massive Jonathan.

For their part, the two brothers who normally would have been very comfortable maintaining downeast taciturnity now occupied themselves and this guest with their masculine bantering charm. It allowed Susan to enjoy her salad, half-listening, but being reminded of the investigation she had paid for almost sixteen years ago for her own missing parent.

Susan read through the article the woman had brought up on her screen. According to National Weather Service Reports, temperatures had been unseasonably warm rising up to the 70s "with withering winds out of the northwest" that swept in "a staggering drop in humidity from a Canadian front".

During the first January winter thaw in the valley running along the base of a mountain to the northwest of Plantation Six, there had been a controlled burn of the lowland blueberry fields. Every other year the owners took out a permit to clear the fields with fire in late winter to replenish the soil. Everything went well, or so it seemed, and the burn finished within its control lines. The field workers raked together the debris into piles, just in time for the next snowfall to blanket the fresh fields until spring.

Susan followed a link to a two-paragraph news report:

Winter is generally a good time to burn large brush and slash piles left over from logging and to conduct controlled blueberry field burns for improved soil nitrogen and mineral content, according to the Department of Forestry. However, as with any control burn, if not properly monitored and extinguished burned piles can rekindle and spark wildfires during thaws or in the spring.

"Winter fires are unlikely to spread as long as there is snow on the ground," said Dale Eaton, with the U.S. Forest Service and a Maine Hotshot. "However, snow, ash and dirt can insulate embers and allow fires to smolder for days, weeks or even months. On a dry, windy spring day embers can fan into flames and quickly become a fast-moving wildfire."

Susan got it: somewhere deep in one of those cooling burn piles out of sight of Plantation Six, an ember must have lingered until the snow thinned, the brooks ran again, and an angry genie escaped. The genie seared the springtime song of birds, the next ten years' crop of the local paper companies, the solid wood frame homes of area residents, and took the lives of two dozen souls in Plantation Six.

For Susan, and she imagined for most people, losses layer upon themselves like tree rings. She almost felt David absorbing the new scene up there in Plantation Six at the same time that he was driven back to the sedimentary rock of memories, too.

Something about the way the whitened woods made it look like Nature had shuffled the seasons from winter back to spring drew Susan back to a small thing sixteen years ago. Until now she had forgotten it, but seeing the topsy-turvied season up there was like absently unmuting a music file and finding that it had, in fact, never stopped playing.

Susan saw that small thing on the first leg of her trip to meet Noklek, the business meeting in Tokyo. Hiroshi was taking her to a luncheon with one of the exhibit patrons for "Hall of the Asian Peoples." As she and her host stopped outside the traditional teahouse alcove to slip out of their shoes before entering, a tiny tree in a celadon green pot caught her eye.

Though the nearly bare stems cascaded like a weeping willow there were buds that opened as tiny feathered petals. It was *yuki yanagi*, or snow willow, and the way it inferred an ambiguous time of year, at the cusp of both winter and spring, remained with her even now.

This time watching David, Susan was back looking at the *yuki yanagi*, the snow willow, and having that same sense of being at a cusp.

Then it was before she found one mother and lost the other mother.

David had lost the living father Aliza had declared dead, but David hadn't yet claimed this new, truly dead father.

When she was done scrolling, David caught her eye across the table. She knew he must be guessing exactly the connection she had drawn about their two very different stories. Later that night, in their room, she referred to this day as his "reunion" with his father. She misjudged his reaction and regretted saying it immediately.

David looked away and she could sense the fury welling up inside him. He looked like he really wanted to find the words to lay her flat. Susan knew it: David must think her search for her missing mother and their reunion of sorts left her naïveté blithely intact.

"He must think I understand nothing," Susan thought. But she remembered every accusation from previous marital spats: that she had that tendency to leap before she looked; that she would consider an option, not all options, then garner moral support from him or one of her girlfriends to act. Only later, once her inner sea was roiled by rising emotion did she begin to look around, take some depths, and realize that not everything happened in her head. Time and again she hit these same shoals, David complained even though he was there trying to beacon her away.

Carrying the lighthouse analogy further, David once told her, signals were never enough. His showing consternation, annoyance, whether through his silence or gruffness, had the opposite from his intended effect. These signals of light drew her like a moth. Far from heeding them as a warning, she received them as an invitation to pull alongside and fire pellet after pellet of questions. David had complained that she would insist on him translating every neuron flinch of his brain into a reasonable expository sentence.

~

As he put it on the eve of their wedding, "Damn, the rigamoral can make you understand the appeal of a mail order bride–at least they wouldn't insist on coherent English sentences."

A very poor choice of metaphor: a white man, an Asian bride. That night long ago a livid Asian-American bride treated her groom to many, *many* coherent English sentences about the concept of white privilege.

~

Now though, Susan imagined that after the cascade of senses and emotions today he would just want to bark at her. And snarl. Susan knew what to do. She sidled up to him from starboard.

She began stroking David's back and he sighed before he could stop himself. He turned and looked down at her. Susan knew her hair smelled fresh because as soon as they put their bags down she showered and shampooed all traces of the putrid smoke of that day. Susan paused and David leaned down to kiss her. She buried her face in his chest and he said with receding exasperation that he wished he had something to kick.

A half hour later he marveled that in this life you really could find rolled into one human the equivalent of man's best friend, an ally at arms and a concubine. Now, lying on his back with her leg resting proprietarily over him, the answer to the question Susan hadn't asked came to him. He pressed his chin into his neck to look down at her.

"You think we should be connecting over both having a missing parent. You think whatever we found up in the woods today is like what adoptees call 'a reunion.'"

"Yes. Yes, David, I'd thought you were in denial all this time about the parallel. That's why you couldn't feel very engaged about unraveling my story, because you weren't ready yet to unravel your own mystery."

"Like you did –"

"Or like others who at least decide to look even if they never find."

"Suzie, I appreciate your trying to make a sympathetic connection. It's one of the qualities that draw people to you. But your birth mother and my father just aren't comparable. Think of the term 'do the right thing.' What do you think it meant for your birth mother?"

Susan thought for a minute, and then answered, "Give your child the best possible start. If you're poor and unmarried in some places and times, that could mean giving your child to a stable couple."

"Now what does 'do the right thing' mean with a man?"

"Man up," Susan answered in her best David voice, "marry your pregnant girlfriend.

Choose a job that allows you to support a family, stick around."

But David didn't respond to her playfulness. Susan settled back into pure earnestness as David continued, "You see, your mother was following society's script by not mothering you, by 'making an adoption plan'–or abandoning you–to a future that was supposed to be better. My father, on the other hand, not only abandoned Ma and Jonathan and me, he did it despite the poverty he must have known he would be condemning us to."

Susan waited as he took a breath and continued, "Sum up: by relinquishing you, your birth mother did the right thing. By staying my father would have been doing the right thing and instead he abandoned us. Their stories, whatever his turns out to be won't be parallel."

20 BACK TO THE GARDEN
2007

The seven hundred acre blaze was all over the news. Within hours of Jonathan and David finding out where their father had been all these years, everyone else had, too. There were news vans parked outside Susan's mother-in-law's home and for three days the phone rang off the hook, as often from curious strangers or reporters as from friends and acquaintances.

Finally, Aliza simply unplugged all the land lines in the house. The rabbi called Aliza on her hand held to see if she or the boys, as he still called them, wanted to hold a funeral or sit *shiva*, the seven days of mourning at home when guests came to offer condolences.

She wasn't sure. A few hours later the rabbi's wife called, offering to bring over dinner and arrange for meals the rest of the seven nights.

Eventually Aliza decided not to claim the

body. He had left her and remarried after all and she had papers declaring him dead already, but she decided there should be something for the boys so she agreed to sit *shiva* for their father, but for two nights only, not the full seven. It is traditional for close family to recite the mourner's *Kaddish* prayer, but none of them could bring themselves to do it.

Aliza said, "I thought about doing it for me, for closure. The *Kaddish* says nothing of Death and nothing of the deceased; it only praises God on their behalf. But even then I couldn't do it."

She cancelled the *shiva* after only one night. Had she asked her two grown sons, they would have asked her not to perform any rite or ritual at all. No one asked about Ramona Graves. The government disposed of both their bodies.

~

The end of sitting *shiva* segued into a long-delayed day trip. Susan and David drove southwest from her mother-in-law's house to the Schoodic peninsula and then David took a circular route that led them on winding roads by the shoreline.

Along most stretches, natural stands of

evergreens curtained the view, but occasionally off to the side of the car they could see white then pink ledges jutting out into the ocean, seeming to slide into the waves. These avenue-wide boulders were quiet now, even though they carried the scars of glaciers from eons ago. Around some bends the ledges joined the ocean less peaceably, and even over the car engine she and her husband could hear the crashing of the waves.

At one point the road turned north and inland away from the roiling open ocean. They slowed it into a gravel parking area that was a corral of white pebbles encircled by fir trees. Even this far inland you could smell clean salt in the air.

Seventeen year old Lily tumbled out of the car as soon as the ignition was off. Today the clouds of teenage moodiness had lifted and Lily danced over to the garden entrance, pausing to point to rosettes of scalloped leaves clumping close to the ground.

"Wild ginger?"

"Yes," approved David, "they're imported but they grow well in this climate."

Lily had the same love of gardening that her father did and that no one else in the family shared. Susan realized that even his mother's neat vegetable garden was an act of economic necessity not love when she noticed that Aliza weeded hurriedly and with a tightly drawn mouth.

Susan let Lily and David run ahead as she struggled with putting shoes back on the twins. Their seven year old cheeks were imprinted with the faux leather pattern from the armrest of the back seat. Wisps of dark, silky hair crisscrossed their nap-sotted faces.

Susan stooped in order to hold each one by the hand across the wide unpaved lot. They had made it as far as the smooth flagstone path where Lily had crouched to see the shiny dark green ginger when Susan heard Lily's voice again, now up in the courtyard.

This garden had been owned by one of the families of the gilded age. In order to maintain it as a tax write-off in recent years, their foundation had to open it to the public, but had managed to limit that to less than a dozen days a year, didn't publicize its existence, and required reservations to wander its grounds.

One of the old ladies in the Corea gardening club had told Susan about it, but not in time to win a coveted appointment last summer. They'd had to wait almost a year for this day. As Susan stepped through an urn-shaped opening in the stone wall, she saw David far ahead, his back toward her as he walked animatedly up a gravel path between two rows of towering stone Mandarin courtiers.

She saw him look over his shoulder at Lily who was near some flox. Susan caught his eye and he ran back to take Noam from her and lead him onto the smoother garden trail.

She realized that she'd found something that woke an old enthusiasm in her husband. She hoped he'd get to enjoy this before being too worn down by the twins wanting to be carried. Susan and David both joked that nowadays they make children a lot heavier and faster than a decade ago when they had only Lily.

"These are supposed to be like the Ming Dynasty statues that line a walk in the Forbidden City," David pointed out to her as they walked with the monoliths flanking them on either side. He had never seen the originals in China but he knew enough to tell her this and to mention the New England botanist, William Smith Clark, who founded the University of Massachusetts at Amherst before moving on to Japan to teach at Hokkaido University.

Susan remembered hearing of him, "I think before he left Japan he made a famous speech that ended with the line, 'Boys, be ambitious,' that's still a catchphrase there."

"Then what?" Lily asked.

"So," David continued, "later generations of his students continued a transpacific cross-pollination between the eastern US and Northeast Asia. They have remarkably similar climates and soils."

David reached down and hoisted the other twin Maya onto his shoulder and said, "At the same time that the United States saw the great emigration that brought the Yosefs and the Pipers, your great-grandparents from Eastern Europe and the Mediterranean, it also welcomed immigrants who arrived after even longer voyages from Asia–azaleas, rhododendron, mountain laurel, bamboo, mounded mosses, holly, hydrangeas, and dwarf maples."

"Cute, Dad," Lily laughed.

He took a breath, "The interwar descendants of German Bavarians worked alongside the descendants of Iroquois and Scots in the park-like estates along the Hudson River."

Susan laughed as he swept his arm across as if indicating a vast landscape, "Whole communities of skilled Italian carvers finished the blocks of granite quarried from the isles of New England. Then these massive blocks were ferried down the coast to pave a golden age of landscape architecture and the new skyscrapers of New York City."

Then he dropped his voice, "So it went for a century until the last block was blasted from the tiny Oceanville quarry south of Corea and shipped to the Kennedy Memorial. The village's cranes and dynamite were laid to rest." Susan and Lily watched him drop his chin in punctuation.

"Be serious, Dad."

"I am, Lily. Seriously, the impact of that era was so complete that today it's almost bewildering to imagine that a Christian catholic president was ever controversial or that any town could have lacked a pizzeria, or that Wall Street was once a low-skylined warren of alleys before Mohawk ironworkers transformed it, or that suburban Westchester County lawns were unwreathed by evergreen ornamentals–until their ancestors arrived from Confucian gardens near Pyong Yang and the snow country of Yamagata."

Susan was feeling poetic, "So this planted garden here in Maine is an extemporization on the resulting New England and East Asian floral patois."

"Mom's trying to be a green geek, Dad," fake-grumbled Lily.

"That's fine," David said expansively, "Even as the great era of migration and assimilation both human and herbal closed, what had been prized imported ornamentals in the late 19th century quickly escaped from the rarified care of the robber baron estates. They found new footholds in the slopes of the Appalachian spine running up the eastern seaboard and sloping down to the shores of the Atlantic, as far from the Korean peninsula or the Japanese islands as one wayfaring plant could hope to roam."

David looked up beyond the symmetrical rows of the English garden with its brick footpath, and noticed trails. Then he looked back over at Susan and before he had a chance to ask, she offered, "You go up there on your own, Lily and I can watch Noam and Maya."

He was eyeing one that promised to meander up a granite-stepped slope. It led off into the woods. and eventually into a sun-dappled clearing. This was really what he had been hoping for after the unremitting scrutiny, and press vans, and well-meaning visitors of the past week. He wanted to pick a single path, quietly and alone, and follow it.

He climbed it a few moments silently and was pleased when he arrived at the end to see that it was a grotto. A bright green moss carpet covered and softened the woods floor and embraced the bases of the trees that grew up from it. The path he followed stippled into a line of gray flat stones that seemed to barely float above the lush rug as they approached a stone bench.

The bench was nothing more than a larger heavy gray slab laid across two smaller stones that had been stood on their sides. The moss accepted no footprints and the visitors before him had taken care to leave no rubbish. He imagined it had looked similar a century ago and hoped it would remain so a hundred years hence. He walked over to the bench and pressing the heels of both palms against its rounded, irregular edge, lowered himself slowly.

He closed his eyes to the green for a few minutes and breathed in the familiar smell of pine and sea. He thought he heard a whippoorwill up in one of the branches to his left. He was mindful of the distant voices down below among the blossoms in the English garden. He even thought he could pick out Susan gently admonishing Lily or one of the twins.

He couldn't help chuckling as he thought this was just the right distance from everything he loved, near enough to know where they were and that they were safe, far enough away not to be called out to for a while.

Later he would rejoin them, taking one of the twins from Susan, and together they would step through a moon gate, a perfectly circular opening in the high eastern wall of the grounds. It had enough diameter for them to pass through together and was meant to frame the sunrise and the moonrise. The scene before them was a clearing of pale ferns. In the center of it, rising from a gilded lotus, was a Buddha with a third eye nestled among stylized curls.

"The Buddha doesn't really share a sensibility with the garden on the other side of that moon gate behind us," Susan noticed. There it was a sunken shade garden dominated less by plantings than by shadows, and by the perpetual tinkle of a bubbling pool at its center.

Susan, echoing a trait of her mother, would try to explain some connection between the two disparate gardens, "Hmmm, from a world of darkness and shadows to a garden of light and enlightenment?"

"It does prepare you for that," her husband agreed.

New Englanders, from the Transcendentalists to the donors of lacquer and scroll paintings at the Boston Museum of Fine

Art, to some inspired stonemason who recreated the towering Ming monoliths here, seemed to have a penchant for mingling treasures from the Far East, both real and reimagined, with their own northern sea-swept heritage.

Her husband had come across a tract about this by Ernest Fenellosa, a Salem, Massachusetts returnee from Japan who wrote after the Civil War, "Fenellosa envisioned the Union being restored with an identity that distinguished itself from Old World nations by becoming a melding of Orient and Occident. Whether the landscape designers or patrons of private estate grounds viewed their own plots philosophically that way–or–or whether they were borrowing indiscriminately from visual motifs and palettes, they seemed to be creating a distinctly North American sense of place."

Susan and he would talk that through later, and he would remember how much he loved being able to riff on almost any topic with her.

But right now, resting his gaze on the calm green fabric of a moss forest at his feet, he thought nothing. He noticed a few brown pine needles that rested on the tips of one clump. He rocked his weight from the heels of his palms to the row of joints at the base of his fingers, enjoying the cool, gray stone. A minute passed, or maybe ten. He wouldn't have minded staying for hours but was surprised to find that he was just as content to return back down to the garden. He leaned forward and rose quietly and left that grotto for the first and last time.

~

Later that night, Susan and David lay heads resting together on their bolster at his mother's house. He turned to Susan and said, "Today was really good. I needed those moments alone up there."

"You weren't gone that long. I knew you would like it."

"Kind of amazing that I never went there before you. I'd heard of it," he paused, "I kinda made my peace."

"Your father?"

"Yeah," then David paused in thought, "Maybe it was more like I found that peace I thought I made years ago."

Susan waited. The lamp near their bed cast light on his hair, almost creating an orange penumbra. His cheekbones and jawline looked hard and chiseled, unmistakably a mature man. It was David's words only that betrayed the fatherless son.

"Today I just remembered how. I remembered what I already knew, what I figured out back in my teens for placing my dad and not letting him make me crazy."

"What was that?" Susan propped her chin slowly on her palm, "I don't think you told me this before."

"Susan, you know we had him declared dead years ago?"

She did. She nodded.

"I suspect that was for financial reasons," David said, "but it let us mourn then. I will think about him when we recite 'who shall live, and who shall die, ...who shall perish by fire.'"

"The *Un'taneh Tokef* poem from Rosh Hashanah and Yom Kippur?"

Susan knew its mournful tone well. It seemed so universal and, in fact, was one of the sources of the Dies Irae in the ancient requiem mass.

We shall cede power to this day.
For it is awe filled and terrible.
Your kingship is exalted upon it.
Your throne is founded on mercy.
Your rule is hallowed with truth.
In truth You are the judge,

The exhorter, the all-knowing, the witness,
God who inscribes and seals,
Remembering all that is forgotten.

....

"Ay-uh," David said, slipping into the Maine-ism he used when he was tired, "it goes back to the time right after Mama had him declared dead. Jonathan and I were staying with cousins for the Sabbath," and then Susan's husband recounted a story he'd never shared with her before.

21 SILVER FILIGREE
2007 (1981)

"Jonathan, our cousin Bill who was sixteen then, and I had a plan. We snuck out to the graveyard on the hill in Bangor. Do you remember it?"

"Yes, but you never mentioned going there," she felt a little like she was tucked in at summer camp and about to listen to a ghost story.

David, Jonathan and Bill had never gone there before at night, and it looked completely different in darkness. The spruce needles were slick with moonlight, as though wet. Their dark spiny canopy was mirrored by the blades of ferns that rose from the cemetery bed.

David was clapping his gloved hands together for the companionable noise as much as the warmth. When he did, the flutter of air dissipated cold will'o'the'wisps that escaped in front of him every time he breathed out. Up ahead he saw two balls of light scale the face of the Angel of Death.

The lights steadied on her lowered eyes and he ran to catch up with his older brother, Jonathan, and their cousin, Bill, who stood with their flashlights aimed at the marble statue above the mausoleum gate. Her head was shadowed under the heavy hood of her cloak, but the sculptor had taken pains to carve the faint crease in each of her eyelids, the flair of her nostrils and almost childishly plump lips between sunken cheeks.

David pulled his gaze away and, meeting Bill's eyes just above the halo from his own flashlight, asked,   "This won't take long, will it?"

There was a rumor at the high school that one of the coffins in the Greenlaw family vault was decorated with silver filigree. None of the boys had thought of what they would actually do with the silver once they had it. They were here nonetheless, each of the three carrying a crowbar to jimmy the clasp on the gates and then pry any precious metal they found inside.

The legend lent at least the perception of rational motive beyond the two entwined adolescent urges to be bad-asses and to stare down their own misgivings about being in a graveyard at midnight.

After a quarter of an hour of Bill, Jonathan and David taking turns with their crowbars, the lock and the twisted iron gates were proving stronger than any of them had anticipated. Suddenly they felt a rush of air and heard just above their heads the flap of wings. It might have been an owl. It might have been a raven, as dark and broad as its wingspan seemed. Then there was a scrambling sound in some alder bows uphill from them, it seemed like it might have alighted there. There was the telltale pair of glowing eyes.

"It might swoop back down again. I heard their talons are like a hand full of knives."

"I heard their beaks can flay a gorilla alive."

"Guess you're worried about that you old knuckle-dragger."

"Enough with 'Discovery Channel' let's get out of here."

"Me, too."

"Ladies first."

"I'll wait for you at the bottom of the road, darlings."

With that they were crashing through bushes and plantings, running down the hill, at some points elbowing each other aside and at other junctures pushing each other faster.

In one narrow shadowy grotto, David could just make out fronds whipping his legs as he tore down its slope in the moonlight. Their height and the stiff cassia-colored reeds that grew in the center of each rosette of ferns told him they were likely cinnamon ferns. As he broke through to a wide slanted clearing the ferns were now a broader species. As the boys trampled them underfoot the damp evening air picked up a scent like a freshly mowed meadow.

"Hay-scented fern," David remembered. It used to grow near the chopping block in their backyard. His father had pointed it out to him one day as he sat, only four or five at the time, cross-legged at the edge of the trees looked up raptly as his father split that winter's logs.

"Hey, do you recognize these?" David called down ahead but his older brother and cousin were in no mind to pause for botany. He re-doubled his pace and caught up with them but with each step he grew more certain of something he couldn't share with them. Their boot heels hit pavement and they followed the winding cemetery road out under the stone arch onto York Street. A few places were still lit and they went in the soda shop to end the evening with glasses of frappes.

What he didn't share with them was that sense, as they say in ghost stories, of a presence. Not there among the tombstones, but somewhere, of his father being alive.

~

In that darkness off York Street only a few years after his father's disappearance, David made the decision then that he recognized again after the wildfire. His father would be dead to him all the while still alive, and no less alive now that he was dead.

To the extent that David had ever had any father, he would mourn that relationship. To not do that would make him feel not human, no matter how angry he was. The timing would always ring false to pick a date of death, a *yahrtseit*, and then say the *Kaddish* prayer daily to observe the year of mourning. It was arbitrary. Last year or next year would have rung just as true.

Instead the communal, that is to say for him impersonal, annual New Year prayer, *Un'taneh Tokef*, was truer to mourning his father.

Susan mused, "It's odd, I've seen *Un'taneh Tokef* translated two ways: as 'ascribing holiness' and as 'ceding power'."

He struggled to put something else into words for Susan, "Ever since that night in the clearing of ferns, I knew I would never say the *Kaddish* for him. When Ma had him declared dead, I was angry with him for disappearing. Now it's years later, and whether my father is living or dead, he will always exist.

"Maybe if he weren't absent the distinction would have mattered more," Susan said.

"The *Un'taneh Tokef* forces everyone to accept a, a certain powerlessness in choosing 'who shall live, and who shall die.' My father leaving certainly made me feel powerless as a kid. And also, the prayer's cyclical the way the memories of him come back to me over the years."

Susan thought she understood, but asked, "Can you explain a little more, honey?"

"It's untethered to any one death. It chants about many losses. And when I say it's cyclical, I mean the prayer is really a liturgical poem tied to an annual event, in this case Rosh Hashanah. All my memories and mourning, if you could call it that, were tied to all the cycles other fathers and sons shared."

"That you missed out on, right?"

"My uncles and my mom stepped in when

they could, but, yeah, it was during father-son things that I felt it: boy scout camping trips, reciting *Kiddush* together over wine on the eve of my bar mitzvah, learning to tie a tie, or to shave, or to drive, my graduations, our wedding, my becoming a father when we had Lily. I didn't need a *yahrtseit* to remember that prick."

"David!"

"Sorry, I know."

"It's okay. That's a longer list than I have, but I kind of have that for, well, not my birth mom–at least not consciously–but for my adoptive mom. I've told you that–how my menstruation and pregnancy and then breastfeeding made her weird."

"Skipping mourning makes you weird. I didn't think of this before, but mourning can take what looks like odd forms if you don't realize you're seeing it," David said thoughtfully, then added, "I'm talking about your mom, not me by the way."

"Okay, man of steel," Susan hugged him, "Hmmm. You did really show good instincts by hooking onto the *Un'taneh Tokef* when you didn't have a death anniversary to mourn with the *Kaddish*."

"It wasn't just about solace," then he chuckled, "It's also got to be the goriest prayer anyone could have imagined, maybe it was my teenage wishful thinking."

Without the prayer book Susan only remembered the first few lines, but her husband surprised her and intoned them all in his quiet, sonorous voice while lying next to her:

> *How many shall pass away and how many*
>   *shall be born,*
>
> *Who shall live and who shall die,*
>
> *Who shall reach old age and who shall die*
>   *too young,*
>
> *Who shall perish by water and who by fire,*
>
> *Who by sword and who by beast,*
>
> *Who by famine and who by thirst,*
>
> *Who by earthquake and who by plague,*
>
> *Who by strangling and who by stoning,*
>
> *Who shall have a home and who shall*
>   *wander,*
>
> *Who shall find rest and who shall be*
>   *pursued,*
>
> *Who shall be at peace and who shall be*
>   *tormented,*
>
> *Who shall be exalted and who shall be*
>   *brought low,*

Who shall become rich and who shall be poor.

Susan was listening, "David, I never knew that."

"All these years, I've been on to you: hinting that I might try searching for my father. But I didn't need to. How about yours, Suze? Meaning your birth father."

"I don't think Noklek even knows his nationality. He was just a *farang*, a white person, to her," Susan thought for a moment more, "I can live with one or two unsolved mysteries."

"Like Ramona Graves."

"Like Ramona Graves."

Susan heard David inhale with a new thought, "It let me think about him without drawing attention to myself. I never liked how at the synagogue my family went to they would call for only the mourners to rise for the *Kaddish*–it was like they were commanding you to fish or cut bait."

"'You're either a mourner or you're not, no wiggle room if it's a missing person.' I see what you're saying."

"A-yuh, I'd rather just blend in with the rest of the congregation like for *Un'taneh Tokef*."

"And you've brought personal meaning to that communal poem."

"Just like how your mother's Passover *Haggadah* gave more meaning to Psalm 113 in Hallel for you."

Susan remembered her mother's note that quoted its verses. The adoptee as the prince of His people, the barren woman as the joyful mother of children, "So all that traveling, whether it was to Piscataquis County or Thailand, just made us better pilgrims in the congregation?"

"Exactly, and the meaning you personally assign to a psalm or a Passover song will be a little twisted." He waited for Susan to hit him.

Once she did, he continued, "But it will have meaning so you can stand there with others who have a really different life story and still be able to pray the same words from the heart."

Susan looked at David, "Okay, are you including your interpretation of the *Un'taneh Tokef* prayer as twisted, too?"

"Sure," conceded David, "But it works for me. Or it helps us elude the alternative, which, Suze, that would be to turn into some Jack Kerouac pair wandering the country in search of Old Dean Moriarty and all we'd find is confirmation that our fathers weren't who we were looking for after all."

"That's from 'On the Road.' How did that end?"

"They never do find him. They just kind of drift and get hip to the cosmic 'reality of being' along the way."

She laughed. He put his arm loosely across the front of her shoulders and she rolled her head in a slow arc, shaking and smothering what had become giggles in his hairy, warm forearms.

"What is the cosmic reality of being?"

"Kokomo in a china cup. The horizontal twist. A thrill on blueberry hill. That, or that you should tithe on time."

22 FINAL ARRANGEMENTS
2006

Gideon Ames lay sunken in a deathbed of pillows there in New York. He knew it was *his* deathbed only until he died, was removed and the hospital sheets changed. His body would be sent back to Maine. They promised him that and he'd made most of the arrangements himself. Just in case, they would try a last hopeful, experimental procedure against his terminal cancer.

The final thing he did before checking into the hospital was log onto his laptop. He emailed PDFs of his notarized last will and testament. Then on a whim he decided to set someone else's effects in order, too.

Gideon looked up Abel Piper online and saw something startling. Abel had already been declared dead in 1981, the same year and if Gideon wasn't mistaken the same month that he had discovered Abel's ruse and confronted him.

Gideon hoped any death certificate had at least freed up some inheritance or benefits payments for Abel's wife and children. For good measure, Gideon decided to look up that invented name "Joseph Piper". Nothing.

Then Gideon went to a survivor notification site that promised to contact next of kin in the case of death or incapacitating emergency. Gideon was stunned at how easy it was to create an account for fictional Joseph Piper. He listed Aliza, Jonathan and David Piper as the next of kin to be notified should authorities ever have the necessity.

23 CONTROL BURN
2007

The hairs standing up on his arms and the back of his neck were what woke him. It was only once Joseph had struggled to consciousness and opened his eyes that he registered the horrifying combination of darkness and unbearable heat. Outside the cabin windows–windows that seemed to warp and run down to their frames–he saw a sore orange-red wall beating outside the eastern window. And the northern window. And the western window. And the southern window. Their little cabin appeared to be entirely sheathed in flames and he dropped to the floor instinctively.

He crawled over to the door and placed his palm flat against its planks. It was like touching the coils of an electric heater, and hot movement in the dark nearby, coming from somewhere near its frame, might have been smoke.

Then he listened. His senses of touch and sight found no outlet for escape. He strained to hear the voices of firefighters, or neighbors from down the hill with a hose, or trucks pulling up nearby just the other side of the flames. He heard nothing but a fierce roar that came from nowhere and everywhere.

He heard no stirring from the direction of the bed where Ramona still lay. She had taken cold medicine before lying down and if she hadn't woken up by now, she never would. He thought briefly of somehow grabbing her and crawling through what were surely flames on the other side of the door. Sometimes headfires like this might only be ten feet thick and there was chance of survival. Then again, they could be half a mile deep.

Briefly Joseph remembered his fantasy of somehow running into a burning building to save his boys, the vision that always reassured him that at heart he was still a good man. He would have risen to the occasion if somehow his boys had really needed him.

Joseph realized now that faced with the prospect of offering his own skin and flesh to this thundering heat, he would not have run into flames. He would have let his boys burn. There was no redemption for what he had done: he had abandoned them in better times, as he would have now, if it would have allowed him to escape this choking heat.

He also knew he could not save Ramona. From where he lay on the floor, he reached his hand for the shovel left propped against the wall earlier that afternoon. Its metal and wood handle was warm but not too hot. To avoid the searing smoke, he kept the shovel in front of him as he crawled on his belly and elbows over to the bed. He felt with one hand to make sure it was the side of the bed.

He shook Ramona gently but couldn't even feel the familiar rise and fall of her ribs in sleep. Raised high up on their bed, she might have already suffocated from the toxic burn of cinder particles in the air. He couldn't be sure so he rose to his knees with the shovel balanced against one shoulder.

He could barely breathe and moved quickly, raising the shovel over his head with both hands and then bringing it down on the slumbering form in the bed. The second time he heard the certain, crisp sound of her skull cracking. He slammed the shovel down one more time to be sure, this time it sounded like liquid. This was the least he could do: make sure she would not wake only to die from the fire. He himself would not be so lucky. He let go of the shovel and collapsed back to the floor trying in agony to gasp.

24 FROM DISTANT KINGDOMS
1992

"Thrice now," the only thing she was enjoying about this was getting to use an archaic word, "thrice now I've sent packages to Noklek that never arrive. And like the last two times, when I send follow-up notes, Noklek apologizes through Kun Sompan that mail carriers are poorly paid, and so are shipping room clerks. This is so frustrating."

"Does that mean we're just supposed to accept that an entire country can't reliably get postal mail?" demanded David, "And that postage was expensive, too!"

"We've sent five other packages that did get through, David. Noklek writes '*mai ben rai*' which Kun Sompan explains as 'que sera, sera."

David wiseguyed with a shrug, "New Jersey-ese would be 'whadya gonna do.'"

Susan continued, "Here's what she writes, 'It could have happened at Suvarnabhumi BKK when the international air cargo plane landed. It could have happened during sorting or at a stop along the trip by truck across those clotted canals and land highways. If not then, it could have gone missing anywhere between leaving on a domestic flight from Don Muang DMK, to its landing outside Chiang Rai, to its sorting again in the central post office at the open air loading dock, or during the last leg of its journey– possibly by bicycle.'"

David shook his head, "I'm beginning to understand your birth mom. She's being thorough in listing all these wonderful opportunities to show compassion."

"Hah ha. She wants us to earn merit and get good karma," Susan smiled up at him and continued, "'The packages could have become exotic surprises brought home one day to a family, or at least shared with neighbors.'"

One time Susan switched from sending packages of goods to mailing more pictures of Lily, of their home and photocopies from her childhood album. She did this only once actually because despite the profuse thanks, the extra-thin aeropost paper that Noklek used might as well have been tear-stained for the returning tone of melancholy, "My Suwan, you have sent me what nevertheless remains lost, that little girl raised far, far from Thailand. I have missed every Songkran (April New Year) and every Lantern Festival with you. You looked happy and well-fed, a little girl who is now gone."

In late summer that year, Noklek's stepdaughter Aimei turned fourteen. Noklek wrote to Susan that this had been her age when she left home, and the age Suwan would have been when Noklek married Jugo, Aimei's father. Noklek sent a paper doll for Lily's second birthday–something Lily managed to tear before the weekend was out.

These were the kinds of exchanges where everyone tried to become a family without any allusions to what had created them, torn them apart, and then brought them back together.

Another year brought the unveiling of the tombstone for Susan's mother and the first *yahrtseit*, the anniversary of her death. These two years of parenting, only one with her own mother nearby then the next with her gone and this birth mother far away, cast new light on parenthood.

The passage of time only confirmed that Masha was Susan's mother. Skinned knees and hugs and bathtime and storytime and cutting food into toddler bites all made this so.

Nothing could deny blood ties, Susan felt, but nothing, nothing made a parent except for parenting. Noklek would never be her mother. That was lost, but Noklek would always be in Suwan's heart. And just as surely, Noklek had turned herself into Aimei and Ailan's true mother.

~

One day, Kun Sompan included a note of his own with notes from both Noklek and Tuptim. Each seemed to be filling in gaps from the others' narratives. Susan and David had seen very short news items on TV and then read a one-column news article below the fold.

Taken together they explained that the generals of the coup last year, the one that had almost delayed Susan's visit, were now refusing to give up their taste of power.

"'The promise of elections had allayed everyone's fears last February. They were to be held after the April hot season,'" David read, "'but instead General Suchinda, one of the klatch now leading the country, is reneging on them.'"

"'Klatch'? Did they really write that?"

"Ay-uh."

Susan slid another clipping closer, "'University students and shopkeepers have been converging on Bangkok for three days now,'" Susan looked up, "What's today's date?"

"May 20th," and then David picked up the sheet.

"'Onlookers report that army trucks came at night and arrested twenty five hundred,'" David looked up and said, "I'm glad you're back home."

Susan kept reading, "'Despite brutal attempts at a crackdown, the crowds have grown by international estimates to two hundred thousand and a leadership structure has emerged'."

"At any rate, I think I realized something about us. Thanks to your trip to Thailand, we're becoming news junkies."

Susan demurred, "No, I hate political news. This is about my birth mother. Although, I wonder how much of this actually touches people outside Bangkok or Chiang Rai."

David read through the rest, "'The royal family became involved and the much respected eldest daughter of the king, Princess Sirindhorn, taped a plea for peace that was rebroadcast throughout the final day.'"

Susan remembered excitedly, "All the

shops we went to had pictures of the royal family hung high on the wall. You saw their portraits at the airport and even in Ban Naan, the little town near my birth mom."

David continued, "'Sometime in late afternoon, they aired a similar speech by the Crown Prince, and finally the King himself ordered the general and the civil protest's two civilian leaders to a state-owned television studio. There His Majesty ordered them over the airwaves to use the parliamentary process.' Susan, I thought you told me he was a figurehead. But look how smartly he played this. He publicly scolds both the leaders of street protests and martial law. He refuses to choose a winner and basically forces an election by invoking the legislature."

Susan got it, "The earlier news articles don't mention the civilian government. It's the King who forces them to use the democratic process."

Susan thought for a minute, "I bet the members of Parliament were the most surprised."

David chuckled, "From this distance it's almost like some kind of dreamscape, with thrones, and kings and coups, and even two hundred thousand marchers. And–," he added with a sigh, "because we're an ocean and a continent away they don't make a single sound."

Susan agreed, "It couldn't be further from home."

~

The following spring Susan received a breathless letter from Tuptim herself. She would be leaving the village with an exciting job offer to go where one week's wages were better than three weeks at the local mill. Oil had been discovered the year before in the United Arab Emirates. The oil rush was on.

Dubai was a boom town. News had spread west across South Asia as far as Thailand, Malaysia, and Indonesia that Arabs were clamoring for butlers, cooks, valets, and maids. Large compounds and villas were going up with demand for a servant on every floor.

These contacts were on the up-and-up, Tuptim assured Susan. They would even accept mature, married women. This trader didn't talk about young girls or use the typical lures of the other life, promises of beauty pageant awards or singing contracts. This would be honest work.

That led to why Tuptim was writing Susan herself: for the time being Suwan might need to wait while Noklek worked things out with her husband, Jugo, before she wrote again.

But, Tuptim assured her, soon she would be able to write to Noklek directly via Kun Sompan. Just in case, and here Tuptim addressed her with Thai familiarity as "daughter," she would send her the new address in the U.A.E. once she was settled.

The next note came a few days later from Noklek, asking her to wait before writing again.

Finally, a month later came a cheerful note from Noklek in which she wrote now about Aimei and Ailan, as well as new chickens Jugo had bought. She wrote that now that both girls had reached puberty, their hair had become thick and glossy and she loved braiding it in the morning before sending them off to school. The farm was doing well enough that they could set aside money for school fees to let both girls graduate.

Instead of drawing Susan in, the letter had the effect of water too shallow or air too thin to stay with for long. How could she respond or follow her mother's narrative which omitted the only ink-worthy change at home: the new knowledge of her own existence in America. She held her own private boycott of this whole situation by not responding to Noklek's letter and putting it aside for a week.

But of course she did write back, and this time asked only one question. She decided Noklek would tell her about the stepsisters' reactions, and her husband's reaction in a way that she would choose. Asking about it seemed heavy-handed and, then, too, there was that adage to never ask a question unless you were ready for any answer.

There were some answers that might be disappointing to read. At this distance Susan preferred to believe that her birth mother's choices were not now being judged. Whether Noklek's family welcomed Susan or shunned her, the rectangle of envelope sheathing rectangles of two or three sheets folded into three neat panes did not betray what was happening in their tiny home.

As Susan re-read and then refolded the letter, sitting in her own house, she calmly felt the distance that might always be there. She was glad she had found Noklek, that she knew the truth of her relinquishment. She sat with the feeling, curious, almost trying to curate it, but failing.

Instead she asked that more urgent question, about Tuptim. The promised note from the UAE had not arrived and, ominously, neither did Noklek's letter mention Tuptim.

~

Noklek's husband Jugo remained silent as he thought through what she had just said this evening.

He imagined standing before a scale, one palm full of cooked sticky rice, one palm holding many more grains of unplanted rice seed. In decisions, the better choice would always be the hand holding more grains even if realizing their harvest would take more effort.

Immediately Jugo knew that in such a landscape the correct choice would be to ask the rich American daughter and her husband for the money for a ride-on rice sower.

Then he did the abacus work of his home: asking for the money would require thinking more about his wife's previous life in prostitution. When he married her, he subtracted from that three facts. His daughters needed a mother. He was only a coolie, a poor ethnic Chinese in a northern plain of pure ethnic Thais like his late wife. Noklek herself was a Thai and was charming in a cheerful, slightly bashful way. This, despite having lived that life. Hadn't other girls, just like her, left the countryside eventually to return and marry?

He counted a few more beads on this abacus: a new tractor would also arouse the curiosity of his own daughters. Would they somehow learn that giving away a child could bring reward? He wiped his eyes bitterly on his sleeve. Even if they brought more wealth, these grains of rice were not ones it would be wise to plant in a field near home.

Sometimes it's better to accept what is, to swallow the rice that is already white and cooked.

The letters would come from America to the house. Maybe no one would ask him about them. The letters would be his wife's business as long as she agreed to keep them from his daughters.

On their wedding night he had admitted to his wife, "I know from the matchmaker that you're not a virgin," and now, just as then, he would let her know that, "I do not need to know any more."

Jugo brushed his hands together, as though wiping away actual grains of rice, both the white and the darker ones, from his palms. He looked at his wife, not unkindly, and said, "They are your business."

25 OLD FRIENDS
1988 ~ 1990 ~ 1999

Farah and Susan had become friends while living on the same floor of their dorm freshman year. Then Susan and David's first apartment was only a short drive from where Farah was living with her immigrant parents after graduation. It wasn't an obvious friendship at first.

Farah started wearing a *hajib* in college and belonged to a Quran study group until the semester she had to focus on organic chemistry as part of her pre-med course load. Farah's parents were delighted that she had a friend like Susan who was already married by her early twenties and had a child.

The two young women were actually closer now than they had been when they went to college parties together. Both women reached out to the other as a kindred spirit from the wider oxygen-filled world to whom they could confide the details of what they called their second life.

It started sophomore year when they had a really good conversation. Farah got the deep obligation Susan felt to her parents because they had gone to the extra effort of adopting her. That, in a way, paralleled the sacrifice that Farah's parents had made when they immigrated to a non-Muslim land.

Their family wasn't like every other one on the block. Adoption, emigration–both were joyous choices that each set of parents embraced, but to the extent that their fathers, Al and Shamir, were worriers, any differences that followed were fraught.

Farah told Susan during an end of semester barbecue about how her father agonized over every invitation, torn between *halal*, the Islamic dietary laws, and his own inclination to accept any neighborly or collegial gesture for what it was.

Susan got it. While her own parents didn't really keep *kosher* at home, the echoes were still there. Her family still avoided mixing meat and dairy at the same meal and didn't eat pork or shellfish. Whether this was because of the biblical religious laws, or family custom, her father Al put himself through the same torture, but double, worrying about what they might serve when he was a guest and then worrying that he wasn't kosher enough for his more observant extended family.

Farah laughed with recognition as they sat down on the dean's lawn with some of their friends. Their paper plates were piled with salad and eggplant parmesan, while the rest of their circle had just come back from the line with roast pig.

~

1990

While Susan waited for word on her search from Fred, Farah was in a predicament of her own, only different from Susan's on its surface.

Farah never tried pork, but she stopped wearing the *hajib* in med school. Partly she didn't like the implication that she was somehow immodest and responsible for male bad behavior unless she wore it. She also didn't like wearing religion on her sleeve every minute of every day, although even during her residency she continued to pray several times daily. That eventually fell away, too.

Her mother, Srifa, who prayed five times a day except during her period when it was forbidden, began to worry that Farah was losing her faith.

"Mother, I think it's becoming deeper. I still recite the *dhikr* remembrance prayer and the personal *du'a'* supplications because they're the most intimate. They're more spiritual than Friday prayers because I'm not relegated to a backroom at the mosque. I can say these anywhere, directly, without an imam."

Farah noticed that her mother's chin was only drooping lower and her face had grown so unreadable she might as well have been wearing a *naqib* over it. It always was worse when her mother put on this game face. Farah would have preferred a scolding, and even paused. Nothing, so she continued earnestly, "I can say these at any time of the month and no one can invoke *tahara*, ritual purity laws, to stop me. I think they allow me to be more spiritual."

To Srifa, her daughter's use of the concept "spiritual" was a code word for lacking community. That night she conferred with her husband, a formality, before signing her twenty four year old daughter up for Muslim dating services and the regional Eligibility Ball which was strictly chaperoned to prevent mixed dancing.

The sister-in-law of the wife of her family's imam was the primary instigator of that first awkward mixer they had Farah attend. It was a group event held in the mosque social hall where too many parents hovered along the walls or the buffets while their twenty- and thirty-something American offspring mingled self-consciously.

Farah explained, "We're supposed to find our *habib roohi*, like in English 'soulmate'. Literally it means 'lover of my soul', but it sounds sweeter in Arabic."

"My family calls it *beshert*, which is either Yiddish or Hebrew. It means your 'promised one' that God meant for you to meet."

Farah sighed, "I like that."

The outlines of each friend's search story notched perfectly with the other's. Where Susan was looking for the missing imagined soul-mate that is a birth mother, Farah's parents were seeking for her the promised soul-mate of an arranged marriage. As their respective searches progressed, they traded stories. Though Susan never introduced them, years later she shared Faith's story with Farah, too, and some of the more successful stories she had heard in the search and reunion group.

Farah's story, it would turn out, played out over the next decade.

~

1999

Shortly after Sukkoth that year, she got a call from Farah. Susan was describing some of her family's amalgamated motifs. When she described how Cousin Tracy always added Christmas lights to the sukkah decorations–it had become a family tradition in the intervening decade, Farah jumped in.

"Oh, no–you, too? We Muslims have started using Christmas lights along with the traditional lanterns for Eid ul-Fitr.

"The end of Ramadan?"

"Right, the celebration that closes Ramadan."

"Welcome to America."

"Amen," they both laughed.

But then Farah's voice weakened and she turned serious, "Do you remember Mohammed?"

"Of course. Until a minute ago I thought this call might be to tell me you were engaged."

"My parents would love that. He'd do it, too, but I just can't marry him."

"Oh. I guess it's better to find that out before things went too far. You were afraid he had the potential to become a little strict."

"Yeah, remember how I thought by refusing to meet immigrants I'd avoid all their issues and rants. At first he seemed really easygoing, not bringing up the M word right away. I really liked that we were both spiritual but not dogmatic. But things got really messed up."

"Farah, I love you. I'm listening."

"In the Muslim community there's this idea that if you're going to be alone with a man, your reputation is so compromised that you....you might as well be engaged."

"I know you've been meeting for lunch, and you've been going out with groups of Muslim friends. Have you been alone?"

"Yes."

"People shouldn't read too much into that. Don't let them rush you."

"How do I explain this to you? It's kind of like, if everyone is going to assume anyway.... And therefore to put it pessimistically, your reputation is shot, it's not like a society where dating is normal. In this country, if you go on a picnic with a guy, or hiking or the movies, that's all it is. But where dating isn't normal, you feel like if you've already broken a taboo by just being alone with the guy, you could go a lot further."

"So –?"

"One thing led to another."

"How are you two doing?"

"Right after, I don't know. I didn't think, I just felt that this decided it for me, this must be my *habib roohi*. We managed to see each other every day after that. I thought I was falling in love.

Farah hesitated before continuing, "No– actually I told myself I was in love before we were alone together. Until then we talked about his work and my classes. Of course we were introduced with the intent of marriage, but it was when we began talking about married life I realized I couldn't be with him. I couldn't see breaking up because he was the one who I had given my virginity to, but I also couldn't see being with him years from now."

Susan waited.

"He wasn't realistic about young doctor's hours and somehow wanted me to do all the traditional things at home," then Farah hesitated again, "I do respect his knowledge of Quran and his Arabic is beautiful.

"Okay–?"

"The more we talked, the more I realized he had no close non-Muslim friends and he really had that lost immigrant mindset: 'us' is good, 'them' is bad, and acknowledging that inside you're a mix of both is somehow weak or confused. It turned out he was brittle, not solid."

"I remember you liked that about him. You called him 'centered'."

"My Islam makes me love Creation and the Creator, and see us all, all of us hyphenated Muslims, like other hyphenated Americans, as His Creatures."

"I know you. You would have told him that. What did he say?"

"He didn't even argue with me. He just slipped into tolerant condescension. My view didn't matter, or he thought it was, I don't know, naïve. He just brushed it away."

"Maybe he's smitten. Any chance he'll accept to your way of thinking?"

"His brand of spirituality takes on all the centuries of xenophobic, misogynist patina. There is so much beauty in Dar al-Islam, literally beauty in mosaic tile work and textiles and architecture. There is calligraphy that makes you shiver with how much it conveys.

"There is so much that, Susan, it can make you ache with its kindness and wanting to serve humanity, I actually believe that. It makes me a better doctor.

"Then there's this, all its opposite: cowardice and hatefulness when offered new ideas, draping and hiding girls and women obscenely with *chador*, or more subtly with *hajib*. Some guy gets turned on if he sees my hair so it makes me immodest? I can study and be chaste, but if he sees my calves suddenly I'm immodest? None of this is beautiful and now Mohammed is letting all that show."

"It sounds like you'd be happier if you broke up with him."

"It gets worse."

"I'm here."

"Susan, I'm pregnant."

The next week Susan did something she thought she'd never do as an adoptee: be involved in an abortion. They found themselves in a waiting room with about a dozen other women and girls one bleak day that they took off from work. Farah hadn't told Mohammed and had been avoiding him for days. She would end the relationship as soon as she recovered.

A nurse came out and offered her valium

in a small paper cup. Farah shook her head silently and held Susan's arm. When they led Farah and a half dozen other women through a pair of swinging doors, Susan couldn't stop herself from weeping.

About a half hour later they called for anyone accompanying, then looked down at their clipboards to find and read the patient's name out loud. They led Susan to a recovery room where she found her friend sitting in a semi-reclined chair, still wearing the surgery gown and looking pale, almost gray. A cotton ball was bandaged to the crook of each of her arms.

Farah refused to lie to her mother or father so she simply did not talk to them. She looked so miserable that her parents assumed Mohammed had broken up with her. They were shocked when they heard at the mosque that he was the jilted partner. To his credit, he didn't expose their liaison to anyone in the community. She was free to find a better match.

~

A few months later David and Susan found out she was expecting. She put off telling Farah until her fourth month when she couldn't hide it anymore. Farah wished her well, but she had medical boards coming up and seemed to get busy–and remote–quickly.

The pre-natal test results told them they would be expecting another healthy daughter. And a son. Twins!

When Noam and Maya were born, Farah came alone to the baby-naming and *bris*, the circumcision ceremony. She gave a check, kissed Susan, but left early. As long friendships are wont to do, this one had experienced a season of warmth and was entering a new one that, while still holding loyalty and affection, also carried coolness and distance. Susan remembered seeing Farah at the *bris*, but didn't notice when she left.

~

A month and a half before that, Susan reconnected with Faith. It took a week of phone tag. It was just before the only support group meeting she would be able to attend before her twins were born. David agreed to put Lily to bed while Susan propped her swollen ankles up on the sofa and pressed Faith's number.

She knew Faith had found her birth mother almost a decade earlier. Faith left her three children with her husband and took a long weekend to visit her in the UK. "It's been years, and she's been travelling extensively– she makes sure to send me postcards from all over Europe. You remember she lives in London, right?"

Susan did.

"Well, she planned and now she's cancelled several visits, and at this point I don't want to leave the kids again to see her. I decided to reach out to other birth relatives."

"Like who?" it hadn't occurred to Susan to ask Noklek much about her brothers and sisters–Suwan's own aunts and uncles after all– nor had Noklek offered. Susan would ask about them in her next letter, "Hope that's going better."

"Yes, it is. I spoke to my biological father. We haven't met yet."

"Really? Faith!"

"I told you I had something to tell you – "Faith continued mischievously.

"Congratulations!"

"–his name is William Yard–I'll save the how-to of tracking him down for the meeting with everyone next week. I also spoke with an aunt by phone, on my birth mother's side."

"What did you get?"

Faith looked thoughtful, "Each one gave me a story about myself that I will always carry within me, Susan, like –"

"Precious gems," Susan offered.

"Yes! Precious gems! Bill told me something interesting. Even though I was born before Roe v. Wade, they visited two abortionists when my birth mother was four months pregnant. One was on Riverside Drive in New York City and the other was in Fort Lee, New Jersey."

Susan stopped herself from blurting out anything about accompanying Farah to the clinic. Instead she said to Faith, "So they weren't too hard to find even before abortion was legal?"

"Nope. They decided against an abortion even though they are both pro-choice. When I asked my first mother for an explanation she says mysteriously", Faith mimicked a dreamy voice, "'Oh, I don't like to second-guess myself.'"

"I didn't even think to ask my birth mom whether she was offered one or not. She never mentioned it." Susan decided to change the subject for now, "What is the other story?"

"Well, I found and wrote to my biological aunt. She told me another story, one about their mother, my maternal grandmother. It happened in the late 1980s. At the time I was arranging the filming of a scene at Bloomingdale's Department Store on Lexington Avenue for a Christmas special.

"My first grandmother got on the Lexington Avenue bus one day about that time. She saw a young woman in her twenties who reminded her of her daughter and as she watched this stranger she felt more and more certain that the woman was the granddaughter that her unwed daughter had relinquished years before. When my first grandmother got off the bus, instead of going home, she went to visit her daughter, my aunt, and for the first time told her about my birth mother's untimely pregnancy and the missing granddaughter."

"Do you think it really was you she saw on that bus?"

"It's entirely possible. I rode it regularly during that time period–and only during that time period."

"Do you remember seeing her?" Susan had heard of adoptees thinking they saw a stranger in a crowd who looked like they might be kin. She'd never had that happen as an international adoptee. Instead, "I was always fascinated when we ran into Eurasians when I was little. I guess I wondered if they were related."

"Sometimes I almost think I do. I'll never know for sure. That grandmother died soon after," Faith sighed, "If only the adoption agency had let me know immediately when my first mother tried to contact me in back in the 1980s I could have met her. I could have told her that I was okay and that my adoptive parents were good to me. I like the thought that she never forgot me."

26 JUST US
1999

Two of the facilitators of Susan's old monthly group had contacted her. Faith had told her to expect this call. They wanted to try something new just for adult adoptees, breaking away from the larger group. They would have a three-part idyll where they could, as Lisa the adoptee facilitator promised over the phone, "let our hair down, think out loud sloppily and imprudently because we won't have the other two sides in the adoption triad."

Christine, the adoptive mom, put it as, "Susan, would you be willing to be one of a handful of activists and genealogists to test out this format?"

"Yes," Susan answered. After hanging up the phone she did wonder if she wanted to spend time–really–in a topic that she'd put on the back burner these past few years.

Tonight would be the first of three adoptee-only sessions. Lisa from the regular monthly group was wearing a stick-on name label and as Susan accepted the marker to fill out one for herself she looked around the room. About half a dozen adoptees sat in a rough circle made from two sofas and several arm chairs.

The monthly meeting facilitator announced, "I think that's everyone. I'm Lisa."

"Betty."

"Sandy."

"Jo-ohn."

"Keyshia."

"Naomi."

"Joyce."

"Faith."

"And Susan."

Darker than the usual meeting place, this was in a hall two counties further away but near the guest facilitator. There was a bow window that stretched the length of what she decided must be an Edwardian sitting room. Susan saw no refreshments–next week she'd bake a fruit loaf. She was happy she had brought a needlepoint frame that held the family tree piece her mother had begun years earlier. It needed finishing and there was enough space next to where her mother had stitched Lily's name to stitch in the twin leaves before the babies came.

The session leader had thick white hair and introduced himself simply with "I'm Alan Cooper." Actually he was an author Susan liked, she almost felt like she knew him. He asked each of them to introduce themselves and briefly describe where they were in their search. She already knew about half the people in the room from the triad group.

Then he spoke again, "Like many adoptees of my generation, I waited until after my adoptive parents passed away before beginning my search. My birth mother had been deaf and institutionalized, and assumed to be retarded."

Susan remembered his memoir, one of the best she had read by an adoptee.

"I was conceived when a grounds worker raped her."

Susan heard someone suck in their breath.

"Yet she recognized me when I found her years later."

Susan said aloud, "I read it," and then more slowly, "I thought of it as a love story."

Alan's smile was genuine. Susan really was a fan of how he infused compassion and humor into his descriptions of every scene.

He continued, "I believe we encounter many soulmates in our lives."

Susan was stunned. This is how she'd described it to Farah.

"My birth mother was one of mine, so actually were my adoptive parents. So essentially I embarked on a quest to find her."

Susan noticed that you could have heard a pin drop.

He continued, "Like any good hero in literature, you all are on a quest, too. If you're sitting here, you're on a quest whether you realize it or not. There are people who will help, or hinder. There are curses. There are blessings. You're not promised a relationship or even a living family at the end of your search. You're promised truth. That's the broader meaning of 'reunion' in the context of an adoptee's quest."

He leaned back now in the armchair and intertwined his fingers, "You've shared your stories and I think you may find, if you haven't already, that 'search' is broader in meaning than the literal definition. It's freedom to finally ask questions. It's freedom to act on the human need we have to know our roots. For some the freedom is just realizing we even have the curiosity, to lift off a cloak of denial.

"Mind you, I don't think everyone needs

to be out there searching now. I think for child adoptees denial is a healthy way of dealing with curiosity for a whole host of reasons."

Susan thought of David's choice not to search for his father. It had taken her so long to understand.

She listened to Alan's story, "I was in denial until my adoptive parents died, and I felt the cost of hurting them was too great. But what a relief, what freedom–when I finally could ask the questions, when I could think the forbidden thoughts."

Susan noticed they all were waiting on his next words. The chord Alan had struck in Susan and the rest of the circle was so pitch perfect that the next few words didn't ring fantastical with any of them, "But I want you to know that I'm honored to be part of your quest, even if only for these three evening. I honor that, I hope to support you on your way. I wish us all God-speed."

The group facilitator, Lisa, added, "I got the sense that many of us adoptees felt constrained from searching–by embarking on what you're calling a quest–by guilt we felt toward our adoptive parents, however much we wanted to search. Then we get hit with a different guilt in the larger triad group by sitting in a room with others who rightly or wrongly express self-pity."

"Right, it would offend or hurt them. It would definitely challenge their version of reality," said Faith

Naomi added, "We'd be accused of being judgmental. Half the time their view erases ours, but we have to sit silent."

"Can I quibble on one point?" Joyce asked, "The term 'guilt' gets thrown around so much, it's an ugly term. I didn't search because there was a sense that you had to choose sides and I loved my adoptive parents. I would describe it as 'loyalty'. Now I realize that my searching wasn't disloyal to them. They were both extraordinary individuals for their time. I think my adoptive parents would have risen to the occasion."

"Well," offered Faith, "also I think some of the silencing that goes on is justified. We were originally a self-help group to learn how to navigate around sealed records. With thirty, forty people showing up, we have to give someone's emotional stuff short shrift. Otherwise, we wouldn't cover everyone."

"I agree with that thought," agreed Susan, "and it seems like over the past couple years we're seeing searchers with different logistical issues, too. Just talking the mechanics of search takes longer."

One bespectacled man who looked like a fluffy-haired John Lennon quipped, "I'd like to go to one of those triad meetings wearing a T-shirt that reads 'Birth mothers are sluts' and just watch the self-serving, revisionist Madonnas squawk."

"Ouch, John," said one of the women.

Alan stepped in, "It's pretty hard to look back at having given up a child. I know some birth mothers feel a lot of shame and guilt. One told me that not a day goes by that she doesn't think about the son she gave away forty years ago. I'm not saying all birth parents do, and it doesn't invalidate what you're feeling, John."

Betty offered, "And let's say it, some just don't give a shit, pardon my French. Now they've hit menopause or they're afraid of growing old alone, so now all of a sudden some of them come back looking after decades away–probably for a caretaker."

"The neediness seems so misplaced. It's so presumptuous. I'm not sure it's that they're looking for a caretaker though," said Lisa.

"Great, so it's still on their time schedule. That's something I hope we talk about more," Betty concluded, turning in Alan's direction. He nodded but pointed at Naomi who had timorously raised her hand like a school girl.

Naomi spoke hesitantly, too, "I really like that you're calling this a quest because of what I'm getting–not so much from birth mothers or other adoptees or the older generation of adoptive parents–but from younger ones. It used to be the older generation took our quest very seriously, to the point of feeling betrayed or threatened by it. The newer ones feel like they deserve all sorts of awards for doing things differently, you know, 'I've told my kid they're adopted so I'm so much more enlightened'. Or, 'I have a picture of their biological brother so they have roots and there's nothing to be gained from searching, I've done it for them, I'm on top of it'."

Naomi turned to Lisa and said, "I think you know what I mean when I say, it seems like some of the adoptive parents think that if they say and buy and even attend all the right things, then their child will never grow up to search."

Lisa agreed and added, "In several states adoption attorneys tried to have laws enacted that would criminalize either adult adoptees or birth mothers who search. They tried to attach mandatory jail sentences. Fortunately, we defeated them."

"You're all tapping into important themes.

I've brought something to give our conversation some structure," Alan pulled a slim stack of papers from his bag and passed one out to each of them, "I've just handed you some stats about relinquishment, "Sandy, would you read first?"

Susan recognized her as an activist. Sandy was tall with china-blue eyes and rarely came to monthly group meetings. Just as Susan and the others arrived Sandy would be leaving an envelope-stuffing session that ran right before the monthly meeting.

Sandy read that "There was a thirty year band of time in the U.S., sometimes referred to as the Baby Scoop Era, when close to five million babies were placed for adoption. Two events, the end of World War II and the legalization of birth control in the early to mid-seventies, bracketed that era. During it, eighty percent of unwed mothers gave away their children, but after it only four percent did."

"I don't think there was anyone telling them they could resist," added Joyce, "a lot of this was before the feminist movement. My birth mother couldn't even get her own credit card. I don't blame my first mum. But I'm every bit as angry as someone who does, I lay the blame on the whole idea that I'm illegitimate. How do you bloody label an innocent newborn legitimate or illegitimate? How is a human being 'illegitimate' and therefore 'awkward' to have in their family of origin? My birth mother had passed on but her brother treats me like I've got the plague. I'm a nice, hygienic person, thank you."

"Yes, you are an excellent person!" laughed Alan, "That uncle may actually be a little mortified that he didn't somehow protect his sister. Wouldn't it be nice if now he were protective of you, his niece?"

There was silence.

"In other words," mused Sandy, "maybe as part of the price of the family's joining the middle class that was forming after the war 'illegitimate' members had to be shed."

Keyshia from the group cleared her throat, "I think these might be white statistics. I don't think blackfolk gave away their children historically. And we weren't entering any middle class much before the civil rights movement."

"You're right, Keyshia, I have to confess I couldn't get numbers for the black population. Anecdotally, it seems like the original mothers with extended family raised children when the father and mother weren't married," said Alan.

"Eighty percent versus four percent!" exclaimed Joyce whom Susan met for the first time that night, "the difference after birth control is seventy-six percentage points? My takeaway is that seventy-six percent of the birth mothers out there didn't want us."

"Okay," added Alan, "Let me share my view as a social worker and an adoptee. This is what I tell birth mothers who come to my practice because their adoptee may either not be willing to meet them for a reunion, or they may cut off communication at some point down the road."

"Because she's a whore," sneered John, and looked out toward the window.

Susan had a hunch and decided to try something, "John, are you opposed to pre-marital sex?"

He looked back and said "Hell, no," then added with a twinkle, "I want to find out how to get more!"

Faith jumped in, "So you're angry enough at birth mothers to call them 'sluts' and 'whores,' but maybe it's not their sexual history that bothers you."

"What are you? The therapist?" and John looked over at Alan Cooper, the only other man in the room.

Lisa started to answer for Alan, then Alan resumed calmly, "Let me finish what I was going to say and I think it suggests one answer. This is how I try to explain to those birth mothers how their adoptee might be feeling, that would lead them to reject their birth mother. I believe this as a clinician, but you're also experts."

Alan waited. Everyone more or less nodded, or looked at him expectantly.

"Whatever social opprobrium a birth mother faced," Alan began, "whatever pressure she was under at the time, strip all of that away and look at the core relationship of mother and child. In that room there is an infant who is completely helpless and all she or he has known for their entire nine months or so is the smell and sound of their mother. That first mother was literally their entire world.

"Only the birth mother, by the stroke of her pen, had the power to end the relationship. The adoptee had no power. Whatever an adoptee understands intellectually about society during the Baby Scoop Era, the reality is that in that moment they were completely powerless. The little power the birth mother had, she used to sever the adoptee's tie to his or her entire known world. That can leave a profound wound."

John agreed, "I'm not completely tasteless. I'm just sick of birth mothers not owning what they did. Of course you hear about adoptees being pissed. And look around the room at those meetings. It's mostly women. Most of us men don't even want to deal with it because it's remembering such a betrayal. Once in a blue moon a birth father shows up. They're just deadbeats."

Susan had heard that there were certain countries that were known as "good" sources for adopters, "I'm from Thailand. I wonder if they were or are experiencing a Baby Scoop Era, too?"

Alan agreed, "I would imagine so. What can you tell us about that?

"Well," Susan thought for a moment, "I remember this one time when I was a kid, 'Miss Saigon' was playing on Broadway. My parents' agency held a fundraiser there at the theater."

Susan paused and shifted after one of the twins jabbed her under her rib cage, "The injustice, the dramatic tension, was all about the imbalance in power between whites and Asians. And yet–there was no self-consciousness about the imbalance in power between the white adoptive parents and the adoptees in the audience. I'm not talking about parents being more powerful than adolescents, trust me, I've got a pre-teen and I know whose side I'm on now."

The circle of people, except for John,

laughed.

Susan was relieved and went on, "What I mean is the Asians in the room, like me, had given up a natural curiosity about their roots to make their adoptive parents feel more comfortable. All the well-heeled, well-meaning theatergoers at 'Miss Saigon' were oblivious to that. At the time we Asian adoptees were oblivious, too. It was buried so deep."

"Susan, thank you for bringing a full perspective to this conversation. I guess my research covers closed domestic adoptions during the Baby Scoop. Keyshia, that doesn't cover much of the black community. I need you both to bring a full perspective to this conversation," said Alan.

As soon as he finished his last syllable, they heard Lisa's voice, loud, reading from the sheet, "Adoption records were not sealed in the United States until the 1920s. Kansas and Alabama never sealed their records so adoptees from those states knew from their original birth certificates who their biological parents were all along. Contrary to the fears of those opposing opening records in the other forty-eight states, there were no great scandals, no lives upended, no reality shows created around reunions in either state," she smiled and then looked up.

Joyce looked carefully past Lisa to Alan and asked, "I always assumed adoption records were illegal to look at. So for the first hundred and forty years in this country they were available to adoptees?"

"Yes, and by the way, the term isn't 'illegal.' All sorts of people, court clerks, social workers, hospital staff, all sorts of strangers are empowered to view your original birth certificate. Only the person it should belong to can't."

Keyshia cleared her throat, "I don't have proof, but what I was trying to get at about in my culture is that you can't correlate it to a middle class. I think it had to do with the mob targeting black communities with drugs. That's what broke up families," said Keyshia starting to get as uncomfortable as she was indignant.

"I think you're sane to get angry about that."

"Thank you. Angry is an understatement," replied Keyshia, "I'm glad we're here. It's just so nicey at that group sometimes. Nothing real gets said unless it's love and bunnies."

Sandy said, "Now you know why I don't stay. I just work on lobbying to restore adoptees rights, that's where I'm called. I know you've accepted Christ as I have. I think some of those women see the world as a vast country club, and some of it is. But the world that engages me is the one that needs healing and recovery."

"Thank you," answered Keyshia, "amen, and thank you. I know the work you do, Sandy."

Alan leaned in Faith's direction, "I think you could speak to the American Indian community. We need to hear from you, too."

"Okay," Faith explained, "First of all, I'm part white and raised all white, just to be honest. But here's what I know: starting around the time of the reservation system, the Bureau of Indian Affairs worked with proselytizing groups of Christians to take Native American children away from their tribes. Children that were being raised by extended family instead of exclusively by a married mother and father were the most vulnerable. It was that 'white man's burden' stuff at its ugliest. Some were sent to boarding schools, some placed for adoption."

Faith leaned forward to take a sip from her water bottle before continuing, "The Indian Child Welfare Act was a reaction to this. This is a law that passed in 1978 and it lets American Indian adoptees reconnect with their culture and families, and going forward it puts adoptions of American Indians in the tribal courts."

"Thanks," said Alan, "Let's continue."

Lisa said, "Here's a statistic that's a good one in replying to the Catholic Church when they try to impose their doctrine on the entire country. They claim that making abortion illegal will create an adoption buyer's market for newborns. Here's a study of women who went to abortion clinics and were turned away because they were too far along."

"There's such a study?" asked Sandy.

"Yeah, I've heard of this study before. It's small, but it should get its authors funding for a larger study. If that gets the same results, it should be a new conversation."

Sandy demurred, "I didn't mean to jump in, please tell us more."

Lisa seemed to know the numbers by heart and managed to keep eye contact through most of the study conclusion she was reading, "Of the women who were turned away, some found other ways or places to end their pregnancies, about as many kept their babies, a roughly even split. Only nine percent turned to adoption."

"So, you're saying ninety-one percent of those women chose to either have a legal or illegal abortion elsewhere, or keep their babies– rather than carrying them to term and then giving them away?" asked John.

"Yes."

Susan shifted her tummy twins a little and said, "Who would go through all this and then give her child–or children–away? Maybe this goes to show that the whole legend about birth mothers being selfless is simplistic. Now that they have more options, like daycare and living wages to support their children, they choose to keep them rather than give them away."

Betty responded deliberately, "I hear you. It gets a little wearisome to sit politely when some of the sketchier birth moms or dads start to contradict themselves. But let's take John's point. What if a woman is the neighborhood bicycle, you know, gives everyone a ride? What if? Even then it seems that being pressured into giving away her baby is cruel and unusual punishment."

Alan nodded but said, "Or more to the point, because it's you the adoptees who we're here to focus on, let's try another 'what if?'. Either way, that baby has experienced a loss. Sometimes with substance abuse or abandonment or mental illness, a parent really can't keep a child. You can argue that adoption was the best answer, but STILL the baby has experienced a loss. We get told over and over how much better off we are."

"That's debatable," mumbled John.

"True, and even if materially we're better off, it's a loss."

Susan realized something, "You know my mom loved scrapbooking. As she got older she really got into genealogy, labeling old family photos, and even started this needlepoint family tree. Looking back, I always felt at some level that adoptees had to give up their family tree and knowledge of any roots. It was payback for winning the financial jackpot, you know, the price of being saved by adoption. If you look at it that way, it makes the adoption–I've heard some activists call it the adoption industry–feel pretty ruthless."

Betty leaned in, "I bet Susan's mother didn't face all sorts of weirdness when she finished her needlepointing like adoptees face when they announce they want to do something similar with a family tree!"

"Uh, no, she didn't," Susan said quietly. She didn't want her mother drawn into this by someone else, even someone conveying sympathy to Susan.

Keyshia added, "People can act like it's even more fragile if you're black trans-racial. And they really assume that if your parents are white that they must have rescued you from a crack house. 'They must be saints.' I'm embarrassed for the adoptees that buy into it, 'Yes, massa done save me by bringin' me up ta the house,' when they should know that they are just as valuable as anyone else. Their parents adopted them because they wanted a baby, not sainthood."

"Amen," joined Susan, "and if you're Asian, it's not a crack house they saved you from, they think we must have all arrived from a Vietnam airlift. And –"

Sandy finished the chorus, "even then you're just as valuable as everyone else. Giving up access to your birth history or your OBC shouldn't be the tradeoff to make up for being adopted.

Alan prompted. It was Joyce's turn and she read, "Men's behavior, as much as women's, was changed in the 1970s by the availability of alternatives to adoption. It marked the end of the Baby Scoop Era. Until that time and reaching all the way back to colonial days, roughly thirty percent of all first children were born less than nine months from their parents' wedding date."

"Interesting," said Sandy.

"Thirty percent?" Faith repeated.

"These are based on studies of parish and

cemetery records," Alan added, "With the legalization of both abortion and birth control happening in the mid-seventies, no one could definitively assign cause and effect to just one factor. But what numbers do point to is a drop in shotgun weddings: the number of first children born 'prematurely' to newly wedded couples declined."

Susan remembered a project she worked on in Philadelphia, "Benjamin Franklin's sister married at age fifteen and six months later gave birth to a full-term baby boy."

John hummed a few bars of Billy Idol's "White Wedding" and then called out, "'Shot-gun wedding,' 'had to get married,' 'honeymoon baby'. It's there in the language."

"John, you have a point. They're something hiding in plain sight," For the first time, Susan thought about those old-fashioned euphemisms and their implications. Alan picked up the thought, saying, "Birth fathers could now rationalize that their girlfriends had options, be it abortion, or raising the child alone. Men could tell themselves that a lifetime of marriage wasn't the only solution to an unwanted conception."

Lisa nodded, "No consensus was ever reached on whether the number of pregnancies outside marriage had gone up or down, and whether abortions had gone up or down. Betty brought that up when we've talked to both pro-choice and pro-life groups. We absolutely think the difference from the seventies was that boyfriends became less likely to 'do the right thing' and mothers were to continue their pregnancies and their parenting–alone."

Susan wanted Faith's take, "What was it your birth mom said about why she relinquished you?"

"Here we go," sighed Faith, "something like, 'I don't like to second guess myself.'"

Alan looked at her, "Knowing her, what did that mean?"

"No idea. It usually means I'm wasting my breath if I try to get any more clarity from that point on in the conversation. She knew my birth father had a steady girlfriend."

"All due respect," smiled John, "you were no accident."

Susan looked at Faith and added, "I don't want to tell your story, but it bugs me that she contacted you and then was so cagey about your birth father."

"Oh, yeah. I asked her to tell me what school he attended before she dated him so I could at least find a yearbook picture of him. She ignored my request. On top of that, for a full decade she led me to believe her–my–ancestry was Czechoslovakian. She liked Prague so she just kind of made it up on the spot," Faith paused.

"She sounds like a bit of a fabulist," John's hard face actually began to soften, "that's a really cruel trick to play on an adoptee. Big f-ing cosmic joke."

Alan shot him a look. Susan was getting a little weary of the profanity, too.

~

Susan's stomach growled and her mind drifted to her pregnancy a decade ago. Back then she armed herself with the certainty of first-time parents about what was right and what was wrong for her child.

She was certain that her daughter would somehow be inoculated from pain because Susan breast fed her and didn't relinquish her for adoption. Susan was equally certain back then that putting a baby on its stomach or side to sleep would prevent sudden infant death syndrome. Crib bumpers were necessary to prevent an infant from trapping itself between the slats of a crib.

Times changed, Susan mused. The baby

experts change, too. Now one was supposed to place a tightly swaddled infant on its side, never its stomach. Crib bumpers were dangerous because a baby might get entangled. You were cheating your child if you didn't give your child DHA in infant formula.

One thing didn't change for Susan, she still felt that somehow the twins would benefit by being raised in the scent and sound of the mother who bore them.

She was certain about one other thing: with twins she would no longer boil pacifiers for ten minutes each time one hit the ground the way she had for Lily.

~

Susan shifted her focus back to the group.

"I think there needs to be a distinction between adoptees born before birth control was legal, and adoptees born after," said Naomi.

Keyshia looked at her curiously, "I can see making a distinction between sealed-record adoptions and open adoptions. Or," she glanced at Susan, "issues for people adopted from overseas instead of domestically. Transracial adoptions are different from intra-ethnic group adoptions, but I've never heard that one. Where are you going?"

Naomi looked nervous but said, "The eighty percent who got pressured into giving their kids away before there was legal birth control are different from the four percent of unwed mothers who give their children away today. The first group was normal, just like the rest of the population. Our generation of adoptees, you know," Naomi paused as though the rest were self-explanatory.

Sandy now leaned in, "What are you getting at?"

"Well," Naomi eyed Keyshia and Sandy defensively before continuing, "the new generation that comes from that unusual four percent isn't the same. There's a lot of substance abuse, a lot of mental health and behavior issues. Now being identified as an adoptee, say at my job, would be bad and not because of what we were talking about before–illegitimacy. I think there's a consensus out there that adoptees are messed up. It's because of the newer generation."

Susan could swear she heard either Keyshia or Faith suck in their breath.

Alan offered, "I can't really speak to the newer generation that's coming of age now. It's too soon to draw conclusions. I think we share that same loss with them. And I don't know if you

intended it, but you pointed out something else–
we share the experience of being stigmatized.
For us it was illegitimacy, for them it's the
unusualness of being given away. In some cases,
but not all, it's compounded with other issues."

Keyshia spoke slowly, "So are you
suggesting you want to distance yourself from
the post-seventies adoptees because they're
lower class?"

"I didn't say that," Naomi said defensively.

"Of course you wouldn't. It reminds me of
what used to happen in the black community
when some folks tried to distinguish between
light skin and dark skin," Keyshia sighed, "White
folk didn't care, nothing changed for the
mulattos any quicker than it changed for people
whose skin was blue-black. The law had to
change for everyone."

"Oh, I agree with you. We need
restoration of original birth certificates for all
generations of adoptees. Legislation has to
change for everyone," Naomi nodded.

Faith shifted to face Keyshia and Sandy,
"It's ironic: just when one stigma gets lifted, we
get pre-judged with this new one. And this one is
basically saying that we've got a bad gene pool.
Our kids come from a bad gene pool, too."

Alan agreed, "Maybe that was the silver

lining to what adoption agencies used to say, that a baby was a tabula rasa, a blank slate. It implied both a stigma but also a fresh start."

Alan began to wrap up. He announced that at next week's session they were going to make a collage about being adopted. Susan would miss this much discussion, but was a little relieved that next time she would be using her hands instead of words.

27 COLLAGES
1999

"Did you ever notice the sets of a lot of the police procedurals on TV are these same dark colors?" Susan pointed this out to Faith in a low whisper as they walked down the high-vaulted lobby. They were early.

Her friend agreed, "The crime scenes are anyway."

The lighting was low, coming from the lamps on end tables. From outside the large bow window the parking lot's sodium lights twinkled through the raindrops. Elsewhere velvet dark greens, burnished mahoganies and sepias shone softly from a row of cushions here, an armrest there, a polished banister, a recessed bookcase.

Two reading lamps had been positioned, probably by Lisa, to pour light across the work table where they would be putting together collages. There was a promising pile of magazines, scissors and poster board.

If it had been daytime, and sunny, Susan would have gone straight to the windows to throw open the sashes or flee the room altogether. If Susan had been alone it would have been a haunting room, inciting grief and brooding. But with others around her the enveloping darkness felt protective, the shadows warm. She could speak plainly. Lisa and Naomi were the only ones there when she and Faith stepped through the double doors but the others soon trickled in. Susan off shouldered her handbag and put down the cake loaf she had baked.

When Alan arrived, he brought a burst of cool air that smelled like earth and rain. By then everyone had gathered and he was friendly but quick in his instructions for the collages. Actually all of them nodded and then seemed to melt away into their own separate nooks to work. Susan perched on a chez lounge with magazines fanned out beside her while Faith sat on the other side of a cherry drop-leaf they had pulled between them.

"Have you ever done anything like this?" Susan asked Faith under the lamplight.

"Yes, at one of the national conferences. There was a workshop called, what was it?– something like 'Superman's Kryptonite' and we were supposed to find pictures or found objects that reminded us of either our heritage or adoption," Faith said quietly over the sound of her shears already extricating an image from a glossy magazine.

"Superman was an adoptee, wasn't he?" Susan smiled.

"If you stop to think about it, there were a lot. The twins who founded Rome, Romulus and Remus. Ophelia in Hamlet."

"Moses," Susan remembered the scrapbook and the Passover *Haggadah*.

"Set afloat in the bulrushes by his sister and mother," Faith was already uncapping a glue stick.

Susan remembered more, "I remember all those girl books my mother and grandmother gave me. Heidi, Rebecca of Sunnybrook Farms."

"Ann of Green Gables."

"Pinocchio."

Out of the corner of her eye Susan saw John doing a circuit of the other works-in-progress.

"How about," Faith thought for a minute, "Nancy Drew was raised by an aunt."

John had heard them talking and was walking toward them. Faith said, "Dorothy in the Wizard of Oz."

John bent down with a grin, "No, she wasn't really an adoptee, her parents were just away in Kansas City living in the back of their van and running a meth lab."

Alan overheard and spoke sharply, "That's only funny if you've decided to be deaf, dumb and blind; there are adoptees who lost their entire family because a birth parent got involved in drugs. John, here's two reasons not to do that again: this needs to be a safe place, and using others' pain for laughs keeps *you* anaesthetized."

John backed off, "I was just kidding." He retreated, embarrassed, back to his chair. He really wasn't all that tough beneath the armor.

Faith whispered to Susan, "I don't know if he really belongs in a group. He's got so much of his own stuff to sort through."

Susan knew what she meant but whispered back, "Obviously he's not handling the deeper stuff yet. Maybe he needs to be in a group for a while first to get that some of the issues aren't just his. Adoptees share a lot of the same stuff."

Susan stopped, sensing someone else walking toward them now.

It was Joyce, "I'm trying to come up with ideas so I thought I'd walk around the room. I'll redeem myself: David Copperfield."

"Good one," Faith looked up, "Maybe all of Dickens. How about Little Orphan Annie?"

"Okay, Peter Pan and the Lost Boys," Susan was running out of ideas and needed quiet now to keep working.

"Last one," Joyce offered, "Batman, or at least Bruce Wayne," then she headed back across the room.

Faith and Susan sat together comfortably as they worked. By now Susan had ripped out several pages that had images that intrigued her in some way. She trusted that there must somehow be an adoption connection, but she would kind of dwell in them as she cut them out and arranged them before finishing up with a glue stick. For her the meanings would probably come last.

She looked at what she had pulled out: a tiny calico kitten, too young to be weaned yet curled up on a braid rug in front of a fire with a golden retriever instead of a mama cat; a woman's arm bedecked in silver bangles, the hand brushing some intricate patterned fabric; a dolphin (from a vacation resort ad); a picture of a tropical sunset; a warm orange-ish picture of an apple pie sitting on a cooling rack; some faces she liked of children; an old woman's wrinkled face under a kerchief; an iron gate in a stone wall; an Ojibwe dream catcher; a picture of an airplane taken above the clouds, gleaming in the sun; a nail polish ad that showed a padlock below the words "lock in color".

Alan gave them the cue to wrap up and then they went around the circle.

John went first, "These red sound waves on the black background are me and my old man fighting about his finally giving me my f-ing information. Then it turns out all he has is the name of the hospital I was born at and the date he and my mom got me from the agency. It was four months after my birth date. Usually they only kept you in foster care two weeks or so. That stayed with me."

John surprised her with his self-awareness.

Susan then was disappointed when he continued with his familiar angry-hurt-boy tone, "I have a picture of a woman screaming–maybe it was an involuntary surrender and they took me away from her and this is her fighting it. Or maybe she thought she could do it but dumped me after four months. Maybe she was too strung out on H to sign the relinquishment any sooner."

Susan caught herself gripping the armrest of her chair.

John was still sharing, "My dad said there were no health reasons they gave for the long stay in foster care–said he hadn't really thought too much about it. It's amazing how little it mattered to them, my info," and then John pointed to one corner of the collage and pivoted it so everyone in the circle could see it better, "so here's ripped up and crumpled pieces I glued on. It's how much thought they all gave to me. And you know I don't mean about 'Oh, but they changed your diapers so many times,' I mean it's clear that saving my background info didn't mean a thing to them," he swallowed, "they're who all my stuff got entrusted to and now I've got nothing."

Sandy suggested, "Maybe afterwards we can talk about petitioning to have your original birth certificate unsealed."

John shook his head, "Joyce and I already spoke about that during the break at the monthly meeting. I really don't have a legal lever. They suck. The baby-sellers got me good. I heard there were some maternity homes. Well, Joyce told me," and he looked over at her, waiting for her to join in.

Joyce shook her head, "It's your collage, you know the story."

"Those homes were first set up for unwed

mothers, to help them find work and be able to keep their babies. Then social workers got involved and 'professionalized' it," he said with a weak sneer, "sounds like what it came down to was brow-beating the single mothers to sign away their kids. They took away our mothers and even our access to finding them. Phase two, finding richer couples–like the married social workers themselves–to buy the babies."

"You don't know which scenario it was. You are mad now, aren't you?" Alan asked.

"Ya think?"

"It's certainly justified. Your reaction to the same set of facts can change over time. Your reading of your collage can change over time," Alan offered, "anger's a funny emotion. It can be a mask for a different one."

John seemed to more than understand, "I'd like to be mad at the social workers–this is the story that justifies that. Otherwise I have to be mad at my birth mother giving me away."

They continued reviewing each person's collage. Faith and a few others had created captions by cutting out single magazine type letters that spelled out messages. Susan ducked her head a little lower each time Alan asked for the next person. She wasn't sure what she would say.

She managed to be last and found herself narrating the collage counter-clockwise, "Well, the airplane and the tropical sunset have to do with mine being an international adoption. I had to fly across time zones and climates, that's how far I've come from where I was born. Then the woman's hand with the jewelry and the fabric– they're both exotic. But maybe if I hadn't been taken away from Thailand they wouldn't be exotic. In fact," Susan turned the poster board around to find the next photo she was looking for, and then flipped it back, "this warm apple pie would have been what seemed like an exotic pastry with strange fruit called 'apples.'"

The room laughed.

"But flipping around the point of view, the warm apple pie is home. Like the kitten curled up with the family dog by the fire, even if I don't match, it's home. I realized recently that the kitten may think she's a golden retriever. It wasn't until I visited Thailand that I realized I'm more comfortable with Caucasians. It's who I grew up with. There were some other Asians at synagogue and at school but it was a real shock when I did my MFA work in Japan. I mean, suddenly *they* are everywhere, those Asians. I actually, in grad school, had to get used to being around people with hair and eyes like mine. I mean it was good, but isn't that weird?"

Alan answered, "No, it's part of your story, being a transracial adoptee."

"Thanks," Susan really did appreciate his saying that. She looked at the collage and resumed, "It's all sunny pictures. Even the one with the padlock has corals and salmon nail polish colors. That and the iron gate, which looks like it's somewhere in the Mediterranean, they both remind me of that early part of my life and my family history being locked off from me. Then we're back at the silver airplane again."

Silver. Susan remembered something, "a while ago my husband told me about sneaking into a cemetery at night. They wanted to steal some silver they heard about."

"David?" Faith was incredulous.

"They were teenagers. They didn't have any plan for it. They really just wanted to see if they could."

"You just wanted to 'see if you could'? Visit your birth country? Find your birth mom?" asked Betty.

"Does it always have to be heavy? There's plenty that's 'deep,' sometimes we need a break."

Betty shook her head, "I don't know if it was just a lark."

"What if it's just an adventure," Susan

persisted, "becoming an explorer for once?"

Faith pointed to a picture at the center of the collage,

"You have one more you left out, Susan."

Faith was usually better at paying attention, but Susan turned it around just in case she actually had missed something.

The dream catcher. She thought of the ghost in the mirror. She told them about the little girl there, Suwan. Susan didn't tell them there were other dreams from her childhood. They had begun returning in recent months, too, but she couldn't make out their mumblings yet.

Susan looked up at the small group, "I just realized something now I didn't think about when I was choosing the images. With this gate or with this 'locked in color' tagline, you could either see it as being locked out–like being locked out of your information. But it reminds me of a feeling I've had since visiting the orphanage and my birth mother's village. That's of being locked in. You know, I have all this new information. It feels good to have it. But it's still locked in that adoptee part of me. How do I apply it in other parts of my life? I guess these images could be about once you have your information, how do you unlock it into the rest of your life.

The only concrete example I can give is that during my first pregnancy I had no medical history and I had to explain why to the ob-gyn staff. For these babies it's different. With new nurses I don't even have to mention I'm adopted."

"You want to hide it?" Betty asked.

"It's personal and I want it to be my call. Before the reunion I felt I had to share my personal history–to explain why a pregnant woman wasn't supplying any family medical history. Most expectant moms aren't forced to discuss their own conception with strangers. With the twins, I have the info that's useful to share, and I can have my privacy about the other stuff. I feel more grown-up."

Betty nodded.

"That's very interesting," Alan smiled with his arms crossed and one arm propped up on the crook of the other with his palm supporting his chin. Then he pulled out his datebook, reminding them that they would be having their last session in two weeks.

"Susan raised a point that I'd like us to explore further for our last session," Alan said, "that's how do you bring it back? How do you take whatever facts you've uncovered about your birth family and the adoption, and make them useful going forward? If you discover injustice, as John has, how do you bring it back to make your life and your interactions better?"

He walked across the circle and every pair of eyes followed him, "If you uncover emotions in yourself as a result of search and reunion, or qualities in yourself that you share, or don't share, with a birth relative–what next?"

"How do we," Joyce offered, "bring the Holy Grail back home?"

"Exactly," affirmed Alan, "when we began, I identified what you are doing as a quest or an odyssey. Odysseus' story is the perfect example. The first half of his quest was the Iliad where he wins a battle at Troy. But the whole second half of his quest, literally the Odyssey, is how to return home."

Alan waited, his eyes twinkling, "This is your quest. I'll lead the discussion next time, but some or all of you are already the unwitting experts: what are the perils of the odyssey after the search and reunion? Hmm?"

"I think maybe," it was Naomi and she seemed to be struggling for words, "even when you are speaking from the heart on a panel to a group of prospective adoptive parents, or to online ob-gyns in the baby business, they can really dismiss you completely. They're in the dark, truly benighted, and say they have a question for you. You start to give them a hard-won answer. But before you know it, they're talking over you."

Faith said softly, "That's because they don't really want your answer. They don't really want the truth."

"Susan," Betty called out suddenly, "you didn't explain the old woman in your collage. Is she the wise old crone that points the way?"

"Oh, my gosh," Susan looked at the photo. She laughed, "I suppose it's someone who's 'been there, done that' on the search. She seemed like a kind of–either a salt of the earth who is comfortable on her land, never immigrated away, never been adopted away, never wrestled with infertility," she was making this up.

She stopped herself, "But then she wouldn't be very wise, would she?"

It was clear Lisa wanted to speak, Susan asked, "What are you thinking?"

"It's your collage, but just a thought. If she's a wisdom guide, she'd be a counterpart to some of the people called 'search angels' who help others with search and reunion."

"'Search angels,'" Susan repeated silently. There were paid specialists like Fred Kouyoumjian, but she'd begun to hear of volunteers: genealogists, reunited adoptees who helped others. A few became friends, too, like Joyce seemed to have become for John.

She looked over and saw Faith was looking content. Faith looked at Lisa, then her, repeating, "search angels."

Alan spoke, "One image, two interpretations: a well-worn face that is 'comfortable' because she has experienced none of the disruptions of the triad. Or, an elder who has 'wisdom' because she has faced a disruption and still found comfort."

Then he held up a peace sign, "two weeks. Thank you each for your stories tonight. Don't forget to take your collage."

28 FOUND
1999

Susan closed her car door and stood still for a moment taking in the pink and lavender twilight, aware that Naomi was walking toward her. The days were getting long enough that it was no longer dark before the final adoptee session.

"Susan?"

"Hi, Naomi. How're you doing?"

"Good. Listen, I know we need to go in, but maybe we could talk on the phone or meet up sometime?"

"Um, sure. I'm not sure where you live."

"I'd drive to somewhere near you. Especially in your condition," Naomi said looking at Susan's middle.

"Okay," Susan said as Naomi handed her a business card. She flipped it over and Naomi had already written her home number on it, "I'll give you mine, too."

"Hey, ladies," Lisa called out, and as though they'd been scooped up, Susan and Naomi walked in on either side of her.

Inside they found Keyshia, Joyce and John. Joyce had brought a little crudité and spreadable cheese. Keyshia was opening and setting out crackers.   John was pulling a pair of cherry soda and birch beer bottles out of a brown supermarket bag. There was an air of busyness that Faith and Sandy joined as soon as they arrived.

Maybe it was because this might be their last chance to share that pithy observation that would reveal their own dash of brilliance. Their last chance to make sure -- to make sure that they didn't miss something, that they didn't leave a pronouncement unspoken, a spiritual alleyway unexplored. There was an urgency that only rose higher when Alan finally arrived. He was on time. All the other adoptees were early.

Once settled, they went around the room. Some shared where they were in their search, others focused on what they'd learned from their reunion. After one speaker, Faith turned toward Alan and asked, "When was your search?"

"In the 1960s."

"The Dark Ages, back 'before Stonewall',"

added Betty cheerily.

"I don't follow," Alan looked pleasantly puzzled.

Lisa chimed in, "It's an inside joke from the regular triad group. Especially among the people that go to the State House to meet with legislators to restore adoptees' rights. We've come to borrow terms from other civil rights movements. Some of the birth moms refer to people who acknowledge being a birth mother as 'out' and those who hide it as 'closeted'."

Joyce shook her head, "But, Betty, I think that being out with decorum is at least as important as having a Stonewall. Smashing things gets you media, but bringing some maturity to the conversation gets you heard by people with power."

"It sounds like you might be saying that there's a continuum in how adoptees pursue their needs. A continuum of behavior, or an evolving maturity?" offered Alan.

"Yes, exactly," Joyce nodded, "Stonewall didn't have any nice old ladies like me. But I can tell you a first-term senator would rather talk with a cookie-baking, grandma adoptee than an angry guy in leather."

"Joyce, you old queen," laughed Sandy, "I think back in the day you threw a few chairs."

Joyce laughed and in a stage whisper, "But the boys in the State House must never know," then she straightened up and turned serious. "I think the more power you realize you have, and you do get that from searching, I did, the less you have to show it off. Or if you don't find it searching, you realize how it's been stripped and hopefully join to restore adoptees rights. Here's the PSA: next Tuesday we're meeting at the church to stuff envelopes, we have letters from the bill's sponsors in both the house and the senate."

"I'm there," offered Sandy.

Lisa tried to direct the conversation back, "Alan, you were saying something about a movement and evolving maturity?"

By now Alan was standing at the head of the circle, "I like where you're going here. You know the saying coined by the feminist movement, 'The personal is political?' Well, for some, their evolution is going to allow for political engagement that will advance the fight for rights. But what I can help us focus on here is the personal. I'd like you to view yourself as the hero of your story, even though the details of the story were hidden from you at the beginning. Your story, your destiny was completely dependent on and controlled by the authorities.

That's whoever arranged the relinquishment, and in some facet, your birth father and birth mother, and then whoever sealed your birthright information from you," Alan sat back down.

Susan had no new insights to share, but an old secret. When it was her turn she hesitated and Sandy said, "You've been quieter than usual."

She had to agree. "Do you remember I told some of you about the orphanage? I couldn't tell if what I thought I remembered was an actual memory, or an imagining of a family story I'd heard over and over?

"Yes."

"I told you about learning what the ghost in the mirror kept coming back for. It was to tell me that 'Suwan' was really me."

"Go on."

"I can tell you that I got to learn the truth, and to accept that I'll never have more about my birth father. But some of the other stuff–I feel like I might be mouthing the search and reunion doctrine," she hesitated, looking at their circle.

"I'm not sure if it's mine or if I've just heard it so much–in the group before I went to Thailand and now in more recent years with the online communities that have sprung up."

"That's interesting," Alan said, "do you

have an example?"

"Okay," Susan thought about it, "I think I have two."

Susan inhaled, "Everyone, and I mean everyone talks about 'seeing someone who looks like you,' but I actually experienced that a year before my reunion. I met my first blood relative when I gave birth to my daughter. That's when."

Betty interjected, "That's true. That's interesting, but you'd never met an adult like yourself who was related."

Susan tried to joke, "Yeah, we have more hair."

She remembered that Betty didn't have kids. "I think it's important, for me, to be tied to the flow of generations. You get that when you get to hold a baby, by birth or by adoption. If you don't have that," Susan wanted to offer Betty something, "I guess you get that when you meet older bio relatives."

Alan looked at her, seemed to understand she was being tactful, and then decided to say nothing.

Susan continued, "The very first time I went to a meeting, it was like the clouds parted and the heavens came streaming in because I heard an adoptee talk about feeling apart from others. I was just like him, I have a great family, but I put it as suffering from 'phantom limb pain.' I'm like an amputee who feels an absence.

"But," yes, she was sure of this now, "but a reunion doesn't give me back the years, it doesn't undo that. And then right after I got home, my adoptive mom dies. I carry that 'phantom limb pain' because she's not here to be a grandma."

She could feel herself sigh, "I may have swapped in one 'phantom limb pain' for the other, or," and then she stopped again.

She shrugged, "That's where I'm at."

It sounded wise to say it that way, better than admitting she had failed at finding an epiphany. No Holy Grail.

Alan kept the room quiet for her. She really had nothing left to say, to perform, she felt. Finally Alan said, blessedly not focusing on her, "The Odyssey unfolded over a decade. I think some of you described plateaus in the early stages of your search. Either roadblocks, or dead ends, or red hearings followed by decisions to pause." He waited a beat, "returning home can have similar plateaus."

Faith stepped in, "My birth mom is making it really difficult to find my birth father. Frankly after dealing with all of it, I'm not putting as much energy into finding him as I could. You're saying it's okay to wait and catch your breath on a plateau."

Joyce laughed, "I like to call them scenic overlooks. At my age you savor them whenever you can. I think psychologists call them 'chances to integrate' whatever you've learned."

"I like your hiking phrase, 'scenic overlook' while pursuing a quest. It's a helpful image, Joyce." Alan smiled, "may I steal it–with credit?"

"Sure."

Joyce looked at Susan, "I sometimes set up an easel with watercolors at a scenic overlook. A real scenic overlook with those blue and white highway signs. You may not be a painter, dear, but I think you mentioned have an MFA?"

"Yes, that's right."

"How do you prepare an exhibit?"

"Well, if it's large I start with the theme and brainstorm it into categories. Then I work to obtain the art pieces or installations we want to fill out the categories of that original theme."

Alan looked at Joyce before saying to Susan, "You've named at least one theme tonight: reunion not 'curing' the absence from your original loss. Instead it brought you a new truth, maybe healed you without curing you."

She liked that. It was beautiful and true.

Alan continued, "I'm stretching things with my next suggestion–it's always a danger when you try to draw connections between adoption loss and other human experience, but, have you thought about a 'reunion' for your more recent loss?"

"What? Are you saying a 'reunion' with my adoptive mom?"

"You'll curate a better term," but he agreed.

Susan was lost. The two things had happened so close together she wasn't sure where one shift ended and the other began.

"With my scenic overlooks," Joyce said, "sometimes I go with my easels and no clear picture in mind. I start to paint. Later I find the themes."

"My work can happen that way, too," Susan agreed, "When it's right, I can start a sketch or a project outline, and the larger plan flows from it. Those are the best moments."

Alan leaned forward, "You've led the quest once, Susan. You know the way back to do it again. You'll know when it's time."

29 SAN JAO THI
1999

Susan had all but lost touch with Fred Kouyoumjian after paying her bill and getting a thank-you call for the spirit house, the *san jao thi,* eight years earlier. She periodically returned to the monthly adoption triad meetings and once in a blue moon she ran into him there. They always exchanged warm but brief updates about her correspondence with Noklek. A few times over the years she referred searchers from the group to Fred.

Susan was less interested in Kun Sompan's explanation of the spirit houses than she was in understanding the real mystery: how Fred Kouyoumjian could have spent any time in that country whatsoever without learning what they were. Something about them sparked her imagination.

One day at lunch with Faith, Susan thought out loud, "Maybe we could somehow use them in an exhibit someday." Susan remembered the replicas sold in upscale gift shops and the one in Noklek's own yard. It wasn't until later that she took a closer look at the two tourist guidebooks she had brought with her on that trip. They were full of *san jao thi* photos.

She held one up for Faith, "One of the books gives a thumbnail description of their relation to the South Asian Hindu Vihara. There are two varieties it illustrates, a *san phra phum* which holds a miniature pointed-roofed temple, or *wat*, and this one here which seems more like a small home, it's called *san jao thi*."

"I'm getting kind of lost here," Faith shook her head, "So, one of them is some kind of temple, right? The other looks like a house and sounds like san-jow-tee?"

"Right," answered Susan., "That's what was near my birth mother's village."

"Susan, you normally don't try to get me to say the technical terms you need for work or something. This isn't a criticism, but I'm noticing a difference. You don't want to say just 'spirit house'. It's like you're seriously trying on the language, trying to use it when you can, even back home."

"Huh, I never thought of that. Yes. I think you're right. It's a little like trying on the silver bracelets in the night market. They're pretty, but I was also trying out what it would be like to dress like other Thais. What it was like to wear their–our–jewelry."

"What it's like to wear your language, too. Maybe someday you could look into Thai language lessons."

They both drank from their cups in silence.

"There's another point."

"About the *san jao thi*?" Faith smiled triumphantly.

Susan laughed, too, "Nice. You see, you or I could have read about them and learned their names from a guidebook. Even before setting foot in Thailand. How could Fred Kouyoumjian not know what they were?"

"It is strange," agreed Faith, "but maybe he just tossed them in as street cred, part of the pitch to get you to pay for his detective services."

"If he hadn't visited, if he hadn't read about them in a National Geographic somewhere, how did he even know of their existence?" Susan didn't want to let go of this.

Faith thumbed once more through the colorful photos of garlanded *san jao thi* and brightly painted *san phra phum* before handing them back to Susan, "The words and the facts don't add up. But he remembered them from somewhere."

"This hardboiled detective has a mystery of his own," and Susan guessed that like those of adoptees or birth parents, its answer lay not with solving a crime or tracking down a missing person. Her lunch with Naomi the following week would confirm that it lay deeper than that, in the heart.

~

"David," Susan turned to him the night after she met with Naomi, "why when I find something that feels sanctified does it always have at least a little corner of it that is off?"

She knew he would remember the idea she had shared with him when she was working on a folk craft exhibit once. There was a concept shared by crafts people from Afghan carpet weavers to Indian potters and Amish quilters that a piece of work should not strive for God-like perfection. Instead, each artisan deliberately created a flaw.

"That little quilt square they call the Humility Block. Beyond that I'm not following."

"Yes. I just had lunch with another adoptee, remember the one I mentioned to you from the three-week group whose parents also had a biological child?"

"Yes. Naomi?"

"Yup, good memory."

"You do seem to attract lost souls."

"David! She needed someone to talk to, 'It's not good to be alone'," Susan quoted the old aphorism from the Talmud.

"People do seem drawn to you. I see that more and more the longer you are involved in the search and reunion thing. I just worry that some of them might confuse compassion with friendship," then David hesitated, seeming unsure.

"I have different friends in different parts of my life. There's also fellowship, that's important, even if they're not friends who share in other parts of my life."

"Yeah, I'm not sure what I'm objecting to. Sometimes broken souls need more than a cup of coffee."

"Sometimes they need both. I do feel needed. Each year it feels like there are adoptees with more kinds of relinquishments, more kinds of adoptive families and, so, more kinds of searches. When I searched nine years ago very few international adoptees did. I have that experience of learning from people who had some details in common with me, but still having to find my own path. These new ones can talk with me for ideas if their adoption was international, but I also respect where they are on their own pilgrimages, no matter how much others may tell them there's nothing new under the sun."

"Honey, Suze, I see all that. It's kind of amazing to watch from the sidelines. Where is this Naomi on her search?"

"It's not so much that, it's something she confided in me about a man who attended the group."

"Okay," David put away what he was reading, "You're very trusting, but I'm taking some of this with a grain of salt. There may be another side."

"Go ahead," Susan didn't mind. A reality check from David was fine, if it was needed, "Before Naomi met her husband, before she even met her birth mother and birth sister, she got involved with someone through the group."

"Was he single?"

"Yes, three-times divorced, recovering alcoholic but that's not the point."

Susan exhaled and continued, "It was Fred Kouyoumjian."

"Well, whadya know!"

"She was interested to hear that he arranged the search for me in Thailand because–the real news is he has an adult son named Carl. That son lives in Thailand."

"Is his son Amerasian, too?" David asked, "Fred Kouyoumjian said during your first meeting that he'd been there for R & R."

"The son is from his first marriage. I just assumed it was here. She didn't say the son was Amerasian but she did say Fred got a Thai postcard from his son Carl, once–no return address in English–just saying he was working for a relief agency. Fred told Naomi they were semi-estranged. That postcard is how he even found out that his son wasn't in this country anymore. He also said something to her about having always wanted to visit Asia."

"He's never been before?"

"Yeah, exactly."

Susan continued, "His telling me he knew Thailand and had been there for R & R might have just been a story. It would have made me more confident in his ability to do an overseas search back when they were uncommon."

"But the reality is that when it came to search and reunion, he really did have some skin in the game," David offered.

"Poignant, right? The estranged father

making all these reunions between other parents and children. Naomi thought he was trying to make amends. AA," explained Susan.

"I learned something else, too," Susan paused to let David know she was about to reveal one more of the detective's own mysteries, "I asked her what was on the postcard. She said she didn't know what it was–but it looked like exotic bird houses."

"Huh. Like the one he had you ship back to him?" asked David.

"I'm guessing so."

~

The next month, Susan and Faith embraced before going into the meeting together. Susan caught Fred Kouyoumjian going in just ahead of them. It was a good session when he was there. He offered tips to people who were searching even though some might have hired him to do the same work.

There were close to forty people sitting in two concentric circles around the conference table. When one of the facilitators called the number Faith was holding, Susan felt excited, too. Faith shared the announcement that she had finally located her birth father. It sounded like all forty people in the room called out "congratulations."

The adopted men and birth fathers were the most enthusiastic. One asked her, "How the hell did you pull that off without your birth mother helping out?"

"Okay, here's how to crack the system," Faith looked peaceful and proud as she began to share the steps, "This happened in two phases–the first was five years ago, in 1994. I started by going to the library to use some software that contained two national telephone directories."

Faith looked over at Susan and Hans Berwanger, born Kim Chung-hee, adding, "I don't know exactly how things will change for international adoptees. Maybe when DNA tests get easier and cheaper, and there are international databases for their results...okay, I hope I'm not getting into too futuristic here, but changes will come."

Hans grimaced, "Thanks for acknowledging it's harder if you're international."

Susan smiled, "I'm hoping Hans won't have to wait for the high tech solution–but–this is your day, tell us about your search."

Faith continued, "I started looking for my father and I was staring at a black and white database screen. One directory was for people east of the Mississippi, the other was for people west of the Mississippi. On a hunch I picked the eastern directory and typed in my birth father William or Bill Yard's name. There were two hundred of them. I circled the William and Bill Yards in the city where he had lived at the time he met my birth mother. There were only three of them."

She cleared her throat and went on, "That night, when I sat down to make the phone calls, my hands shook. Of course, I thought, they should be shaking. This is the first I'll be speaking to my birth father and I don't know what I'll find. Of course I would feel shaky before calling my first father. Why shouldn't I?

"None of the three matched up with what I knew about my first father. Then I tried several other ways of tracking him down. Have you ever heard of ICWA, stands for the Indian Child Welfare Act of 1978? I stumbled across it in a Barbara Kingsolver novel."

Susan heard laughter but it sounded sympathetic.

Faith smiled, too, before continuing, "That meant a lot because one thing the adoption agency was able to share with me was that my birth father was part Indian, part European-

American. Turns out that under that law I had the right all along to have my OBC, original birth certificate, and background information."

One man asked, "Is that why you're adoptive parents kept it a secret?"

"I don't think my adoptive parents knew, I think the agency withheld that to make me, I don't know, more marketable," Faith concluded.

"And it sounds like the adoption agency sure didn't act on it," the facilitator who was a birth mom added.

Faith nodded, "Among other provisions, the ICWA gives Indian adoptees access to their original birth certificates with their first parents' names on them. Despite that, I got an imperious scolding from someone who answered the phone at the Indian Museum in Manhattan –- that I had no right to search because I, apparently as an infant, had 'legally agreed to protect' my first mother's confidentiality."

"I think she was speaking off the cuff. Sounds like she wasn't even educated about the ICWA," said the adoptee facilitator, "the museum has never taken a stand against adoptees' rights legislation."

Faith jumped in, "I was able to work around them and didn't need them for my search, but I think it would be helpful to engage them. I'd be thrilled to call back and send them one of our position packets on adoptees' rights."

Faith paused and looked over at an adoptee activist in the group, Barbara Cohen, "Barbara put me in touch with the attorney who helped draft the ICWA. He in turn put me in touch with a tribal historian on the Iroquois reservation in upstate New York. She told me that a lot of Iroquois moved to the outer boroughs of New York earlier in the 20th century. They became construction workers on Manhattan's skyscrapers. So that matched what I knew about him being in New York. She also told me that Yard was a surname found on the reservation and she would ask around," Faith paused to deliver a little drama for the group, "But, no luck there.

"My birth mother did mention once where he worked at the time. She had been impressed because he designed music LP covers for CBS Records–Sony Records by then. So, I called up William Yard's former employer. Someone in the office there was sympathetic to me and promised to find out what she could but I never heard from her again.

"Yet a few weeks later I happened to contact a William Yard in another city and his secretary laughed when I asked her if he had ever worked in the art department of CBS Records, 'The man doesn't have an artistic bone in his body,' she explained, 'We can't even read his handwriting. But you're the second person this month to call and ask that."

"Whoa," Susan laughed, "So who do you think the other phone call was from?"

"Maybe either the sympathetic woman I had spoken to at the music company or the Iroquois historian. Anyway, this William Yard's secretary put me through to him. It turned out he was seventy-eight years old (too old to be my first father), but at the end of our conversation he told me–really sweetly, 'Don't worry, I'd adopt you any day.'

"After I made a few more creative attempts that led nowhere, Rita helped me out."

Eyes turned toward the petite blonde woman sitting about two chairs over from Faith. Rita was the head of Adoption Crossroads, another adoptees' search and support group, "Rita found a William Yard that fit the information from my birth mom," Faith said.

"The Mormons maintain a national death registry," explained Rita, "they help regardless of your religious background."

Oohs, aahs, "Good to know," came from the circle of listeners around them.

"But," continued Faith, "he died in 1987."

Now the group responded with a warm shower of "I'm so sorry." "Did you learn anything else?" "Maybe you'll find brothers or sisters."

"All I could get now would be a copy of a government document he had filled out. I sent away for that and planned to put that in my family album as a memento."

The facilitator who was an adoptee then asked, "Where were you emotionally then, Faith?"

Faith looked down, "I was disappointed that I did not feel grief. Instead," she looked up at the group, "I felt satisfied at having tracked him down. Yes: satisfied. It's hard to explain but I also felt a kind of contentment at having survived one of my forebears. It made me part of the flow of generations. Just as Bill had probably survived his parents, I survived him and so, I hope, my children will survive me."

Susan reached for some crudité, and noticed that a few other people were reaching for snacks. Introspection and food went well together.

Faith continued, "In a few weeks the document Rita ordered for me arrived but when I scanned it I saw the box for race was marked 'Negro' and, uh," she deadpanned, "I am more or

451

less white."

Some laughed while others tsked in disappointment for her.

"I had the wrong William Yard. I ran out of leads so I decided to let matters rest for a while. I put my energy instead into phoning and writing state legislators to try and push through our bill that would give adoptees at the age of eighteen in our state access to their original birth certificates," then Faith caught the eye of one or two adoptees in the room before concluding, "so others will be spared the kind of quest my birth mother and the system sent me on."

An adoptee who was still searching said, "Really–you're helping out the rest of us. I've literally been taking notes."

"That's happy ending number one," laughed Susan, "There's more."

Faith inhaled, "Ending number two is that I borrowed an old mobster technique."

A few people laughed nervously, while others knew Faith well enough to take the reference in stride and waited as she went on to explain, "I hired Fred Kouyoumjian who had a sympathetic cop run a DMV check. Then Fred spoke to my birth father to confirm he'd found the right man and to give him a heads up."

"So you found him, after all!"

"What did you say to him?"

"When I picked up the phone, I introduced myself and told him my birth date. I asked if it had any significance for him. He said it did and that he'd been waiting years for this phone call."

"Have you met yet?"

"We're having lunch next Wednesday. As it is, we spoke for almost an hour."

The room hummed, almost in unison. Susan noticed that Rita, Barbara and Fred all looked like proud parents as others congratulated Faith and there was a tinkling of "good lucks."

30 MEZUZAH
2001

On her way home from work, Susan picked up the package waiting at the post office before entering her day-end routine of driving to daycare and bundling the twins up to go home. She set something to defrost in the microwave for dinner before she ran back to the front hall and pulled out the contents of the package and left its large empty box, bubble wrap and packing tape strewn over a chair near the front door.

It would catch David's eye when he came home and followed his usual routine of sorting through the mail. He would be late tonight, catching up with everything at the office so she wouldn't be able to start this project until after putting Noam and Maya to bed.

She carried this wonderful package, the size of a large bakery box up to the project room. She was surprised at its weight, and that actually made it feel more precious to her.

Susan opened the last layer of wrap and finally lifted a Thai spirit house onto a drop cloth. This one had a steeply pitched roof and carved eaves that curled up ornately at each corner. The walls looked like fine teak and the roof was carefully shingled with bright ceramic scales. High domed windows had been cut into each tiny wall and they gleamed with tiny gilt sills.

She brought a small hammer upstairs with her to her project room. She knew tapping her work into place with the hammer was quiet enough to let the twins slumber, but she knew when David got home and heard it well past the hour he usually read to them he would come bounding up the stairs. He would see Susan with her back toward him, bending over something with a hammer.

Susan didn't notice when David walked in. She was intently attaching something infinitely small to where the door would be. Before focusing on whatever new adventure his wife was about to draw him on, David smiled at how nice she looked from behind.

"Your mother?"

She turned around and looked at him with eyes almost tearing with appreciation.

"You get it!" she nodded, "Yes, it's for her."

"*For* her? Selling coals to Manchester aren't you? They probably already have plenty of spirit houses in Thailand. And the postage will easily tip a hundred dollars."

"No, not that mother. My *mom*."

Susan stepped back to let him see what she had so patiently been tapping to the front of the spirit house door.

He found himself asking the obvious, "Are you putting a *mezuzah* on that door?"

"It's what she would have wanted." The *mezuzah* even had a tiny letter "shin" in Hebrew.

Susan knew that David would eventually realize they weren't talking about the same mother, "a tribute to my *mom*, and the family 'traditions' of gefilte-sushi, or Moon Festival *sukkahs* or Asian Hebrew calligraphy."

He laughed. Of course.

"Do you remember that detective, Fred, asked me to buy him the spirit house, the *san jao thi,* from Thailand?"

"Ten years ago, yup."

"I bought one on eBay for myself. Don't worry, free shipping."

He waited for more of an explanation. She was enjoying the suspense.

"Susan, why now?"

"I don't quite know yet. It's my version of

mixed media art, it's..." and her voice trailed off.

David offered, "The media are your adoptive and your birth heritages, mixed together in one piece of 'art'."

"Was it that obvious?" Susan asked, disappointed.

"No, I know you. I also know that it won't be just static mixed media. You're working on something, just like you say the pieces in the exhibits you produce at work are springboards for thoughtful people who view them. This'll be a springboard to something else, something next."

They both leaned in for a kiss, and then he went to their room to get changed.

Susan put the hammer down. It was dark enough now that the streetlights were shining through the window on the other side of the spirit house. She walked over to the door and turned down the light switch. Now the glow from the lights outside formed a faint halo around the *san jao thi*. She rubbed the *mezuzah* just to make sure it wasn't loose, and then sat down on the floor. She waited a beat, and then deliberately began to imagine her mother's face.

Now, ten years after her mother's death she was finding words and a symbol for her mother's life, or at least part of her connection to it.

No one was there to hear Susan, but a still small voice spoke anyway, "There's a present I wish I could have brought back to you, Mom. But I ordered it online now and this is it. They had these small alters all over the countryside in Thailand near anything beautiful in nature like an especially old tree. And every house had them, too. They look like miniature Thai houses, like tropical doll houses raised up on poles. At first I thought they were something for ancestor worship, something Confucian. People decorated them with incense and garlands and tiny dishes of food.

"But it turns out that these things–they are called 'spirit houses'—aren't for ancestors at all. They're tended by every family for the spirits that were in that place before them. There's no blood tie. Everyone kind of adopts these spirits to make sure they get attention and care. Wouldn't it be nice if I had brought one home for you–I couldn't because I was keeping the trip a secret from you," Susan paused. Maybe that was still the right decision.

"Either way," she continued again, "it could have been a way of saying, 'You may have been the one who adopted me, but I adopt you right back.'"

If there were such things, the spirit of Susan's mother surely rested with her a while there.

The true story of Noklek, and Susan's conception and relinquishment made her adoptive heritage, just as it was, complete.

Susan didn't need her mother's holidays that strenuously combined the Jewish and Asian in attempts to give Susan the *shalom*, the wholeness, her mother had wanted for her.

Susan had needed to make this quest on her own.

She had needed mentor-friends like Faith and Farah, and even the scary monsters along the way that took form in some of the stories at the group, or in discord with her mom.

Susan had needed something real, not just those metaphorical holidays, and had found it in being able to undo the arrangements of secrecy that others had made for her.

Susan continued gazing at the details of the exquisite spirit house. She remembered her mother's voice telling her a bedtime story almost in whispers, "There was a shepherd named Jacob who had been away from where he was born for many, many years. When he decided to go back and visit, an angel held him, Suzie."

Susan hadn't thought about this Bible story in a long time: Jacob wrestling the angel.

"They tugged and tossed, they 'grappled,' Suzie, all night. Then Jacob won and the angel gave Jacob a prize, a blessing."

Susan, too, had wrestled the angel and won the truth by touching and hearing and seeing her birth mother and then–just as heroic– by still being able to return home and resume her role in her adoptive family. Her quest had allowed her to love both families, adoptive and birth.

She remembered how her mother ended the story, "After that night Jacob's name was changed to 'Is-ra-el,' which means 'one who wrestles with the sacred.'"

~

She and David were closer now that they had found the truth of his father. As much as Susan might like to imagine herself an adventurer, she'd learned that some mysteries don't get solved, no matter how earnestly she might seek. Her father-in-law's heart would remain a mystery to David and Jonathan, and Aliza, the mother of his children.

Ramona Graves was a case of ashes to

ashes, dust to dust with no known history and no kin to claim her. Susan didn't see a way to track down her own nameless, faceless birth father either. Like many others in every generation, he would be lost to posterity. From her view of the family tree, he was the leafless branch. Even without him, her family tree finally had roots.

She called David. He came back in.

"David, I'm ready to tell Lily."

"How will you do it?"

"She's been asking me to take her out to the ice cream shop for a mango bubble boba smoothie."

David interrupted, "Why of course, how obvious."

She backed up and began to explain, "Boba are actually called tapioca pearls, little nubs of the root."

"You're going to tell her about them being cassava farmers? So your adoption and reunion story is going to be told from the perspective of the tapioca supply chain," he chuckled.

"I wouldn't exactly put it that way," she let out a melodramatic sigh, but added, "Do you think I'm trivializing it? Or, is this making it goofy?"

"No, I understand what you want," he wiped the snarky grin off his face, "You're drawing tangible connections, finding some that are light. You can't bring your mother back, and you can't bring this other grandmother over easily either, so there's loss. 'Just a spoon full of boba helps the medicine go down'..." That launched him into whistling the "Mary Poppins" tune.

She brushed off her lap, rocked back on her heels, and stood up in a fluid motion that she knew David always appreciated. As she started to pass him he put his thumbs and forefingers on her hips. She let him pull her in for a peck before she went to find Lily.

He was left looking down at her syncretic creation, the spirit house with the tiny *mezuzah*. He tapped the outside of the little case to find it contained a parchment. He didn't have to look to remember the poetry of the *Sh'ma* blessing and the "And you shall love" prayer, the *V'ahavta*, that would be written on the parchment of the tiny *mezuzah*.

> *Hear, Israel, God is our God, God is One.*
> *Blessed be the Name of God's glorious*
> *   kingdom for ever and ever.*
> *And you shall love God, your God, with all*
> *   your heart and with all your soul and*
> *   with all your might.*

And these words that I command you this
day shall be in your heart.
And you shall teach them diligently to your
children, and you shall speak of them
when you sit at home, and when you walk
along the way, and when you lie down
and when you rise up.
And you shall bind them as a sign on your
hand, and they shall be for frontlets
between your eyes.
And you shall write them on the doorposts
of your house and on your gates.

The melody was one that was always simple and comforting, weaving together the tropes for Deuteronomy 6:9 and Deuteronomy 11:20.

Susan, down in the kitchen, remembered to call up to him to take a look at the essay she had written. She had left it on an ottoman for David to spot. Susan ran up the stairs and her long, dark hair swung across the door frame as she peaked in. He was already holding her single-paged print-out.

"You remember I had that dream from childhood about the ghost in the mirror, and how now, since the search, it ends okay? You can skim that one, I won't be hurt. But, David, that's happened with two more dreams. I write about how the reunion is a kind of 'Dream Catcher' because, well, you'll see."

He nodded and began skimming her writing.

Dream Catcher

Even if my first mother hadn't been living in a distant, misty kingdom, it would still have felt like a call from a faraway land. It lured me back to a landscape of dreams, the recurrent dreams of my childhood. In the first year or so of our reunion, these dark nocturnal messengers returned, but now their messages were gentle, persisting into daylight.

The first dream was not a dream of childhood but a dream of adolescence. There was mumbling going on in the house, I couldn't make out the thread of conversation. Still confused, I followed my parents on an airplane trip to an island wreathed in fog off the northwest coast.

We walked over grassy bluffs, passing thigh-high, white marble tombstones as we went. Through the fog they appeared forever; it was a graveyard. We finally stopped in front of one and I stood back watching as my mother knelt down. From behind the grave she pulled out photo after photo of a teenage girl I had never seen before.

Whenever I woke from this dream I felt washed over by her grief and by my own desolate jealousy and deep confusion.

Now, more than a decade later, I can look back clear eyed and say, the girl in the photographs was the one who would have been in my place, she was their never-been biological child.

There is one more dream after which I always awoke feeling tender and sentimental, but not knowing for what.

It begins with a narrow flight of maroon stairs. They lead up to an attic where my mother has her sewing studio and in waking hours I am forbidden from going up there because of the danger of tangling yarns, scattering quilt scraps, unwinding bolts of cloth or pricking my finger like the princess with the spinning wheel.

But in this dream I do climb the steps and as I round the landing, I see, not her studio, but something from a child's Easter fantasy.

A giant Easter egg made of pastel sugar (in some dreams pink, in others blue or yellow) and decorated with white baker's icing waits for me with a small opening through which I expect to see the usual diorama of rabbit and egg or little girl in a spring bonnet picking flowers.

Instead, kneeling on green plastic Easter grass under shaded pastel light from the crystalline walls is a woman with dark hair and dimples like mine. A small boy and girl with glossy black hair and dovelike eyes snuggle against her casually.

At least in my dreams, the sewing room that held the secret of my real adoptive mother's creating also held the mystery of a first family. Now I climbed the stairs on my search as an adult, and I knew with new clarity the nature of the longing that led me nightly to that staircase so long ago.

~

Susan looked back in and saw David skimming the retelling of the third dream. This was the ghost child in the mirror who now resolved back to Susan's lost name, *Suwan*. She had looked up its Thai meaning, "garden."

David noticed her and held out an arm to let her nestle in.

He inhaled and then kissed the edge of her hair, "Suze, this is good writing. I didn't realize all this was going on," then he smiled, "evening's dream catcher may be daylight's spirit house."

31 TURNING AND RETURNING
2001–2011

At the end of their summer 2001 visit to Susan's mother-in-law, she and David got back home to the tri-state area, carried the twins up to bed and then unpacked the cabin of the car.

As she always did when coming home after being away, Susan went to check prompts and data beeps on their voicemail as though opening a treat. This time there certainly was one. It was a message from Farah.

Susan checked the time. It was late and they had more to unload from the car now that David had loosened the tarp and bungee cords that lashed their remaining bags to its roof.

Susan calculated that it had been almost a year since they'd heard from Farah. Things were different years ago, then Susan invited Farah to Lily's first birthday without hesitation. Now with the twins' birthday coming up, she wavered because of the different paths their lives were on.

With this new phone message, Susan's indecision evaporated. If the package of children's invitations adorned with balloons and giraffes had been near the phone, she would have reflexively filled one out for her childless, and probably unattached, friend. If nothing else, Susan wanted to seize this occasion to include Farah back into their lives. But the invitations were up in the project room.

Instead Susan dialed the phone number she had never forgotten and literally bounced on her toes when she heard Farah pick up.

"There's someone I want you to meet. His name is Fahdi. I think he's the one. Maybe. But I want you to meet him and I've told him so much already about you and David."

They agreed on Sunday brunch, kids in tow, since Farah hadn't seen them since the naming and the *bris* almost a year ago.

As Susan and David walked into the restaurant, she could see Farah and a man waiting for them in a sunny corner. He had a medium build, light caramel skin and a shaved head. His eyes twinkled and he had dimples, but before Farah and Susan could embrace each other and introduce their men, David stepped ahead of her. He grabbed the stranger by the shoulders.

"Fahdi, really good to see you again."

"Who woulda thought. Farah, Dave works at one of my accounts."

"Fahdi's a sales engineer–one of the good ones."

Both men had worked on high clearance projects together, which piqued Susan's interest, but David was loath to discuss security issues outside of work. Other topics were not off limits. Having grown accustomed to the closeness Farah shared with her family, Susan wasn't surprised that Fahdi brought up his in this first conversation.

"My dad is old-school. He doesn't trust young men to make their own decisions, he actually said this: 'If I had been left to my own devices when I was young, I probably would have chosen someone I couldn't love for a lifetime. I love your mother, and now that I'm middle-aged, I realize my middle-aged parents knew a thing or two about people. But this I tell you, son, if I had known Farah's parents I would have arranged a match for you with her.'"

"What!" David laughed, "The ultimate stamp of approval!"

The light in Farah's eyes danced, "Imagine that, I'm good enough for an arranged marriage."

Between dinner and dessert, Farah and Susan went to the women's room. The new couple's joy was contagious and Susan just laughed at the expected when Farah confided that she thought Fahdi would propose soon, and that she would say "yes".

"You've finally found your *habib roohi*!"

"Yes, I've found my soulmate. He's fun, he's a great kisser, he's smart and kind and liberal. He embraces tradition and family, AND this crazy mosaic America."

"I'm so happy for you, Farah."

"Thanks, but there's one catch."

"Oh?"

"He's pretty secular, calls himself a 'cultural Muslim'. He doesn't believe in a soul. I finally found my soulmate, and he doesn't believe in a soul," then Farah added with a laugh, "Yet."

"You'll have a lifetime to try and save him."

"Knock on wood," then Farah turned the light mood even lighter, "Look at this. These are those infinity sinks. No basin. They're beautiful."

Susan watched the running water cascade down its four sides for a moment, and then pointed out the neat row of burnished and lined metal baskets along the counter between the faucets, "And look at all these give-a-ways. Makes you think about planning wedding favors."

Farah laughed and then, looking more closely at one of the toiletry baskets, said, "Or we can leave the guys out there and have our own spa night in this restroom. 'Pink sangria' give-away candles, lavender sachets, jasmine hand cream samples, 'mint julep' mouth rinse."

Susan looked at her friend, "These sure are better times."

Farah paused mischievously, "When we were in college, before you met David, I think you thought finding your other mother would be like finding a soulmate. Was it?"

Susan did remember, and laughed, "Well, David, yeah, he's it, if I had to pick one. I told you that before the wedding. With three kids and work it's easy to forget that and get distracted by other things. But maybe he's one of my soulmates. We've had fights, but basically he's got my back at a party."

Susan paused and picked up a small packaged purse mirror from one of the baskets before continuing, "Noklek? She's–I love her, I'm glad I found her and there's something so familiar about hugging her. But honestly, there's so much we haven't discussed, and everything is so different in our worlds–I can't call her a soulmate. On the other hand, being able to meet her and see my ancestry with my own eyes makes me feel like I have more in common with the rest of humanity. Noklek isn't my soulmate, but being able to hold her has made me feel connected to all the souls that are out there."

Susan and Farah both thought about that for a moment. It was one of those times, Susan realized, where you answer a question out loud that makes you give a name to something, or think a thought you hadn't thought before.

"I can really be happy for you now, Susan." Farah had put the awkward baby-naming behind them.

Susan understood, "I've missed you."

~

Neither Noklek nor Suwan heard from Tuptim, still years went by. Her husband could locate neither her nor her handlers. Someone at the UAE consulate, overhearing him, actually said cryptically "wait seven years."

When she read this in Noklek's letter, Susan wrote back that in *halakhah*, Jewish religious law, there was a concept of a sabbatical year when servants in debt bondage were allowed to go free. It might or might not be the same in Muslim religious law, *shari'a*. She would ask Farah.

"At any rate, the person that told Tuptim's husband Durek this was not an official," Noklek wrote back. She digressed slightly, "Seven years from now would be the turning of the new millennium on the Western calendar, or 2543 BE (Buddhist Era) on our Thai calendar. You should know that our culture has a calendar."

At some level all kept hope, but Thai officials promised they could only wait and see because *shari'a* upheld slavery and the UAE government seemed too preoccupied to choose justice over jobs. The seven years passed. The new century arrived, but neither Tuptim, nor even word of her, arrived.

Then one day Suwan found a double-thick packet in her mailbox. There was a note from her mother that Kun Sompan had translated with something he usually eschewed–exclamation marks and dashes!

"In this 2546 BE, or 2003, Tuptim managed to make her way into the Thai Embassy in Dubai.

"There they have grown used to stories like hers so it did not matter when she showed up and could offer neither Thai passport nor other form of identification. They believed her when she told them that the Arab family had taken her passport and working papers, held her wages as 'rent,' and kept her in a windowless utility closet when she complained!

"As the carrot to that stick–they also continued promising her her full wages at the end of her bond.

"She should have been freed at seven years but they kept her about another year–until she stumbled outside. Tuptim had nothing but the clothes on her back–no reading knowledge of Arabic–and only a few memorized spoken phrases, including,

'I am Thai, please help me to the Thai Embassy!'"

~

After nine long years, the village was welcoming back their Tuptim, but one forever changed. As Noklek put it, "for the first few days Tuptim was very silent, wept on seeing an old friend or even an acquaintance."

The news that came through the village parabola antenna appeared to reinforce the inevitability of Noklek's and Tuptim's stories. In the elections that year politicians seemed to perfectly reflect the acceptance of what happened to both of them in girlhood.

Susan read Kun Sompan's handwriting and imagined Noklek's voice, "The chairman of one of the coalition parties declared in a press interview with The Nation, that 'if there were a crackdown on politicians involved with prostitution, my party would be unable to field enough candidates to keep the coalition in the majority.' This is a reason to let such a practice continue?"

"In this interview, he also said amazingly, 'what is the problem with keeping a mistress or two,'–he called them "little wives," *mia noi*–'as long as it didn't interfere with family or public life?'

"There is more. One broadcast announced, 'A seventy-six-year old elder statesman, Kun Tavick, admitted fathering the child being carried by a fourteen year old prostitute who worked across the street from the Parliament.'

"Tuptim turned her face away from the image. The rest of the villagers noticed but no one said anything until one of the grannies hit the ground hard with her walking stick and cursed the politicians," then wrote Noklek, "many of the elders muttered bitterly. They have seen this for generations. They are more enlightened than us with their years, but even they let themselves be angry.

"This was my age when I left Ban Naan, Suwan! Another party is now playing money politics by successfully running Chuwit Kamolvisit. He is known as the 'godfather of prostitution' as he is the rumored owner of a chain of brothels across Bangkok and other Thai cities."

Noklek was furious.

Through her letters, Susan surmised that the friendship between Noklek and Tuptim had shifted slightly. When Susan had met them those many years ago, it was Tuptim who seemed to defend and sometimes speak for a reticent Noklek. Now Tuptim seemed to have lost her voice, at least for a while. Noklek wrote that she herself was beginning a campaign against trafficking and prostitution.

It was a campaign of stuffing envelopes with flyers. Sending letters to the editors of print, online and broadcast media. At first it was Noklek alone when her girls were away or asleep and when she wasn't working in the fields. It was a very slow process with a few minutes stolen here, a half hour there, before she gave into sleep and the next dawn's round of chores.

Soon the angry granny began to help.

Then others joined, sometimes with slow arthritic fingers, over the next three years. Then Tuptim joined in, too. Although it was extra work, Durek sat with her at the end of his long days.

Susan noticed that plainspoken Noklek was now naming things differently. In her letters Noklek began using terms like "human trafficking" and "debt bondage," or more bluntly, "slavery."

By 2008 Noklek had good news to write to Susan. She and Tuptim had become helpmeets of the growing army to defeat Chuwit in the election that year, "Legislators are beginning to listen to us who came from the life and to our allies the Buddhist nuns and other activists."

"Nuns?" Susan remembered the orphanage.

When they succeeded in passing the country's first Anti-Trafficking in Persons Act, Noklek wrote, "You see what happened to us as girls in Bangkok and again to Tuptim as an older auntie in the UAE. If you unfold the paper doll, you see it has happened to girl after girl after girl. There are many of us to fight this now."

~

One day in 2011 David called Susan to the computer screen. A news show was running jittery footage of several hundred people kneeling in central Bangkok and in the foreground was a plain-faced country woman in a pointed straw hat being interviewed. David read the caption and said, "I know you said it's a common name over there, but...?"

Susan leaned in and squinted, straining to filter out the jangle of the video.

"'Tuptim'!? That's her! She's in Bangkok there!"

According to the yellow subtitles, she was "laboring in prayer for Bangkok" with an anti-slavery group. It called itself ExodusCry: A Prayer Movement to End Slavery. She was reciting numbers in Thai that appeared in translated subtitles.

"Why our country?" Tuptim asked.

Tuptim quoted some numbers, to Suwan they seemed staggering. One percent of women or girls in the USA are involved in prostitution, and possibly as much as one and a half percent in Western, Eastern and the former Soviet Europe, but in Thailand it was about nine percent. In the rest of Asia it was only two and a half or so percent.

Tuptim looked pleadingly, "What has happened to my beloved country? What is happening to our beautiful daughters, our children, boys and girls?"

An activist named Carl K. whom Tuptim explained she had met on the way home from bondage first told her those statistics. Now the reporter introduced that same Carl K.

He was a millennial Caucasian aid worker with curly hair. He stepped forward and leaned into the reporter's microphone. He guessed that the ratio was higher in Latin America at seven-point-four percent and in parts of Africa four-point-three percent--still not reaching that nine percent of Thailand. The bottom of the screen now identified him as Carl Kouyoumjian.

Susan and David looked at eachother and said in unison, "Carl Kouyoumjian?!"

David started to switch on his camera, "It must be that detective's son!"

With the prayers still heard in the background, the interviewer now stood in the middle of a clutch of aid workers for a news analysis.

Susan felt lightheaded.

She tried to focus on what Carl K was saying but instead ricocheted between the realities of Tuptim, that nine percent of girls in

Thailand who had worked in prostitution like her birth mother, and the appearance of Carl, yet another connection between her, Fred, Tuptim and Noklek.

Carl spoke earnestly, "it had to do with being near the Vietnam, Cambodian and Laotian wars at the same time that Thailand was not directly a battlefield. Instead this country became a regional destination for waves of men who were far from home and seeking relief from the fighting, which often included patronizing brothels. By the time fighting had ended," he concluded with a hand gesture that reminded her of Fred Kouyoumjian, "the sordid infrastructure of human trafficking had insinuated itself into the frayed social fabric of border towns and famine-haunted farming villages."

This was hers and Noklek's story that Carl K was expounding on. When they cut from his face to the next video image it would be the last Susan saw of him.

The voiceover identified the next face as a visiting Southeast Asian sociology scholar. Susan listened to the academic as he suggested that even Islam might be a contributing factor to the unquenchable demand for female sexual exploitation; its endorsement of polygamy long after Buddhism had pretty much abandoned the practice meant that there were many poor Malay men who were cursed to never have a wife or children of their own, turning for pleasure instead to prostitutes. Susan remembered Noklek talking about all the Muslim johns in southern Thailand and did some mental extrapolation: that would have also been true for many poor men in Muslim Indonesia, and beyond Southeast Asia as far as the Mediterranean Sea.

David's voice drew her back, "Good for them. A little quixotic, but…"

"No, look!" and Susan found herself letting out a sound almost like a cheer.

The camera had panned to the scene just over Tuptim's shoulder and then focused in on the brothel owners. They were being led away in handcuffs.

Then they cut to a black man above a dateline of Cincinnati, Ohio, Underground Railway Freedom Center, talking about using the lessons of the African diaspora to fight modern day human trafficking.

"Twelve to twenty seven million people today are caught in a form of slavery around the world," he said.

The reporter must have wanted to focus the direction of his answers and asked, "How much of that crosses between countries?"

"...between six hundred thousand to eight hundred thousand are trafficked internationally."

Now he leaned into the mike, "with the opening of civilian air travel, first north Asian, and finally Middle Easterners and Europeans arrived at Suvarnabhumi BKK on international sex tours. We believe that this more than anything has contributed to the steady flow of international trafficking in recent years."

Back to Bangkok and a black minister exhorting the worshippers to "press deeper into prayer" as the crowd around them grew and earlier horn-honking died down, either in resignation or support.

Susan noticed that on a retaining wall alongside a roadway, a group of about two dozen white and gray-clad Sisters were sitting. They had that look Susan had seen before of resolve without belligerence. Their sleeves sloped down to upturned palms as strong and pliant as lotuses floating on the folds formed by their bent knees. They didn't chant, but seemed to draw light towards them.

Suddenly, the side door of the brothel opened again and a clutch of crying, scantily clad young girls were led from the building. They looked around blinking at the bright sunshine.

"Oh, my God! Oh, my God! Oh, my God, David!" cried Susan.

A female police officer and what looked to be volunteers or social workers led them away as a clean-limbed black woman leaned down to hug Tuptim.

David had already managed to click a few pictures of their screen with his webcam, framing Tuptim's triumphant face. Both Tuptim and the woman who appeared to be from the church were crying and laughing. Later Susan would send these photos to her *Kun-mae* to share in the village.

32 OH, FREEDOM
2011–

"What's going on," eleven year old Maya leaned into the family room to ask.

David answered first, "We just saw something amazing. We just saw people able to free slaves."

"Like Harriet Tubman and Moses?" asked Maya.

"Exactly," Susan smiled at her daughter and wiped away tears, "they all looked so happy."

Noam was now standing beside his sister, "Where?"

"Thailand. And your birth grandma helped," David began to swipe back to the photos to show his kids.

Noam startled Susan with his vehemence, "That is such a different country, with canals and royalty and pirates, and now slaves."

She startled herself with the swiftness of

her reply, "You can't follow the national news at home without hearing about slavery right here, too. Sweatshops. Undocumented workers who are afraid to go for help, or even legal ones whose bosses take their passports."

David was right, this reunion had turned her into a news junkie, or better put, someone who was awake.

There was a flush rising from her heart, warming her arms and legs as she digested where her own vehemence might just take her. Alan had said she would recognize her quest again when the time came. Maya was regarding Susan wide eyed from beneath her straight black bangs, "Mom? Are you doing anything about it?"

David and Noam were looking at her, too, now. This wasn't the only part of her life, Susan was realizing, where people were waiting on her. She was on the congregation's Women's Network board and being asked by the president for an agenda. Her old friends in Japan at the Nikko "Hall of the Asian Peoples" had politely intimated that it was time for a new exhibit.

She found herself answering, as if addressing them all at once, "I'm going to try and push through an exhibit about transpacific human trafficking for the 'Hall of the Asian Peoples," and get the Women's Network involved here at the state level. And....," her mind was racing,

It was true. She had heard from a friend at the Jewish Federation that human trafficking was lucrative enough that some drug traffickers had switched to it.

David was the first to speak, "Great. When did you start on all this?"

"Tomorrow morning."

The twins looked at each other and laughed. But later that evening as she was cleaning up at the kitchen sink, Noam came down and leaned into her to show her his screen. He had pulled up the Federation site with contacts for lobbying against trafficking.

"There's something about getting fundraising for a statewide hotline to report signs of trafficking," Noam flicked to another tab, "Then there's the 'Polaris Project' which helps victims. They're also trying to get the governor to pass some kind of bill. Get this–The Junior League is getting involved–your kind of people," he laughed.

"Funny man," but she did think dismissively that all they did was drive SUVs with tinted glass and play golf.

"And," Noam looked proud to inform his mom, "the office of Homeland Security has identified New York-New Jersey as a transport key in the infrastructure for trafficking."

"Here?" Sometimes she couldn't believe Noam was only an eleven year old.

"So you and Homeland Security can rock it with the ladies who lunch."

Susan was about to give him a lecture about the importance of civic organizations, even by–or especially by–sometimes obliviously privileged ladies of leisure.

Instead she looked at Noam, "thank you, honey."

He really wanted his mom to be an idealist. He really was a good kid, she thought. She could do this.

A memory from a decade ago came back to Susan. It was the group of Thai girls she saw being led through the airport when she was getting ready to catch her flight out of Thailand.

She remembered the little boy with the angelic face and the sinister slip of paper.

She didn't do anything then, maybe she couldn't have, but now she could. She turned on the dishwasher and went to her screen to read and collect contacts. She put together a list she would use to begin planning the exhibit tomorrow morning at work.

During lunch she would call the Women's

Network president to pitch the idea of their getting behind the trafficking hotline effort, or lobbying the governor. Susan had a premonition that this will have been a turning point in her life.

~

A few days later Susan got a letter from Noklek inquiring the name of her Twitter account. There had been massive floods that year, starting up near their village Ban Naan and all the ones like it on the plains that spread like a skirt around Chiang Rai. Further downriver Bangkok, Noklek reminded them, "was nicknamed by the tourist industry as the 'Venice of Asia' for its canals. It is at the delta of three rivers–certainly a flashpoint for the approaching floods."

Yet as the head waters rose near Noklek's village, the government remained silent. An independent anime video, she wrote, explained the flood by equating the water to fifty million whales coming down to the delta and washing across the *Krung Thep* metropolis of Bangkok before finding the sea.

David pulled it up on YouTube. Blue whales flooding through the city, piling up and covering buildings. David chuckled.

Noklek's letter went on, "But that isn't the only social media Thais are turning to. As water tables rise, even people in rural areas are buying text-only devices."

David interrupted, "so the average person is using Twitter as though it's instant messaging. Huh, that's different but it works, I guess."

"I can't telephone her, but she wants me to tweet?!"

David surprised her, "Just do it. And let her know that you've joined their fight."

"Against trafficking?"

"Yes. It's their cause, but just watching from the sidelines I think I see something else. It gets at the heart of their being victims. Noklek didn't give you away because she didn't care. She did it because human trafficking gave her only horrific choices. This would be a way for you to acknowledge that."

Susan nodded and set up an account. She sent her first tweet to Noklek. Then Susan looked up Lily's username and sent her second tweet to her oldest daughter, living in a college dorm.

~

By summer of 2012 Noklek typed that

Tuptim and Durek had moved down to Bangkok. Tuptim had accepted a job at the planned Regional Support Office of an international movement called the Bali Process. Noklek missed both Tuptim and Suwan, she tweeted to Susan, using effortful translation plug-ins. But she was proud to see the opening of this haven in Bangkok.

Wasn't it an auspicious-sounding year, 2555 CE, too? Noklek summarized it in a neat 140-character package:

> Tuptim and my dream. RSO will help return and so scare trafficker and make hope for slaves of sex, fishing and housemaid networks. Even more good: ministers meeting in Indonesia next April for Bali Process.

"The Bali Process," Noklek wrote, "was established to reduce irregular migration in the Asia Pacific Region."

In other words, her next tweet said, "the Bali Process enlists international aid workers, local activists, and former slaves to discourage human trafficking by creating 'data base exchanges', 'funding lifelines' and 'procedures for repatriation'."

David cocked an eyebrow, "They usually discuss this out in the tapioca fields?"

"They do now" Susan said proudly. He smiled at her.

"You're smart," David said and seemed satisfied, "why wouldn't Noklek be a quick study, too?"

Susan agreed, "When you think about it, what made the big differences between me with my graduate degree and *Kun-mae* being sold at age fourteen, are the differences between my adoptive dad and her father. I hope he realizes how much of a difference he made."

Through another chain of tweets, Susan learned from Noklek that Tuptim had spoken with economic aid workers who tended to see the problem as having economic roots. Thailand's men, women and children were too rich and too poor. For a long time Thailand was poor, especially in rural areas where farmers didn't enjoy the opportunities available days away in Bangkok. Prostitution paid better cash than the mills, fueled by wealthy Bangkok businessmen and sex tourists, so girls went there or were sent there.

Noklek added a Chinese saying she heard from Jugo, "It is never good when a man is too rich, or a woman too poor."

"I wonder if Jugo is finally taking an interest." It bothered Susan after all these years that Noklek seemed to keep her at arm's length, at least when it came to Jugo, Aimei and Ailan.

David was looking at her.

She picked up the device and saw, "Then as Thailand became the richest country in the region," Susan put down the device full of Noklek's messages and continued on her own, "its infrastructure for human bondage would have–easily–accommodated desperate or shanghaied young women and men. They say they come from as far away as Burma, Siberia, Nepal or North Korea. It's became a giant switching station."

"Meaning?"

"It's simultaneously a source, a destination, and a transit stop for traffickers. They rob victims of their identity papers, just like with Tuptim's passport at the maid job. Also, David, a lot of the people around Chiang Rai if they're from the hill tribes don't read Thai. Neither do girls brought in from outside the country. So here they are, and they can't speak the language of the local police and others wherever they're sent."

Susan really felt like a part of this now, too.

In her own messages she described the links that were being uncovered at home between human traffickers, identity thieves and gun smugglers.

Susan typed to her birth mother, "Some women prefer a quiet life at the country club. Their vision of heaven is mixed drinks at a cocktail party. I think I enjoy this more. It has meaning, and it's exciting like finding you, *Kun-mae*."

Noklek made an oblique reference to the lie that Susan had caught her in during their meeting over a decade ago, she wrote, "Tuptim records the stories of returnees, though sometimes they lie. You must understand that it's an acquired habit that helped most survive and many escape."

Susan thought she read a flit of chastisement from across the ocean. *Kun-mae* concluded with, "Tuptim, Durek and I marvel at how far away from home they have been, how improbable and blessed their return."

Noklek then changed subjects, writing that, "Durek, on the other hand is at his wife's side for different reasons. He happily handed over the fields and their little thatched farmhouse to his son and daughter-in-law. He has now moved down to Bangkok to be with his wife. In his retirement he volunteers in the Regional Support Office itself. Occasionally Durek picks up paid contract work from Carl K. The nine years apart from Tuptim were hard on him. He intends to be together in their remaining years."

As Susan finished reading this last message to David, she stood up, "I love you. I don't want us to be apart like that."

She was rewarded with one of those broad-shouldered hugs that David used for making the world warmer, safer and theirs. They leaned together like that for a few moments before she turned back.

"You wouldn't believe how mainstream, how commonplace it is to see this, David. It's frightening how societies or parts of societies can shift into really dark forms."

David considered for a minute before saying: "Think of Europe and the ten years of the Holocaust. For most of history Germany itself was one of the better host countries for Jews in exile. For most it stopped even being an exile and became home for generations. They really were Jewish Germans for over a millennium, and then for one decade everything shifts. The lands of Mendelsohn and Einstein turn into charnel houses for their Jewish citizens. Then everything shifts back."

"Well, Noklek seems to think they'll get it to shift back for Thailand, too. Tuptim is fighting the good fight," Susan said hopefully.

"Suze, you're fighting the good fight here, too. Even with your job and the kids, you're doing what you can about trafficking–in our society."

By that April 2013 there were forty-some signatories to the Bali Process, including the UN High Commissioner for Refugees. There the shift that David talked about continued, and after twenty years as a chief destination for slaves, the United Arab Emirates finally joined the Bali Process, too.

A few weeks later Susan and the rest of the women from her local chapter were invited to the State House to watch as the governor signed an anti-trafficking bill. Susan wept a lot that month, tears of joy. She imagined that half a world away her birth mother did, too.

~

This spring was unusually early and

unusually warm, forcing the twisted, woody lilac bushes by the screened porch into early bloom. One particular afternoon the warm air was full of their perfume. Bees flew languidly from the lilacs to the impatiens along the brick walk and around the clematis climbing the lamp post. David had taken the twins to the local playground for a half hour so she could finish some weeding and pruning before dusk. Susan decided to light candles in their room that night.

The flickering of candles almost made David think of what it might be like to make love on a boat, lights moving rhythmically across the ceiling, not knowing if it was the earth, the sea or their torsos that cradled and shook the world. Usually the excitement for him grew in the center of his body, but tonight the sensations raced dizzyingly up and down his legs and the movement of hers, and the sound of her breath, and the feel of her soft skin, and the glimpse, even by candlelight, below her lifted shirt made him feel wilder than he had known how to contain since his adolescent awakening.

He covered her, and there was no way to plunge deep enough, no way to sink hard enough, and nowhere as warm and safe and wet as this place that they shared. Her arms stroked his back and almost without thinking he moved in the way they had laughed about once, and he laughed when he heard her gasp with recognition. There's nothing better than understanding the one who understands you, too.

From the other side of the room Susan's device pulsed blue and made a humming sound.

"No," he said in mock defeat.

"I have to check it this weekend. I'm sorry," Susan sighed and pulled her pajamas in front of her like some kind of ineffectual fig leaf.

She did look cute, David thought. Something puzzled him, "since when are curators on call? I thought that was only for us IT security shmoes."

"They are working on the heating, ventilating, air conditioning system over the weekend. If anything goes wrong, we and the preservation unit need to mo-bi-lize," she explained and then something else seemed to catch her attention. He tucked his head under the pillow until from the other side of the room came her delighted squeal.

"David!"

He rolled over. The blue light glinted off the scaled roof tiles of the little spirit house waiting in a corner on the floor. They'd already picked out a spot for it near the garden, and pouring the concrete for its post was on his honey-do list. Susan unplugged the device from the charger and carried it back across the room to their bed.

As its blue light glowed toward him, she said wondrously, "It's Aimei and Ailan! My birth mother's stepdaughters just requested me!"

VOCABULARY

Ab ob nuat – *Lit.,* "bath and massage;" the business conducted at a massage parlor.
Aninut – The twenty four hours following a death, within which arrangements are to be made and a funeral held.

Baht – The currency of Thailand.
Beshert – Sometimes translated as "soulmate," *lit.,* "your promised one".
Boba – Real or artificial nubs of tapioca root, also known as cassava root. Served as a dessert topping or as an addition to a beverage such as "bubble tea". Also called "cassava nubs" and "tapioca pearls".
Boddhisattva – A being who on the verge of enlightenment instead turns back from Heaven in order to lead others also toward the light.

Chai yen-yen – *Lit.,* "Stay calm".

Chevra kadisha – A corps of volunteers from a congregation who wash, dress, and watch over a body; *lit.*, "a holy circle".

Farang – Foreigner, derived from the word for "French".

Haggadah – The book containing the story and home-centered ceremonies of Passover, lit., "the telling" (plural: *haggadot*).

Halakhah – Religious law based on rabbinic interpretations of the Torah that fundamentalist Jews call the Orah Torah.

Hallel – *Lit.*, praise, a specific prayer consisting of verses of Psalms.

Israel – *Lit.*, "wrestler with God," or "God-wrestler," the familial name for the Jewish people and for the patriarch Jacob after he wrestled with the angel.

Kaddish – A prayer on behalf of the dead which does not mention death; recited during the year of mourning and then on the *yahrtseit.*

Ketubah – A marriage contract, usually in English and Hebrew calligraphy. Often illuminated with hand painted ink and acrylic and framed.

Khopkun ka/Khopkun klap – "Thank you". *Ka* is used by females and *klap* is used by males as endings.

Kiddush – *Lit.*, "sanctification," a specific prayer said over wine at the beginning of a gathering.

Krung Thep – Bangkok, the capital of Thailand.

Kun-mae – Used when addressing your mother, third person uses "mae", lit., "mother".

Mai ben rai – *Lit.,* "can't do anything about it"; the nuance swings between the pessimistic to the hopefulness of "*que sera, sera*".

Mai rong hai – *Lit.,* "Don't cry".

Mezuzah – A case that is affixed to doorways and which traditional Jews kiss or touch as they enter and leave. It contains a parchment with two liturgical poems [Deuteronomy 6:9 and Deuteronomy 11:20].

Muang (Muang Thai; "Muang USA") – *Lit.,* "the community of" often used by Thais talking about "the people of Thailand".

Nam pla – *Lit.,* "fish sauce" a common fermented condiment.

Namchai – Human kindness, thoughtfulness, *lit.,* "water for the heart".

Prik – Small hot peppers.

Rachamim – *Lit.,* "compassion," same root as *rechem* or "womb".

Rechem – *Lit.,* "womb," related to the word *rachamim* or "compassion".

San Jao Thi – See "Spirit house".

Sawasdee ka; Sawaskee klap – traditional greeting for any time of day, both to welcome, arrive and bid farewell. The ending of *ka* is the polite form used by women and the ending *klap* · by men.

Seder – *Lit.,* "order;" refers to the ordered ritual and meal with which we celebrate Passover.

Shalom – *Lit.,* "peace" and "wholeness".

Shehecheyanu – A prayer said over something new or when experiencing something for the first time.

Shiva – The seven days of mourning after a funeral, typically held at the home of the deceased or a survivor, to which respects are paid by bringing food and joining in recitation of the mourners' service. *Lit.,* "seven" as in the Anglo-Hebrew: to sit *shiva*.

Shloshim – The first thirty days of bereavement during which mourners do not entertain or celebrate.

Spirit house – A miniature house, *San Jao Thi,* or

temple, *San Phra Pum,* mounted on a pole or shelf to contain offerings that nourish the spirits that came before. Unlike Confucian alters there need be no blood connection to these welcomed spirits.

Sukkah – A booth large enough to serve a meal in during the holiday of Sukkoth. Two other key requirements are that it be impermanent and have a latticed roof that allows a view of the full moon.

Suwan – Garden.

Torah – The five books of Moses which also correspond with the first five books of the Christian Old Testament; this is distinct from the *Tanakh* which is comprised of the *Torah*, the *Nevi'im* (the Prophets) and the *Ketubim* (Writings such as Psalms, Proverbs, etc.). "Torah" also can be used abstractly for the tradition of religious study that includes both the scriptures and the Talmudic commentaries.

Tuk-tuk – Taxis like diesel golf carts.

Un'taneh tokef – A prayer for those who came before and for those who may pass away in the coming year, recited annually on the Jewish New Year. *Lit.,* "and you shall cede" or "and you shall ascribe". This prayer is the basis of the popular song "Who by Fire".

Wunsen – Good street vendor food. A stir-fried "cellophane noodle" dish.

Yahrtseit – Anniversary of a loved one's death. *Lit.*, "year's time".

TOPICS & QUESTIONS FOR READING CLUBS

1) How would the novel's emphasis have been different if told mostly from the perspective of David? Faith? Masha? There is a passage or chapter from each of these characters' points of view. What do these add that we the readers would not have felt if told from Susan's point of view?

2) Susan talks about "phantom limb pain" resulting from the loss of being relinquished. The football captain talks about always being in exile. At other times Susan, Faith and adult adoptees talk about being disempowered or infantilized by sealed adoption records or "closed adoptions." Are these conditions necessary to protect the integrity and stability of the adoptive family? Are

adoptive families less cohesive in "open adoptions" where the child adoptee has contact with birth relatives? Are adoptive families less or more cohesive after a reunion with a birth relative or relatives?

3) David talks about societies shifting. His example is the ten years of the Holocaust when Germany shifted from being a place of relative tolerance among European nation states, to murderous intolerance, and then back again. David offers this as a possible model for seeking to shift societies where human trafficking seems entrenched. Can you offer other examples that support or refute the idea of societal shift?

4) Some reunions are not pursued, some mysteries are not solved (the identity of Susan's birth father, Fred's son, Ramona Graves' history). Should Susan, David or the detective have dug deeper? In each case, would the costs or the benefits have been greater in pursuing a search?

5) "Joseph" challenges Dr. Ames' drawing a distinction between his freedom from

responsibility as a sperm donor and his responsibility as a married father. Should it be black and white as Dr. Ames suggests? What, if any, are the responsibilities of sperm donors, egg donors and the facilitators of these reproductive technologies to the progeny? What are the rights of the progeny once they are adults? What, if any, rights to search should progeny have? Should donors have any?

6) It's said that more than ninety percent of international adoptees who search fail to find their first family. As the Buddhist abbess noted, most adoptees end their search with a visit to the orphanage. If Susan failed, would her character have been as strong?

7) Paid, trained professionals in Homeland Security, the FBI and local law enforcement have worked together against people trafficking in the USA. Is the participation of traditional civic volunteer groups like the Junior League and the Jewish Federation impactful?

8) In the Jewish oral tradition it is said that God, in return for Pharaoh's daughter adopting Moses, adopts her. The rabbis give her the name "Batyah" or "daughter of God." She and other Egyptians chose to join the Hebrews and Moses when they left Egypt. How does this change your view of the Exodus story? Of Tapioca Fire?

9) Reviewers have sometimes described a novel's hero as being a Christ-like figure. Susan can be described as a Moses-like figure. Where do you see this in her returning to Thailand or reuniting with her birth mother? Where do you see this—or not—in her following Noklek's and Tuptim's politicization?

10) Readers have reacted strongly, both positively and negatively, to the scenes between Susan and Masha around fertility. In the end, how would you characterize those scenes and the relationship between mother and daughter?

11) Do you agree with Susan's suspicion about her parents' marriage, that the bond between a couple who adopt is different from a couple who have biological children? What insight does Noklek's first marriage add?

12) It is not until after the wildfire that David is able to put into words his feelings about his father. How might his feelings be similar or different from the emotions described by adoptees? In light of this, should either the husband or wife have been more supportive of the other's decision to search or not search?

13) Susan wonders at some of her own possible moral lapses: not responding to the little boy in Bangkok or the girls at the airport, participating in an abortion, even leaving her infant daughter to find her birth mother. Are her justifications sufficient? Alternately, was she accepting too much responsibility?

14) In the garden chapter David mentions an idea from 19th century intellectual history: the young United States could

differentiate itself from old European society by becoming a cultural melding of East and West. To what extent has that vision been realized?

15) The concept of the Baby Scoop Era describes the period from the return of World War II veterans in 1945 to the legalization of birth control and abortion by 1974. During that period adoptable babies were plentiful. Today the stigma of giving away a child, the thinking goes, is greater than raising one alone. That combined with more daycare options and jobs for women means only 4-6% of unwed mothers in the US place their children for adoption. Is it better for children to be raised by single mothers, or surrendered for adoption to more materially successful adoptive parents?

16) Susan, Faith and Lisa attend an adoption triad group and an adoptees-only group. Based on the reunion stories you hear in each, what do you see as the relative advantages and disadvantages to the two kinds of self-help groups?

17) Several dreams, daydreams and memories are mentioned. Susan has the swan, the ghost in the mirror, the daughter on the island, the candied Easter egg, and the false memory of the crib. Faith remembers the stone arches at the Upper East Side adoption agency and the haunting old woman on the Lexington Avenue bus. How are these important to each woman's identity? Does it matter whether these are false memories, actual memories or dreams?

18) Masha tries to incorporate elements of Susan's East Asian ethnicity into family holidays although neither adoptive parent is East Asian. Susan turns down going on a "Heritage Tour" to her birth country. Did Masha and Al have an obligation to provide this? What do adoptive parents owe transracial adoptees? Should adoptive parents try to "acculturate" children into their birth culture or should the children be raised in their adoptive parents' authentic culture only, possibly to learn their birth culture on their own?

19) Susan, David and Masha draw on common prayers and poems that capture their dilemmas or hopes, in some cases reinterpreting them with personal meanings. Is this an authentic deepening of spirituality?

20) In the latter third of the book, connections happen in or near real-time over the Internet and satellite feeds. This is a contrast to the years adoptees and detectives spent searching in the 1990s and earlier. The Internet has given rise to "search angels" who offer to help adoptees and birth parents search online, as well as ads by adoptive parents who want to "rehome" their child by giving them to a new set of parents. What, if anything, has been lost or gained by the increasing velocity of this kind of networking?

More reading club ideas:
https://www.facebook.com/TapiocaFire

ABOUT THE AUTHOR

Suzanne Gilbert is my birth name, which was also my name in foster care. I share many of the hurdles of international adoptees because my birth mother lives overseas. We have only met a few times. I met my birth father exactly once before he died. It was through reunion with them that I learned my ethnicity is Cherokee, Irish, Iroquois and Jewish.

The protagonist of *Tapioca Fire*, Susan Piper, was adopted from Thailand. This is a country whose multifaceted role in human trafficking I witnessed when I was married to a Thai journalist for eleven years. I have also worked in journalism in Tokyo, Boston and New York.

More at:
amazon.com/author/suzannegilbert

Made in the USA
Lexington, KY
18 August 2014